OECD ECONOMIC SURVEYS

1999-2000

Japan

OECD

ORGANISATION FOR ECONOMIC CO-OPERATION AND DEVELOPMENT

ORGANISATION FOR ECONOMIC CO-OPERATION AND DEVELOPMENT

Pursuant to Article 1 of the Convention signed in Paris on 14th December 1960, and which came into force on 30th September 1961, the Organisation for Economic Co-operation and Development (OECD) shall promote policies designed:

- to achieve the highest sustainable economic growth and employment and a rising standard of living in Member countries, while maintaining financial stability, and thus to contribute to the development of the world economy;
- to contribute to sound economic expansion in Member as well as non-member countries in the process of economic development; and
- to contribute to the expansion of world trade on a multilateral, non-discriminatory basis in accordance with international obligations.

The original Member countries of the OECD are Austria, Belgium, Canada, Denmark, France, Germany, Greece, Iceland, Ireland, Italy, Luxembourg, the Netherlands, Norway, Portugal, Spain, Sweden, Switzerland, Turkey, the United Kingdom and the United States. The following countries became Members subsequently through accession at the dates indicated hereafter: Japan (28th April 1964), Finland (28th January 1969), Australia (7th June 1971), New Zealand (29th May 1973), Mexico (18th May 1994), the Czech Republic (21st December 1995), Hungary (7th May 1996), Poland (22nd November 1996) and Korea (12th December 1996). The Commission of the European Communities takes part in the work of the OECD (Article 13 of the OECD Convention).

Publié également en français.

Table of Contents

●●●●●

Boxes

Tables

Figures

BASIC STATISTICS OF JAPAN

THE LAND

Area (1 000 sq. km), 1995	377.8	Major cities, October 1996 estimate (10 000 inhabitants):	
Cultivated agricultural land (1 000 sq. km), 1995	51.3	Tokyo (23 wards)	796
Forest (1 000 sq. km) 1994	251.4	Yokohama	332
Densely inhabited districts[1] (1 000 sq. km), 1995	12.3	Osaka	260
		Nagoya	215
		Sapporo	177
		Kobe	142
		Kyoto	146

THE PEOPLE

Population, October 1999 estimate (1 000)	126 740	Labour force in per cent of total population, October 1999	53.7
Number of persons per sq. km in 1999	335	Percentage distribution of employed persons, 1999:	
Percentage of population living in densely inhabited districts in 1995[1]	64.7	Agriculture and forestry	4.8
Net annual rate of population increase (1988-99)	0.3	Manufacturing	20.8
		Service	26.0
		Other	48.4

PRODUCTION

Gross domestic product in 1999 (billion yen)	495 145	Growth of real gross fixed investment, 1999	–1.2
Growth of real GDP, 1999	0.2	Net domestic product of agriculture, forestry and fishery, at producer prices, in 1998 (billion yen)	6 819
Gross fixed investment in 1999 (per cent of GDP)	26.1	Growth of industrial production, 1999	1.0

THE GOVERNMENT

Public consumption in 1999 (in per cent of GDP)	10.3	Composition of Parliament, October 2000:	House of Representatives	House of Councillors
Current public revenue in 1998 (in per cent of GDP)	31.6	Liberal Democratic Party	232	112
Government employees in per cent of total employment, 1999	8.4	Democratic Party	129	58
Outstanding long-term national bonds in per cent of GDP (FY 1999)	69.5	Peace and Reform (*Komei*)	31	24
		Liberal Party	22	5
		Communist Party	20	23
		Others	46	30
		Total	480	252
		Last elections	June 2000	July 1998

FOREIGN TRADE AND PAYMENTS
(1999, billion yen)

Commodity exports (fob)	45 794		Exports	Imports
Commodity imports (fob)	31 779	Percentage distribution		
Services	–6 151	OECD countries	60.8	50.3
Investment income	5 696	*of which:* North America	33.7	24.8
Current balance	12 174	Far East	31.8	34.5
Exports of goods and services in per cent of GDP	10.4	Other	7.4	15.2
Imports of goods and services in per cent of GDP	8.7	Total	100.0	100.0
		Crude material and fuels (SITC 2, 3, 4)	1.0	24.0
		Semi-manufactured goods (5, 6)	17.5	16.8
		Machinery and transport equipment (7)	68.7	27.5
		Other (0, 1, 8 ,9)	12.8	31.7
		Total	100.0	100.0

THE CURRENCY

Monetary unit: Yen	Currency unit per US$, average of daily figures	
	Year 1999	133.9
	October 2000	108.4

1. Areas whose population density exceeds 5 000 persons per sq. km.

Note: An international comparison of certain basic statistics is given in an annex table.

This Survey is based on the Secretariat's study prepared for the annual review of Japan by the Economic and Development Review Committee on 9 October 2000.

•

After revisions in the light of discussions during the review, final approval of the Survey for publication was given by the Committee on 2 November 2000.

•

The previous Survey of Japan was issued in November 1999.

Assessment and recommendations

The economic recovery has been under way since the spring of 1999, although the statistics are difficult to interpret

At the time of the last *Survey* in the autumn of 1999 it appeared that the economy was recovering, but that the situation remained fragile. One year later, it is evident that the recovery is stronger than anticipated although uncertainties about its robustness and about future growth prospects have remained large, with opinions diverging widely. The Japanese economy entered a recovery phase around mid-1999 supported by expansionary macroeconomic policies and export growth, with the trough of the current business cycle officially dated as April 1999. While expenditure-based quarterly GDP showed two-quarters of negative growth in the second half of the year, a range of other indicators showed a consistent strengthening of economic activity. There are concerns about weaknesses in the statistical base for quarterly GDP estimates, particularly regarding private consumption and public investment, and the official review currently under way should eventually lead to improved estimates.

By mid-2000 activity seems to be becoming more self-sustained, and deflationary concerns are receding

Although there were fears in late 1999 that, with fiscal stimulus weakening, the recovery would peter out going into 2000, indicators of production activity have continued to improve, and in the second quarter the index of aggregate activity expanded at an annualised rate of some 7½ per cent, which is the sixth consecutive quarter of growth. Moreover, there appears to be a broadening of activity to include the service sector. Driving the upturn has been a marked recovery of business profits, which has led to increased business investment. At first this was confined to the IT sector, but by the second quarter rising investment orders had spread to other sectors. The upturn is also reflected in rapidly rising vacancies and an increase in overtime while the unemployment rate has stabilised, albeit at a high level. By mid-year the key question dividing policy makers and observers had become the degree to which household incomes have recovered and whether this will lead to increased consumption. In the three months June to August, the Survey of Employment was pointing to rising basic wages and overtime earnings while summer bonuses had increased moderately in comparison with the previous year. In addition, purchasing power will be underpinned this year and next by the maturation of a large volume of postal savings deposits. Although consumer prices have continued to decline, this has served to support real household disposable incomes, and price declines are not simply due to demand weakness but to a number of regulatory changes. The domestic wholesale price index, although buoyed by higher oil prices, points to a weakening of deflationary pressure, although the domestic demand deflator has continued to decline moderately in the first half of the year.

However, uncertainties remain large as to the robustness of the recovery and future growth prospects

In the unusual conditions facing Japan, there are both short-term and more medium-term risks. In the short term there are still large differences in judgements, magnified by conflicting statistics, about the robustness of the on-going recovery. Some emphasise the dependence of the economy on public works, the weakness of consumption and the possibility that bankruptcies will rise in a disruptive manner. Under these conditions, a slowing of activity is foreseen at some time during the second half of this year and continued macroeconomic policy stimulus is judged to be necessary. While constituting a risk, the OECD does not judge this scenario as the most likely and projects growth to continue at an annualised rate of some 2 per cent in the second half. Looking beyond to 2001 and into 2002, uncertainty and risks increase markedly. There are the usual risks associated with the international economy, but in the case of Japan a great deal depends on judgements about how restructuring will continue to unfold, especially in such troublesome sectors as real estate and construction. The OECD judges that growth is reasonably well established but that restructuring will continue to be a drag on the economy. The fiscal package from November 2000 should temporarily raise the rate of growth in the first half of 2001, but thereafter growth is likely to slow into 2002 to some 2 per cent with deflationary pressures subsiding gradually.

The zero interest rate policy has served Japan well, creating easy monetary conditions

The zero interest rate policy, which was in force from February 1999 until August this year, has served to underpin the recovery of economic activity. But faced with other deflationary pressures such as exchange rate appreciation and declining wage costs, the full impact will take some time to become apparent. The money base has grown rapidly this year often exceeding 10 per cent, year-on-year. Banks' lending attitude has continued to improve and market interest rates have remained low on all maturities. However, other indicators present a different story: growth of the broad money stock has remained limited to 2 to 3 per cent, and the monetary conditions index (MCI) has deteriorated due to the appreciation of the exchange rate. But with interest rates close to zero, the implication of this last point is that policy should have sought to weaken the exchange rate directly or indirectly – and indeed many commentators argued at the time for such a policy *via* large foreign exchange interventions. In the event, a large and sustained intervention did not take place.

Lifting of the zero rate policy should be viewed as a small correction with monetary conditions remaining easy

In the course of the year the Bank of Japan (BOJ) prepared markets for an eventual change in the zero rate policy, so that when the time did come in August, the quarter point rise had been largely discounted by the market. The BOJ explained the move as the lifting of a policy which had been explicitly characterised as temporary. In their judgement, deflationary concerns had been dispelled: Japan's economy was showing clearer signs of recovery, and this gradual upturn, led mainly by business fixed investment, was likely to continue. Moreover, with the overnight rate close to zero, the lack of liquidity management on the part of banks had become evident, suggesting the need to raise costs for them somewhat. However, the rise in the overnight rate attracted strong criticism and the government had been strongly opposed to it since it viewed the economic situation as being more fragile. While the case against the change in policy focused on risks to the recovery, there were also fears that the monetary authorities might be led to remove a significant volume of excess liquidity from the system and that the move would be seen as a signal for further increases in rates and thus dampen the business atmosphere. Although there are indeed different views as to the strength of the recovery, it is nevertheless clear, given a large output gap and deflationary pressures that are receding only slowly, that monetary policy should remain easy. With respect to draining excess liquidity, it is as yet too early to form a judgement. However, an important experience from the period of deflation and low interest rates is that the closer the rates are to zero, the more quantitative indicators of policy, such as broad liquidity and excess reserves, need to be monitored. With respect to the need to control expectations of further rate increases, it is imperative for the BOJ to move quickly to establish an explicit policy framework to guide expectations in what amounts to a new regime.

A new framework is needed to explain continued expansionary monetary policy for some time to come

In raising rates by a quarter of a point, the Bank of Japan has shifted from one clearly defined situation into an area less well defined and in which broad statements about the need to preserve price stability might be insufficient. Moreover, for some time to come, the economy will be subject to strong headwinds from non-performing loans and from restructuring, not to mention fiscal consolidation, and this will require an easy stance for monetary policy. The challenge will be to set a new framework, which will signpost how monetary policy will react as the economy exits from the serious post-bubble crisis. This will require greater clarity about objectives and about instruments than now exists. First, it would be important for the bank to give more concise form to its inflation objectives in terms of specifying what inflation rate or range is considered appropriate. This is not necessarily the same as targeting projected inflation, but it is necessary that, as deflation recedes, markets can anticipate when a policy response will be forthcoming. Other details such as which price index to use and over what time frame are of second-order importance in comparison with clarification of objectives. With respect to instruments, the last few years of very low interest rates have confirmed the findings in the academic literature that they will need to be chosen eclectically and that a focus on only the overnight rate might prove insufficient. In practice, this would suggest the need to monitor closely various monetary aggregates and act appropriately where they indicate that overall monetary conditions might be tightening. The recently issued document, *On Price Stability*, and the decision to publish semi-annually the *Outlook and Risk Assessment of the Economy and Prices* – in which Policy Board members' growth and price forecasts are indicated – are both welcome steps towards a better understanding of the Bank's views on the evolving situation as well as the main risks involved.

Fiscal policy has been stimulatory but is set to become neutral this year

Although fiscal policy was intended to stimulate the economy in FY 1999, it became increasingly clear through the year that public works spending at local government level was lower than anticipated. In order to prevent this unintended contraction, and in what was judged to be a fragile economic situation, the government introduced an additional stimulus package in November 1999 including additional public works worth 6.8 trillion yen. But delays in implementing the package meant that its effects were not felt fully until into the second quarter of this year. In forming the initial budget for FY 2000, the government has tried to make realistic projections for the activities of local government and has kept public works at broadly the same level as in the initial budget for FY 1999. Some budget items such as social expenditures are expected to grow rapidly. However, even with the carry-over effects of public works from FY 1999, total general government expenditures could decline this fiscal year. At the same time, revenues are projected to surge this year and in 2001 as deferred tax payments are made on interest income from 106 trillion yen (20 per cent of GDP) of maturing postal savings deposits. This surge in revenues gives the misleading impression that fiscal policy is tightening this year and next. Adjusting for these exceptional payments, the OECD estimates that the structural deficit is likely to remain at around 6 per cent of GDP in CY 2000 so that the fiscal stance would be neutral.

Deficit financing is becoming more market based...

The fiscal situation is sometimes said to be only an issue for the long term since high rates of savings in Japan make financing the deficit at low rates of interest easy. While there is some truth in this, the situation is changing faster than is often realised. Market-based financing is rapidly eroding the managed arrangements of the past. Accounting reforms and regulatory tightening have made banks and other financial institutions much more sensitive to their exposure to the traditional 10-year government bonds, and the maturity structure is already shortening as a result. Moreover, the postal savings system is less able to fund government activities, while the "Big Bang" financial market reforms are opening new possibilities to households and to investors. The government recognises the profound changes that are underway and is taking steps to increase the depth and liquidity of the bond market, although further steps will still be necessary. In sum, market forces and market sentiment will be much more important in the future in setting interest rates for financing the public sector and this will make it even more important to avoid an unsustainable spiral of debt.

... making it all the more important to maintain a sustainable level of debt

The current level of gross debt in relation to GDP is already the highest in the OECD (well over 100 per cent), and just to stabilise it at a significantly higher level in ten years would require a substantial amount of fiscal consolidation (possibly 10 percentage points of GDP). The net debt ratio is very much lower at around 40 per cent, but the financial assets of the general government sector are certainly overvalued. The bulk of the difference between gross and net debt is accounted for by assets held by the social security system, which amount to some 50 per cent of GDP. However, some 50 trillion yen of these assets (10 per cent of GDP) are in fact held by corporate pension funds while about 30 per cent of the funds (about 15 per cent of GDP) have been invested in government institutions requiring heavy subsidisation, which reduces their value as a financial asset. Finally, if future liabilities are taken into account, the corresponding levels of gross and net debt would be substantially higher than the current levels.

Fiscal policy needs to remain neutral in 2001 but then to move to consolidation in a medium-term context...

In view of the seriousness of the fiscal situation, the authorities need to take a number of short and long-run policy decisions. The immediate issue is the fiscal stance for FY 2001 which is currently under consideration. While there are significant downside risks to the economy in 2001 and 2002, central projections point to a continuation of moderate growth, albeit subject to headwinds due to ongoing restructuring. Against such a background, the objective for fiscal policy in 2001 should not be to provide further stimulus but to maintain the structural budget deficit at the same level as expected for this calendar year, excluding the effects of the one-off payments of tax on maturing postal savings deposits. This will require that the FY 2001 budget be based not on the initial budget for the previous year as is the practice, but the final budget outcome for FY 2000 including the supplementary budget adopted at the end of 2000, which the OECD estimates will raise spending by some 2½ trillion yen (0.5 per cent of GDP) in CY 2001. A slow but steady consolidation should get under way after that, if the recovery remains sustained by growth in private domestic demand. However, the full benefit of such a moderate consolidation path might only be reaped if the authorities establish a medium-term consolidation plan. Such a plan need not rule out flexibility against future shocks, although it would be worth recalling that the preferred policy tool in such a situation is monetary policy not fiscal stimulus.

... supported by structural reforms

In approaching the challenge of fiscal consolidation, expenditure control will be an extremely important component but, as noted in last year's *Survey*, revenue increases will also be unavoidable. Important in this respect will be a broadening of the base for both income and consumption taxes, so that necessary increases in tax rates will be associated with minimal economic losses. Nevertheless, it will be necessary to pursue and sustain cuts in public spending, especially so since there are strong upward pressures in a number of areas including social welfare, pensions, and health care. Efficient public choice under such conditions will require a clear specification of objectives and knowledge about the opportunity costs which the public expenditure system faces. It will also require a systematic analysis of policy options which are available to meet objectives. However, important weaknesses are apparent in a number of aspects of the public expenditure system.

The public expenditure system is not giving value for money

Public expenditures are not high by international standards, yet fiscal consolidation in the future will make it all the more important for the system to deliver value for money. This it fails to do at present. The budget process lacks transparency and does not have a well-defined medium-term perspective. This has meant that policies and projects have been implemented where the longer-term consequences are unclear. The process also pays too little attention to the public sector as a whole, as is evidenced by the lack of importance given to consolidated accounts and the insufficient oversight and control of the operations of a wide but poorly delineated network of public and quasi public organisations. At the end of the day, a key problem is the weakness of the institutional/political process when it comes to specifying overall objectives and balancing them with the associated tradeoffs. On the contrary, the electoral system seems more attuned to specifying and pursuing local interests in an inefficient manner. The structure interacts with insufficient project planning which further increases the potential for local interest groups to exercise undue influence over resource allocation. This is reflected in considerable waste and corruption in executing public works. Inefficiencies in government spending are also related to the fiscal federal structure which allows local authorities little leeway to specify expenditures which suit local preferences, and little authority over revenues which would make the economic tradeoffs clear to the electorate.

Profound public sector reforms are required, covering both the setting of policy objectives and policy implementation

These problems have become a source of concern to the authorities. The need for reform of the public governance system has been recognised for quite some time, leading to a general reform of government ministries and agencies next year and to the setting-up of policy review groups in each new ministry. Moreover, there have been moves to strengthen tender procedures for public works and to review and to cancel some of them. However, more basic and systematic reform is required in a number of areas:

– *Improving the coherency of policy.* The reform of government strengthens the role of the Prime Minister and creates a Cabinet Office together with the Council on Economic and Fiscal Policy. The objective is to strengthen political responsibility for expenditure priorities and this is welcome. However, its relation to another policy council comprising officials and leaders of the ruling party remains to be clarified, as does the relationship of the government to the political parties.

- *The public sector needs to be more clearly delineated and its governance tightened.* The public sector, including public companies and their subsidiaries, is very broad indeed. It is important to define more closely the operating conditions and the governance system in this extended public sector. The reform of the FILP, which will come into force next year, is intended to tighten financial discipline of public bodies. This reform goes in the right direction but it will be important that government guarantees do not simply replace the old system of financing and that market financing be facilitated by clear commitments about subsidies where they are necessary.
- *The financial relations between levels of government need to be reformed.* As part of its decentralisation plan the government has made some progress in reforming grant financing but it will also be necessary to increase local tax revenue if the opportunity cost of decisions is to be made clear to the electorate. The present system may also work as a disincentive for local financing initiatives since, in principle, the general grant is reduced if lower levels of government are successful in raising their own revenues.
- *Cost effectiveness needs to be improved.* A focus on programme objectives needs to be brought to bear on spending decisions. Too often objectives have been set without the cost effectiveness of programmes to achieve them being investigated. Cost-effective auditing and feedback on policy formation need to be strengthened as part of the overhaul of governmental institutions. Tendering procedures are in urgent need of improvement, particularly at local government level. However, progress here will only be achieved once the objective to support local SMEs is brought more fully under control and made the

subject of cost effectiveness considerations. More systematic use of cost-benefit analysis can be instrumental in improving the focus on achieving objectives efficiently.

– *Improving the budget process.* Fiscal transparency needs to be improved. As expenditure priorities are to be set by the new cabinet process, it is an appropriate time to introduce multi-year spending plans as part of a budget overhaul. In addition, the annual budget process needs to be reformed so that it accurately reflects the overall fiscal situation in the previous year. The disclosure of implicit and contingent liabilities should be improved.

Pension reform has taken a step forward but more radical solutions still need to be considered

A crucial area of public sector reform is the social security system which is in need of a major overhaul, especially in view of the ageing of the population. An important step was taken in pension reform in March 2000 with the passage of a bill which, once fully effective, is designed to cut benefit payments by some 20 per cent. The reform commits the government to raising the share of payments by the state for the basic pension from a third to a half by 2004 and this would seem reasonable if the intent is for the basic pension to play a safety-net role. But financing measures to realise this have not been identified yet, and decisions about this financing will need to be taken soon. However, even taking account of the new reform, the contribution rate will still have to increase substantially, as shown in the official 1997 Actuarial Valuation, to finance gross liabilities (including future liabilities), which on a present value basis are estimated at 2 140 trillion yen or 4.3 times as large as GDP. Moreover, corporate pension schemes are already under severe pressure from low returns in the market, resulting in a rising rate of fund dissolution. Further reform thus needs to remain on the policy agenda. The issues are indeed complex and the debate is quite an active one with varying proposals for redefining the basic pension and for more radical moves towards a more fully funded system. A number of schemes involve greater use of tax revenues making it even more important to broaden the tax base along the lines recommended in last year's *Survey*.

Reform of the health system has been delayed but needs to be pushed forward

Reform of the health system to place it on a sounder basis to handle the already rising demands of ageing population has taken a step forward with the entry into operation of long-term care in April of this year. What is now required is close monitoring of the development of specialist institutions and of whether official prices for long-term care are having the desired effect on resource allocation. In the health system more generally, the control of health spending *via* pricing regulation has led to a number of pernicious effects. For example, the combination of price control and fee for service payment has resulted in extremely short times for, but a high number of, consultations and a large volume of drug prescriptions. Relative prices between broad categories of care have remained rigid with fees for traditional ambulatory services remaining high compared with in-patient services and high-technology medicine. Hospitals are also paid on a mix of fee-for-service and per diem payments for in-patients which stimulates long stays. Fundamental reform is required and some promising initiatives have been taken by the government, although implementing legislation has been delayed in the Diet. Reform efforts need to move along several fronts. Government regulation needs to be reviewed so as to ensure that it helps the proper functioning of a market mechanism. Apart from a more flexible adjustment of the fee schedule, information provision for patients on the quality of health care needs to be improved. The health insurance funds should also be firmly established as an agent for patients. Consolidation of many fragmented health funds will not only help them to play this role but also reduce inequities in terms of large differences in premiums borne by the insured. Finally, resolving a serious deficit problem of the whole healthcare system will require a broadening of financing sources, as in the case of old-age pensions, and more diversified payment arrangements.

A great deal of progress has been made in deepening and widening the regulatory framework for the financial sector

Over the past year substantial progress has been made in dealing with the balance sheet problems of the financial sector and in further developing the regulatory framework and the safety net. Tighter supervision is now being extended to smaller regional banks and to credit unions/ co-operatives. More importantly, a restructuring system for the insurance industry has been put in place, which allows promised returns on policies to be reduced in the case of bankruptcy. A safety net has also been set up which, although relatively small in comparison with the public funds available for the banking sector, has at least established a framework which could be expanded if the situation were to deteriorate. Restructuring in the banking sector has proceeded with a number of bank mergers while three previously bankrupt banks have been sold. In addition, a normal functioning of financial markets has been restored, and there are indications that the corporate bond market is starting to better reflect risk in pricing securities. On the other hand, the universal deposit guarantee for all banks which was due to expire in March 2001 has now been extended, for current accounts until March 2003. While the delay might have been warranted for small banks, there was concern about extending the measure to large banks since the new law already makes special provisions for systemic crises. This decision was criticised by market participants.

There is still some way to go before banks have fully dealt with non-performing loans and become fully competitive

There is, however, a long way to go until the banking sector can be pronounced healthy and functioning efficiently. In some cases time is required, but in others further policy improvements are necessary. Non-performing loans remain a problem especially so as balance sheet restructuring in the non-financial sector enters a new phase with demands for debt forgiveness rising and bankruptcies on the increase. Moreover, banks continue to hold a large volume of property collateral against bad loans exposing them to possible secondary losses. To encourage banks to deal with their non-performing loans, the authorities should continue to insist on strict rate-of-return conditions to be met as part of the restructuring plans which were submitted at the time of re-capitalisation. For the newly merging bank groups, tight criteria will also need to be set. At the end of the day it is important that public funds will either be repaid or the authorities will be able to recoup part of the costs by exercising their right to convert the debentures to ordinary shares and to sell them. Several banks remain under public control and will either need to be liquidated or sold. In the latter case, it is important for the government to be able to use all possible instruments in writing an efficient contract including more flexible risk sharing arrangements with the new owners, which are currently not permitted. With respect to property disposals, one reason for limited progress in this area has been the hope that real estate values will recover. However, another important factor has been serious deficiencies in the legal procedures for enforcing foreclosure rights on property with illegitimate tenants often in possession. It will be necessary to more closely delineate tenant rights to cut down abuse and to simplify costly legal processes such as valuation. These measures would also help foster a more efficient real estate market.

Regulatory changes to promote enterprise restructuring are welcome and are also influencing the system of governance

In order to promote enterprise restructuring, the government has introduced a number of important measures; these include simplifying the procedures for splitting and merging firms and transferring employees, and lifting the ban on holding companies. Restrictions on the issue of share options have also been eased, even though the flexible use of them for performance-based pay remains limited. Moreover, the new reorganisation law is a major step forward in facilitating restructuring in comparison with other procedures. It allows simpler filing, the protection of vital assets from secured creditors by paying the assessed value of the asset and more effective implementation of agreed restructuring plans. Only half the creditors need to approve a scheme as opposed to two-thirds for other bankruptcy options, which has delayed the approval of restructuring plans in the past. However, it will be necessary for the authorities to monitor closely the implementation by the courts and take appropriate action to overcome legal bottlenecks. These measures to aid restructuring are also serving to change the system of corporate governance in subtle ways towards greater transparency and monitoring by outsiders. The corporate governance system is in any case in a period of transition following changing patterns of share ownership and the reduced capacity of banks to operate management-friendly debt restructuring, financing and forgiveness programmes. Moreover, accounting reforms are having a profound effect on management while increasing transparency for outsiders. What is now needed are additional reforms to underpin this general move toward a governance system with more external monitoring. To this end, the commercial code needs to be reformed placing a greater emphasis on the role of external directors.

The institutional structure of the regulatory system needs to be further refined

Last year's OECD *Review of Regulatory Reform* concluded that "… the lack of a coherent concept of the role of the state in a period of market-led growth has left regulatory intervention fragmented, incoherent and vulnerable to a host of special interests" and recommended a sharp break with past regulatory practices. These conclusions remain appropriate in a number of areas. In the telecommunications field it has been difficult for the relevant Ministry to separate (and to be seen to separate) its ownership responsibility for the incumbent operator, and its macroeconomic concerns, from the need to promote consumer interests. Such a conflict of interest needs to be avoided. While specific ways in which this might be achieved vary among countries, promising approaches include the introduction of an independent regulatory body (with strong firewalls if located inside a ministry) and the strengthening of the competition policy authorities. In the electricity and gas sectors, the Fair Trade Commission and MITI have been co-operating to specify rules of conduct for dominant incumbents. Again, the relevant ministry could face a conflict between its role in formulating energy policy and that in policing competition. In the financial sector, the Financial Services Agency has taken over the financial services policy unit of the Ministry of Finance, and at the end of this year the Financial Reconstruction Commission will merge with it, which will add to the Agency responsibilities for the oversight and sale of nationalised banks and the monitoring of banks' restructuring agreements. Although firewalls have been put in place, it will nevertheless be necessary to ensure that they are effective in the event of conflicting interests between the Agency's supervisory and ownership roles. In other cases, institutions are being called to carry out duties ill suited to a modern market economy. For example, to obtain benefits under the Industry Revitalisation Plan or to take advantage of easier share issue regulations, restructuring plans and share issue plans have to be approved by MITI. Such regulations fit poorly with a dynamic market economy but are a function of vague laws, which require excessive administrative interpretation. As part of the reform of governmental institutions to take place next year, the secretariat of the Fair Trade Commission is set to come under the authority of the Ministry of Public Management, Home Affairs, Posts and Telecommunications, which will also take over the current Ministry of Posts and Telecommunications. It will be important for the Commission to retain independence when it comes to staffing policy of its secretariat. Finally, the move from a regulatory system characterised by administrative guidance to one based on universal rules requires a strengthening of the legal profession. Reforms are required to stimulate new entrants and deregulate the legal system as recommended by the government's Regulatory Reform Committee.

Reform of the network industries, in particular telecommunications, needs to be accelerated

Telecommunication issues have become more prominent during the past year as the government has specified the rapid dissemination of IT as a policy objective. Nevertheless, the opportunity to develop further a competitive telecommunications market has not been fully exploited. Interconnection charges have been lowered steadily in recent years, although they have remained high by international standards. Following discussions with the United States, interconnection charges for regional connections will be cut significantly during the three years to FY 2002 and an access charge has been set for the local loop. To achieve the government's IT objectives, it will be important to take a number of regulatory and structural measures in addition to those mentioned above. First, as stressed in the OECD *Review of Regulatory Reform*, the regulations on rights of way and on facility sharing, such as underground tunnels, need to be reviewed with the objective of promoting market entry. Such a review should not be confined just to the telecommunications industry since similar issues are likely to be important in the broadcasting, electricity and gas sectors. Second, consideration needs to be given to a full restructuring of NTT.

The holding company approach with two dominant regional companies and a mobile operator has failed to stimulate competition, confirming a fear raised in last year's *Survey*. At a minimum, the mobile operator should be made independent and allowed to enter other markets and the two regional companies should be restructured under separate ownership and permitted to compete with one another. Steps should also be taken to encourage effective competition at the level of the local loop.

The labour market is increasingly affected by serious structural problems

Despite indications of an improved situation, as noted above, serious structural problems are becoming evident in the labour market. The age profile of the employed has become increasingly older and given the very steep age/wage profile this has driven up wage costs. When such older workers lose their jobs, which given the rise in bankruptcies is now more often the case, it is difficult for them to find employment since their reservation wages are generally higher than their productivity. Their average duration of unemployment is high and is helping to drive up the overall rate of joblessness. With lifetime employment practices still important, enterprises have cut employment of new entrants. In addition, both job mismatch and voluntary unemployment are increasing among young workers. As a result, youth unemployment is high compared to previous Japanese experience, with reduced access to jobs with on-the-job training after graduation.

The increasing emphasis given to employment promotion needs to be closely monitored

With lifetime employment practices and a steep age/wage profile a fundamental cause of the evolving labour market problems, it is quite difficult to identify a direct role for policy. Nevertheless, policy has had a key role in reinforcing the position of insiders (*i.e.* those already in the lifetime employment system). Strict interpretation by the courts of vague employment protection legislation and traditional labour market policy, especially the resort to employment subsidies and more generous unemployment benefits for middle-aged workers, have both served to reinforce the position of insiders. Raising the mandatory retirement age also favours insiders. The authorities should consider adopting measures which would encourage the reservation wage to fall. In responding to the new labour market challenges, the authorities have announced numerous active labour market measures over the past year, describing these as a shift from employment preservation to job creation and a reduction of job mismatch. For example, employment subsidies are available to enterprises for new workers in one of fifteen designated growth sectors. Nevertheless, the take-up rate of new programmes has so far been exceptionally low. If the authorities are to continue to expand active labour market measures it will be important to establish close monitoring to determine the dead weight costs (whether participants would have been employed anyway) and their substitution effects (whether all that changes is who is employed rather than total employment). Greater attention will need to be given to promoting training opportunities for youth, perhaps even by some type of voucher scheme.

Summary

Following the sharp downturn in 1998, the economy has entered a period of recovery although its underlying strength is clouded by conflicting statistics. The upturn has been underpinned by a strong rebound in profits, which has led to a marked rise in business investment. Household incomes are now starting to improve, not only due to overtime but also to a moderate rise in basic wages. The recovery is now expected to lead to a strengthening of private consumption although statistics are, for the moment, contradictory. Efforts are being made to improve the statistical base, which are welcome and need to be followed through. Looking ahead, moderate growth is expected to continue, although the economy will face strong head winds as restructuring gradually gathers pace in such difficult sectors as real estate and construction. Moreover, the banking sector still has a way to go before the problems of bad debt and low rates of return are finally resolved. Whether restructuring will continue to evolve smoothly or develop in a disruptive manner constitutes the greatest risk to the outlook, even though external risks cannot be totally excluded. Under these conditions, monetary policy has a key role to play in sustaining growth and should remain expansionary. With the lifting of the zero interest rate policy, it will be essential for the central bank to be more forthcoming about the framework which will guide their decision-making in the future. The greatest challenge, however, will be to take measures to confront the serious fiscal situation, especially given the risks entailed by the fast increase of public debt and the context of a rapidly ageing population. Although fiscal policy should remain neutral for the time being, it will need to shift to moderate consolidation in the near future, if the recovery remains sustained by growth of private domestic demand. To gain full credibility, the fiscal consolidation should be pursued in the context of a comprehensive medium to longer-term programme. Essential in this respect will be continued reforms of both the pension and health systems as well as measures to increase the efficiency of public expenditures through, *inter alia*, improved budget procedures and more effective project selection and implementation. To enhance growth prospects, the authorities will have to renew their emphasis on regulatory reform, deepening it to include institutional changes. In sum, immediate prospects for the economy have brightened even though risks remain significant. Policy priority will now have to be shifted from short-term stabilisation issues towards addressing more directly a number of future challenges, both macroeconomic and structural. With such a framework, Japan will finally be able to find an exit from the decade-long stagnation of the post-bubble nineties.

I. Recent developments: recovery and adjustment

Using a wide range of indicators, the EPA (Economic Planning Agency) has set tentatively the trough of the down-turn which started in 1997 as April 1999. Although statistics are diverging, on balance it seems that activity picked up through the second half of 1999 and by the third quarter of 2000 the expansion appeared to be widening with increasing investment orders characterising a greater number of sectors. The rate of unemployment remained high at around 4.7 per cent, but vacancies were rising strongly as were new hires. With profits increasing and labour incomes rising gradually, there were indications that consumption was set to make the upturn more broadly-based. Moreover, short-term indicators such as projected capital orders and expected industrial activity have been strong, pointing to robust activity continuing in the fourth quarter. In normal circumstances, such a constellation of indicators would lead to a relatively optimistic view of the economy by most observers, certainly a year ahead if not beyond. However, in the case of Japan the usual business cycle is superimposed on an economy still adjusting to massive imbalances, not only from the asset price bubble of the 1980s but also from the past policy approach of heavy *ex ante* regulation which deliberately slowed adjustment. It is the interaction between cyclical processes and structural adjustments, as well as serious problems in interpreting short-term statistics, which makes the situation so difficult to judge. This chapter first reviews recent developments, seeking to highlight the forces at work, and then presents the outlook and associated risks.

The current recovery

The recovery appears to be similar to previous episodes, though with some differences

Although the recovery is still in its early stages, comparison with previous experiences suggests that it appears to be a normal cyclical upturn with structural factors, at least at the macroeconomic level, not particularly marked. The most obvious difference is the behaviour of public investment, both before and after the trough, while GDP itself and private consumption seem weaker than in past recoveries (Figure 1). However, quarterly GDP, both in 1999 and this year, has diverged from supply indicators such as industrial production and tertiary sector activity, which have developed in a more customary manner (Box 1). The weakness of private consumption is also not quite consistent with the strong growth of domestic consumer goods shipments (and import volumes) (Figure 1).[1] Development of other demand components in the current expansion, particularly business investment, is comparable to those in previous episodes, but export and import volumes are relatively stronger. The distribution of income in this recovery is somewhat different from that in others: the recovery of corporate profits has been very strong, while employment has tended to decline suggesting a change in corporate behaviour. Other differences should also be noted: in particular, bank credit has declined in this recovery and money supply growth has been weak (Chapter II).

Rising profits have driven a recovery in business investment...

Profits recovered markedly despite a continued fall in wholesale prices in 1999, as total real compensation declined (Figure 1) and the inventory cycle unwound (Figure 2). The profit recovery was spread across all sectors, and in non-manufacturing profit levels in the first quarter of 2000 were as high as in 1990, the peak of the bubble period. Higher profits have in turn led to renewed business investment. At the disaggregate level the situation has been quite diverse indicating an important role for Information Technology-related developments (Table 1). A few sectors have accounted initially for the recovery of business investment, which has been visible since the fourth quarter of 1999. Investment by the electrical machinery sector was an important driving force thanks to buoyant demand for IT, and indeed this sector has been the main contributor to the rise in industrial production. Increasing activity in the tertiary sector is dominated by mobile communications, and this branch might have made a disproportionate contribution to profitability helping to lift investment by the services branch.[2] On the other hand, special factors have also played a role. For example, the rush by the wholesaling and retailing sector to invest in new stores in the early part of 2000 might have been related to implementation of the revised large scale retail sales law in June (see Chapter III).

The pattern of investment up till the end of the first quarter of this year appeared to mark the early stages of an IT-led upswing whereby producers must first invest in capacity and then investment by other sectors will – and is expected to – follow. Indeed, by around mid-year there was increasing evidence of this. Orders for investment goods rose strongly in both the second and third quarters and were spread across more sectors (Table 2). The forward indicator of investment goods orders was also extremely strong for a number of sectors.

Figure 1. **Features of the current economic expansion**
Trough = 100

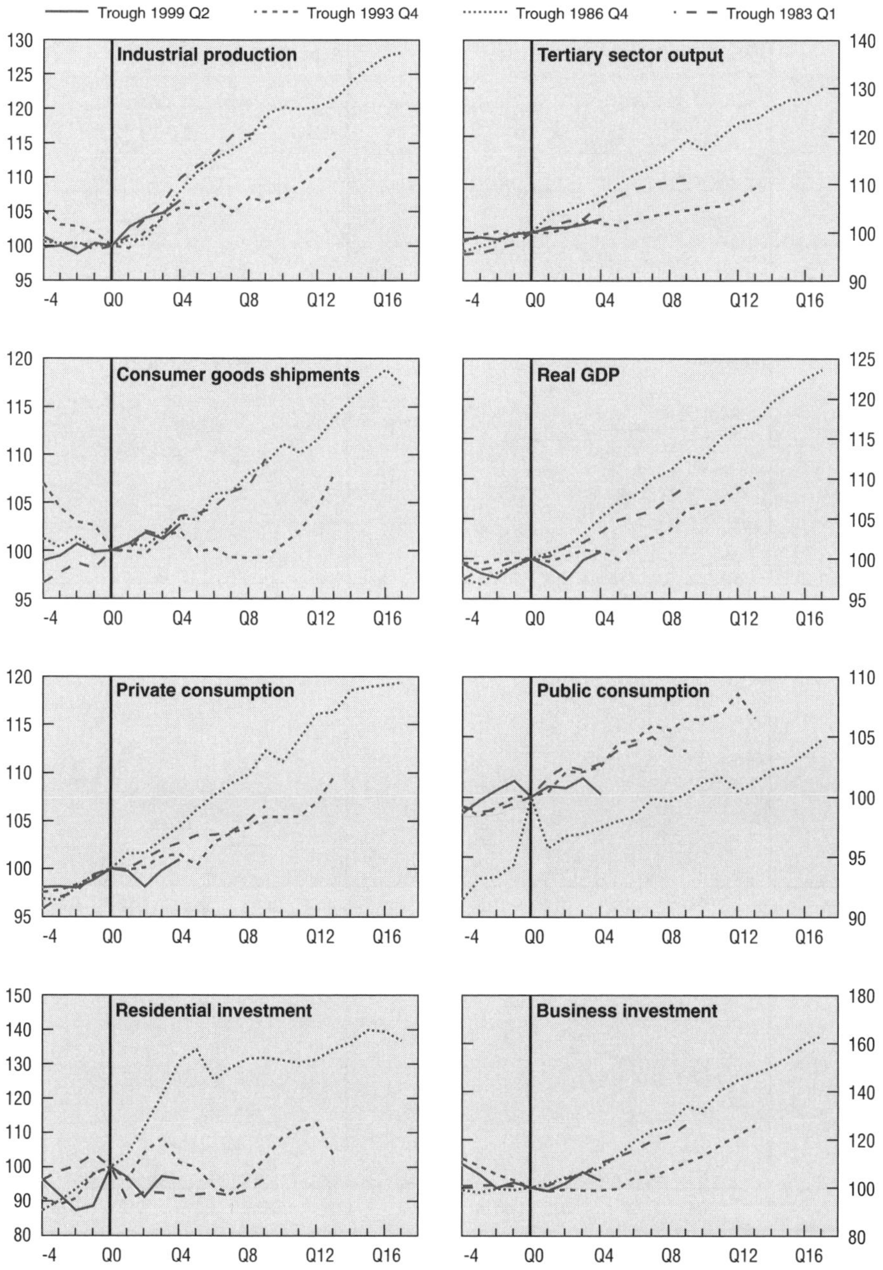

Figure 1. **Features of the current economic expansion** *(cont.)*
Trough = 100

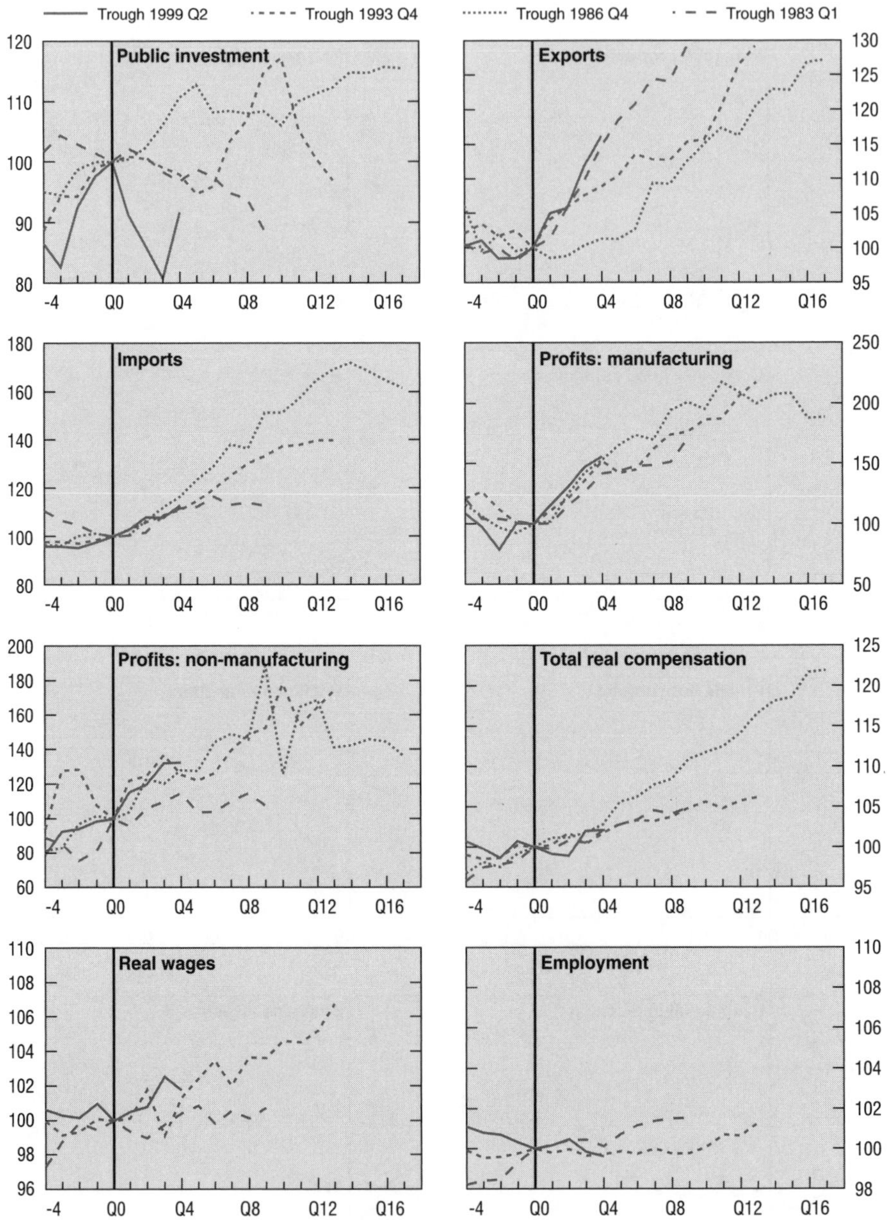

Source: Economic Planning Agency and Bank of Japan.

Box 1. Statistical issues in assessing the state of the Japanese economy

Different types of statistics have pointed to diverging economic trends since the beginning of 1999. For the most part, expenditure-based estimates have been very volatile compared with key supply side indicators, such as the index of tertiary sector activity and industrial production. For example, the expenditure-based estimates pointed to two quarters of negative growth in the second half of 1999, and then a first quarter of 2000 rebound in activity of 10 per cent. However, such supply indicators show a smoother rebound for growth. The index of aggregate production points to continued growth in the second half of 1999 and through the first half of this year. The GDP estimates for the second quarter indicated a slowing of growth to 4¼ per cent.

The main concern with the GDP estimates appears to be in the critical area of private consumption, the bulk of GDP. Unlike most other countries, estimates are constructed from the household survey. The information is, however, based on a rather small sample (8 000 households) which may not be fully adequate. The survey also excludes single-person households, whose consumption grew rapidly in 1999. There are also problems with other indicators of private consumption. The sample for retail sales appears to be biased toward large stores and supermarkets, which have been losing market share to new operators such as speciality and convenience stores, and discount operators.

As for statistics on public investment, the information concerning the expenditure on public works programmes, most importantly by local government, which comprise a significant part of the total expenditure, is limited. Survey-based construction indicators on progress in public works are published on a monthly basis but cover only 80 per cent of GDP-relevant public investment. However, in recent years there has been a tendency for actual expenditures at local government level to diverge markedly from plans and from the survey information.

The method for removing seasonal patterns has also been subject to criticism. The EPA has so far used X11 for the quarterly GDP estimates without adjusting for trading days which, in combination with a long data series, appears not to fully identify the evolution of seasonal patterns during the past decade. The decision of the EPA to stay with this procedure was based on a study in 1997, which showed no statistically significant effect of trading days on private consumption.

Concerns over deflation have focused attention on the deficiencies of price statistics. The CPI is based on the weights calculated from the household survey (changed every five years), and currently excludes a number of goods whose prices are decreasing rapidly such as mobile phones, new telecom operators, and computer equipment. This might lead to an under-estimation of deflation, one study suggesting by as much as 1 per cent per year although the degree of uncertainty is great. On the other hand, a comparison of the CPI and the WPI for a comparable set of goods prices suggests that the outlet bias could be small. The BOJ and MCA have been examining issues related to price indices.

Box 1. Statistical issues in assessing the state of the Japanese economy (*cont.*)

In light of the above mentioned concerns, the EPA established a working group of statisticians in April 2000 to recommend improvements, which were implemented when the EPA shifted to 93SNA and re-based the national accounts in October 2000. The main changes include:

- Utilising the current quarterly survey of single-person households to estimate their consumption expenditures rather than using a proxy.
- Introducing a trading day correction *via* the X12 ARIMA procedure for original data and calculating the new correction factors from a shorter time series.
- The working group has also started to discuss the methods used in estimating public investment, and to this end, the EPA has begun to collect more accurate data on expenditures by central and prefectural governments and major cities.

Moreover, the interim report of the EPA and Management and Co-ordination Agency's (MCA) joint committee suggested introducing a new supplementary household survey to cover large outlays, such as for motor vehicles and some expensive consumer durable purchases, and which would also cover gross expenditures and incomes.

Figure 2. **Industrial production and inventories**

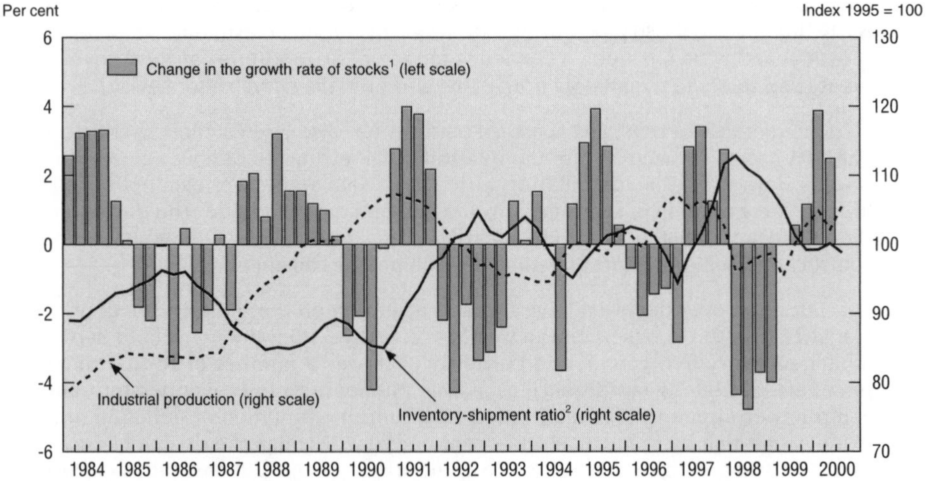

1. Change in the year-on-year growth rate of stocks of finished products in manufacturing industry.
2. The inventory-shipment ratio covers finished products of manufacturing industry.

Source: Ministry of International Trade and Industry.

Table 1. **Business investment by industry and firm size**[1]

Year-on-year growth in per cent

	1995	1996	1997	1998	1999	1999				2000	
						Q1	Q2	Q3	Q4	Q1	Q2
Industry, total	1.7	8.3	7.4	–11.6	–8.7	–10.5	–13.4	–9.6	–0.7	3.3	2.2
Manufacturing industry	7.4	7.0	9.0	–2.6	–18.4	–19.1	–24.6	–20.2	–8.2	–6.1	3.4
Materials	1.7	0.7	2.5	–2.2	–22.0	–24.3	–21.6	–25.4	–15.1	–16.8	3.5
of which:											
Chemicals	–0.1	9.3	15.5	–3.0	–20.7	–21.9	–21.4	–24.6	–13.1	–12.9	–3.4
Iron and steel	2.8	–14.5	–13.3	3.0	–14.6	–17.7	–8.6	–12.8	–18.5	–18.8	–20.6
Processed	10.6	10.2	12.0	–2.8	–16.8	–16.7	–25.7	–18.1	–5.0	–1.8	3.3
of which:											
Industrial machinery	10.0	13.5	10.2	17.8	–23.9	1.5	–38.5	–48.2	14.8	–35.9	–2.7
Electrical machinery	28.8	5.6	6.3	–7.2	–12.0	–24.6	–25.1	0.2	12.9	18.9	18.0
Transportation machinery	2.7	14.1	30.0	6.4	–20.3	–14.3	–27.8	–19.7	–21.7	–14.0	–16.8
Large firms	7.8	6.2	5.8	1.1	–20.3	–22.3	–25.0	–19.1	–13.3	–5.0	2.1
Medium-sized firms	6.0	9.7	14.3	–13.7	–13.0	–16.0	–26.4	–4.0	–4.3	–2.8	18.1
Small firms	7.0	7.8	16.5	–6.9	–15.3	–6.7	–21.6	–31.9	7.3	–13.0	–1.7
Non-manufacturing industry	–0.8	8.9	6.7	–15.9	–3.3	–5.8	–6.6	–3.4	2.9	7.7	1.6
of which:											
Construction	–4.3	–13.3	–7.0	–16.7	–3.2	3.4	–15.1	1.5	–4.6	11.5	–8.9
Wholesale and retail	1.5	5.9	7.5	–15.9	–8.0	–22.6	7.1	–23.2	13.1	31.2	–5.6
Real estate	–9.0	21.1	–11.2	–10.8	–2.0	39.9	–5.2	–13.7	–33.3	–8.9	38.1
Transportation and communication	3.4	6.9	15.9	–18.4	0.9	13.2	–11.8	–4.7	0.5	–16.5	–13.2
Electric utilities	–8.4	1.3	–7.5	–7.9	–10.6	–18.2	4.1	–11.0	–11.3	–7.1	–13.6
Services	2.3	19.4	13.8	–19.1	–0.9	–15.9	–13.4	11.2	17.2	32.7	17.3
Large firms	–2.1	4.1	4.1	–8.0	–6.6	–6.6	–8.7	–5.8	–5.5	5.1	–4.2
Medium-sized firms	0.4	23.7	0.3	–12.3	–6.4	–0.1	–12.5	–9.3	–5.5	–15.0	–0.2
Small firms	1.6	11.5	16.3	–33.4	7.8	–7.7	3.1	6.0	33.4	34.2	16.2

1. Firm classification: Large firms are those with a capital of 1 billion yen and over, medium-sized firms: 100 million to 1 billion yen, and small firms: 10 to 100 million yen.

Source: Ministry of Finance.

Table 2. **Recent monthly indicators**

Year-on-year growth rates

	1999		2000			2000	
	Q3	Q4	Q1	Q2	Q3	Aug.	Sep.
Household consumption expenditure (all households, real)	–0.4	–3.1	–1.4	–0.8	–2.1	–4.1	0.4
Retail store sales	–2.0	–1.5	–1.9	–2.5	–1.1	–1.3	–1.5
Auto sales (including compact cars)	1.1	–3.9	2.5	3.8	0.6	5.0	–0.8
Household appliance sales	8.2	4.3	7.6	3.7	2.1	–11.4	8.1
Consumer sentiment index	40.2	41.5	42.2	43.1	43.3	–	–
Housing starts (s.a.a.r. 1 000 units)	1 241	1 171	1 254	1 234	1 201	1 219	1 220
Machinery orders (s.a.)[1]	2.3	8.7	4.9	3.1	8.2	26.6	–16.5
Public works contracts	–8.2	–12.7	–7.7	–12.6	–11.7	–7.1	–10.8
Exports volume (s.a.)[1]	4.6	2.5	5.8	0.0	–0.1	7.5	–2.9
Imports volume (s.a.)[1]	1.7	6.0	1.2	3.4	–0.2	10.3	–5.9
Production (s.a.)[1]	2.7	1.4	0.8	1.7	1.6	3.4	–3.4
Inventories (s.a.)[1]	–1.1	–1.7	2.4	–0.1	–0.8	0.3	–1.0
Inventory/shipments (s.a. 1995 = 100)	100.9	99.0	100.0	98.5	99.0	96.0	99.0
Tertiary sector activities (s.a.)	0.7	0.3	0.6	1.1	0.5	1.2	–1.1
All sector activities (s.a.)	0.9	02	0.3	1.8	0.3	1.3	–1.5
Job offers to job applicants ratio (s.a.)	0.47	0.49	0.52	0.57	0.61	0.62	0.62
Unemployment rate (s.a. per cent)	4.7	4.6	4.8	4.7	4.7	4.6	4.7
Overtime working hours	–0.3	1.4	3.5	4.0	3.9	3.3	4.2
Number of employees	–0.4	–0.4	–0.4	0.4	0.7	0.2	0.8
Total wage payments	–0.9	–1.2	0.6	1.2	0.4	1.0	1.0
Domestic wholesale prices	–1.3	–0.7	–0.1	0.3	0.2	0.2	0.1
Consumer price index	0.0	–1.0	–0.7	–0.7	–0.7	–0.8	–0.8
Money supply (M2 + CD)	3.6	3.0	2.2	2.3	1.9	1.8	1.9
Number of bankruptcies	–13.2	4.5	44.0	21.3	20.5	18.5	16.4

1. Change from previous period.
Source: Economic Panning Agency and Bank of Japan.

While an acceleration of investment activity is underway, it is also necessary to bear in mind the negative factors which were described in last year's *Survey*: excess capital stock and an investment share of GDP which is much too high for an economy facing a potential growth rate of only around 1½ per cent. The cumulative decline in business investment by more than 13 per cent between 1998 and 1999 has alleviated the level of excess capacity, but it could still remain a serious problem. Using managers' judgement about capital stock in the *Tankan* Survey, the EPA (2000*b*) estimated that the size of excess capital stock (measured in 1990 constant prices) peaked at 56 trillion yen in the first quarter of 1999 before declining by some 7 per cent to 52 trillion yen at the end of the year. This estimate is not so different from that obtained by comparing the actual capital/potential output ratio with an extrapolation of its past trend: some 55 trillion yen at the end of 1999 (Figure 3). This excess capacity is likely to be a drag on investment, although the magnitude depends on various factors, including expected future growth and the speed of adjustment. According to an EPA (2000*c*) survey, most of the managers of major companies think it will take two years or longer to adjust their company's production capacity[3] to its optimal level. Moreover, they judged that the economy will grow by 1.3 (1.5) per cent per annum on average for the next 3 (5) years. Combining the simple estimate of excess capacity of some 55 trillion yen with these perceptions in the business community implies that business investment would be stagnant for some time. For example, if the adjustment period and the real GDP growth rate are assumed to be 3 years and 1.5 per cent, respectively (*i.e.* slightly more optimistic than the managers), business investment could grow only marginally at 0.9 per cent per year. Shortening the adjustment period by 1 year would reduce the growth rate to –4.5 per cent per year.

Reconciling these two forces – an investment recovery with evidence of substantial excess capacity and an excessive investment/GDP ratio – is not easy and accounts for the widely differing views about future developments. Structural

Figure 3. **The ratio of real capital stock to potential output in the business sector**

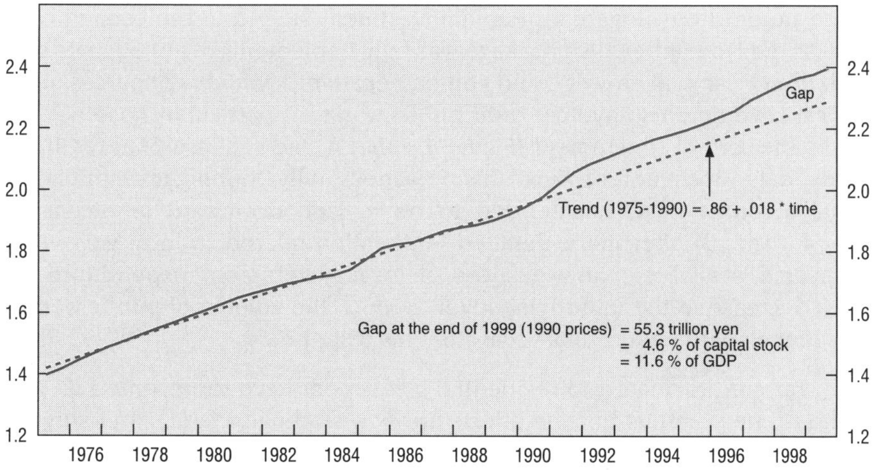

Source: OECD.

change is an important element to be considered in the reconciliation. A salient feature of the present situation is that the pressure on individual sectors to restructure is much greater than before. An index of differences in productivity growth across industries, which can be considered as a measure of pressure for structural change, is now substantially higher than in previous periods of adjustment as in 1972-74 and again in 1985 (Matsuoka and Calderwood, 1999). Moreover, a dispersion index of stock market prices is now twice what it was in 1985 at the height of pressures to adjust to a strong exchange rate.[4] In these circumstances, it is reasonable to suppose that investment will be driven by some sectors and branches, and that the aggregate measure of excess capital stock (in a putty-clay view) may indicate very little about the behaviour of investment. Production capacity fell by 2.5 per cent in the second quarter of 2000 from its peak in the fourth quarter of 1997, even as investment increased. Some industries will run down their capital stock by failing to replace it, but this will not directly lead to a decline in GDP, although it may well be a serious problem for the financial sector if the associated debt needs to be written off.[5] Expanding sectors and branches need, however, to invest for expansion while others may indeed do both. Some sectors report a decline in capacity at the same time that investment intentions and activity have risen.[6]

... although the fiscal stimulus was not strong

Public sector demand gave an important impetus to the recovery in the first half of 1999, but thereafter the contribution to growth has been negative. Government consumption was flat in the second half of 1999, while public investment plummeted by 19.3 per cent (s.a.a.r.) as the effects of the November 1998 package petered out (Figure 4). Public investment surged in the second quarter of 2000 as the November 1999 package was fully implemented, although its overall contribution to annual growth could still be negative. A variety of sources indicate that local governments have cut their public works, in particular those not subsidised by the central government (Figure 4, Panel A, and see also Chapter II). Since monthly data does not capture this weakness fully, public investment on a national accounts basis has tended to be revised downward in recent years (Figure 4, Panel B) after more detailed information related to local governments has become available. The weakness of local government expenditure could imply a decrease in the underlying level to which the volume of public works will return after all of the additional fiscal stimulus disappears.

Tax credits related to residential investment have represented an important short-term stimulus but the effects are now starting to fade. After surging by more than 10 per cent in the first half of 1999, residential investment has remained flat during the following twelve months. However, as housing starts show (Figure 5), there have been a number of changes in the composition of investment.

Figure 4. **Public works and public investment**

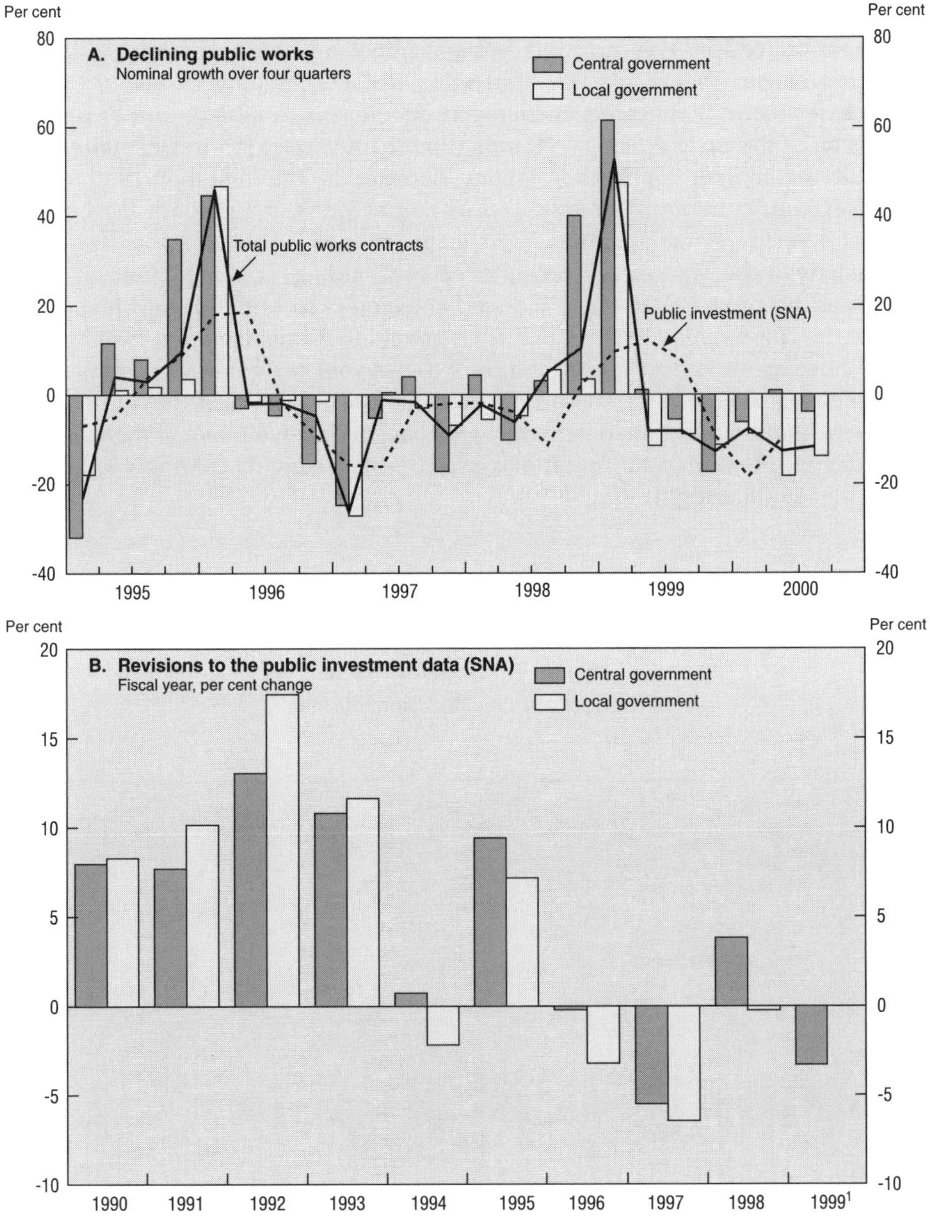

1. Revised estimate is not available.

Source: Economic Planning Agency.

Construction of owner-occupied houses, in particular ones financed by the Housing Loan Corporation (HLC), has fallen but this has been largely offset by a significant increase in starts of housing for sale such as condominiums. The tax credit introduced in 1999 not only brought about a boom in building of owner-occupied houses, but also stimulated sales of condominiums in the first half of 1999. A decline in inventories encouraged developers to initiate further projects. Extension of the tax credit by 6 months to mid-2001 (decided in December 1999) has left the market for condominiums buoyant in the first half of this year. However, with condominium starts appearing to peak, a 13-month lag between start and residence registration,[7] and stagnant loan applications to the HLC's programmes,[8] the stimulatory policy effects are fading. Looking ahead, it is evident that the programmes have induced consumers to bring forward investment so that the combination of the stock adjustment mechanism, current over-capacity of the housing stock and fewer members of the younger generation may lead to weak housing demand for some time to come. Introduction of fixed-term rental contracts (implemented in March) may only have a positive effect at the margin on investment in buildings for rental purposes because existing contracts will remain in force[9] (see Chapter III).

Figure 5. **Housing starts**
Seasonally adjusted, annual rates

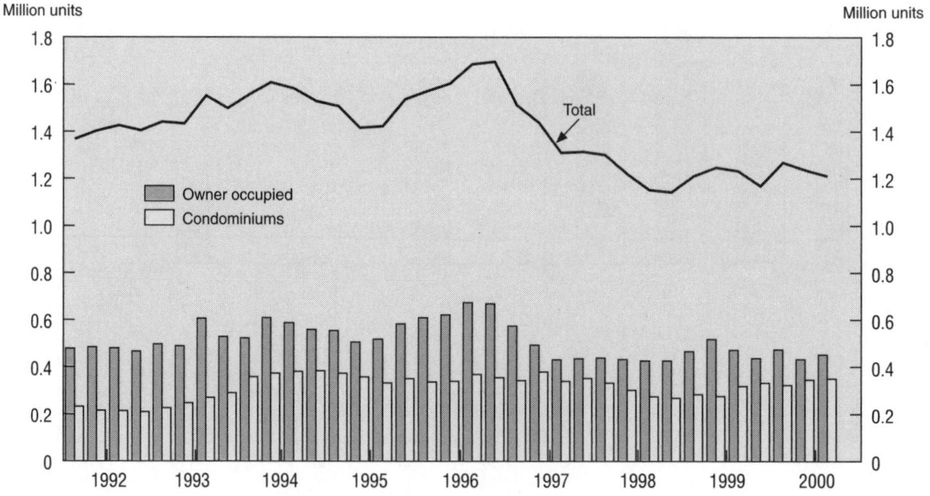

Source: Ministry of Construction and Economic Planning Agency.

Labour market adjustment has continued

The pressure to cut the level of employment has eased during the past year. According to a survey by the Ministry of Labour (MOL), the share of companies adopting measures to decrease employment toward desired levels peaked in late 1998 or the first half of 1999 and has since declined.[10] Moreover, based on managers' judgement in the *Tankan* Survey, the EPA (2000*b*) has estimated the number of excess employees to be 1.4 million persons (about 2.2 per cent of total employment) in March 2000, down sharply by 42 per cent from 2.4 million persons in June 1999. Again, the estimate is not far from the result of a simple calculation. Figure 6 shows that the labour share in GDP, which surged in the mid-1970s, has fluctuated in the range between 53 and 57 per cent. If the deviation from the average since the mid-1970s (54.9 per cent) is assumed to be "excessive" and that a correction is made only through cutting employment, the necessary reduction would be 2.7 per cent of employees.[11] Figure 6 also shows that the failure of wages to adjust downwards fully to cope with the costs of ageing may be largely responsible for the necessary adjustment: wage payments themselves are almost equal to the long-term average. Contributions to social security and to other funds have increased in line with ageing of the population, from 5 per cent in 1975 to 8.5 per cent in 1998. Cutting personnel costs is likely to be more time consuming than

Figure 6. **Labour share in GDP**

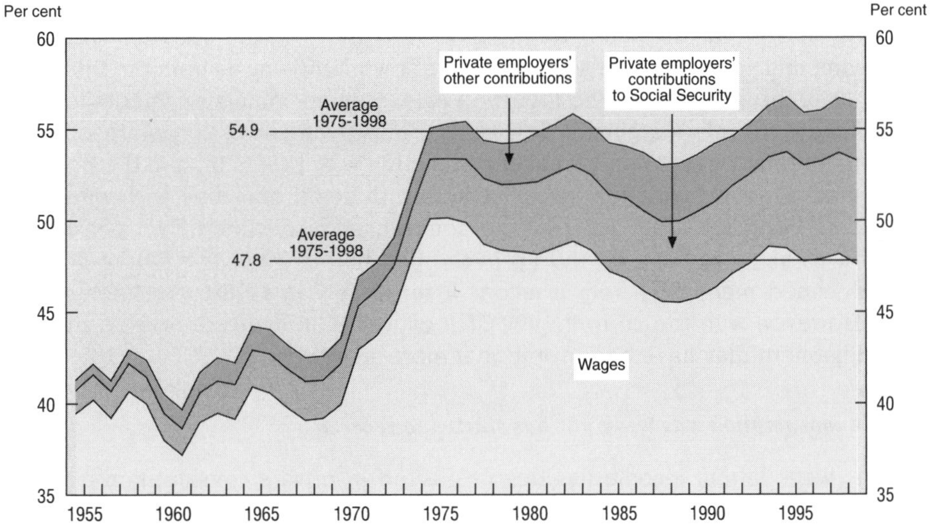

Source: Economic Planning Agency.

other costs. According to EPA's (2000c) survey of managers of major corporations, about 45 per cent of them think it may take more than two years until labour costs are reduced to optimal levels and nearly a half of them judge the required adjustment to be some 5 to 10 per cent. Adjusting the number of employed may take somewhat longer: nearly 60 per cent of them think it would take "more than two years".

Despite the existence of aggregate excess employment, there are a number of expanding companies and sectors whose labour demand has become more pronounced and which signals the need for a reallocation of labour. The actual number of employed was down 0.4 per cent in the third quarter, in comparison with 1999, while the rate of unemployment has remained at a high level,[12] temporarily rising to a record high of 4.9 per cent in March 2000. But overtime hours started to increase in the third quarter of 1999, particularly in manufacturing, and in the non-manufacturing sector part-time employment has risen rapidly. Employment of specialists has increased 3 per cent year-on-year, while that of management has fallen by 4 per cent and by the third quarter total employment had risen for three consecutive months. Signs of employment mismatch, which might prove temporary, have increased. Rising labour demand has led to an increase in job offers of some 24 per cent in the third quarter of 2000 relative to a year earlier and the ratio of job offers to applicants has also risen by about the same proportion.[13] The ratio of vacancies for part-time workers to applicants rose to 2¼ in the third quarter, much higher than around 0.6 for all workers.

Payments for overtime increased rapidly through 1999 and into this year, but the development of total wage income per worker was dominated by another sizeable decline in the winter bonus in 1999 (Figure 7). The situation has been improving this year with total wage income per worker rising as from the first quarter of 2000, the first time in the last two years. Summer bonus payments for 2000 have increased only marginally despite the improvement of corporate profits.[14] Overall, there appears to be a weaker connection with profits than in the past and there is also a wide variation across sectors with some branches and companies paying no bonuses at all. Total labour compensation declined by 1 per cent in 1999 but is likely to have picked up in the first half of 2000. The labour share of GDP declined marginally from a record level of 56.7 in 1998 to 56.4 per cent in 1999. However, with the current 1999 GDP estimate likely to be revised upward, the adjustment may have been somewhat more significant.

Private consumption was weak but has started to recover

Weak labour income has been reflected in private consumption although whether it remained stagnant or actually fell in 1999 is unclear. The national accounts measure, which is derived largely from the Household Survey, indicates that consumption fell at an annual rate of 1 per cent in the second half of 1999 – with a

Figure 7. **Wage and salary developments**
Enterprises with more than 5 employees
Per cent change over four quarters

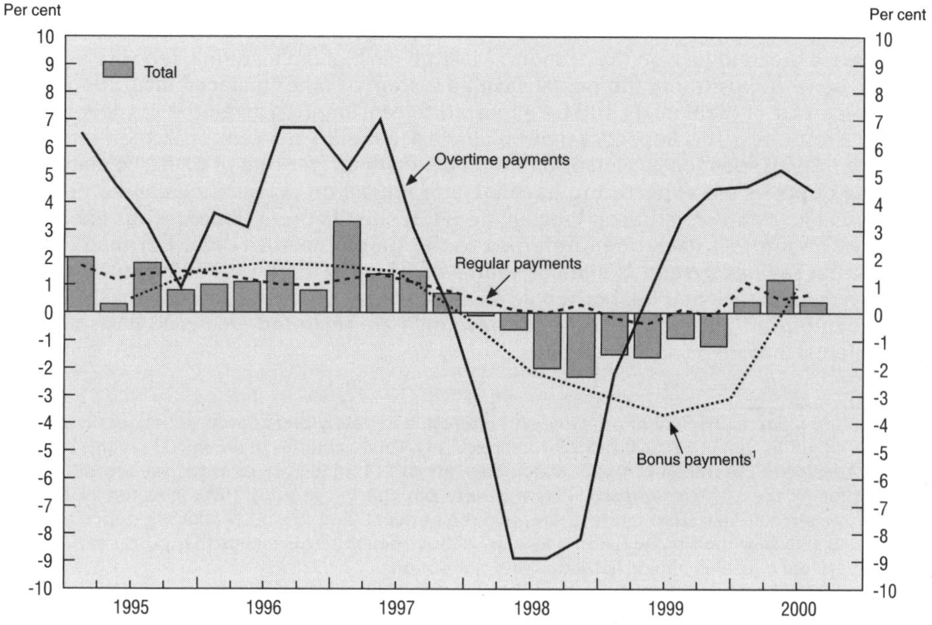

1. Only summer (June to August) and winter (November to January) bonuses are plotted.
Source: Ministry of Labour, Monthly Labour survey.

dramatic fall in the last quarter – while shipments data show a gradual growth (see Box 1). Expenditures on durable goods were weak because of stock adjustment and a fall in the winter bonus.[15] However, consumer sentiment has continued to improve, reflecting an improving labour market, and the propensity to consume (in the Household Survey) has shown some recovery since the second quarter of 1999. Weak incomes were thus responsible for lower consumption rather than an exogenous increase in the propensity to save. With labour incomes recovering, private consumption has started to pick up in the first half of this year, growing by some 3 per cent with car sales surging by about 15 per cent. Consumer sentiment and the propensity to consume have continued to improve further, despite a significant rise in the number of bankruptcies in the course of the first half. In addition, maturing postal savings accounts are expected to give some positive impulse to consumption this year (Box 2).

Box 2. Withdrawal of postal savings

About 106 trillion yen (21 per cent of GDP) of 10-year term deposits in the postal savings system will mature in FY 2000 and 2001 and this is expected to have a broad impact on the economy.[1] Even if most of the maturing deposits were to be re-deposited in the postal savings system or other financial institutions,[2] some part of them might still be allocated to consumption given the low level of interest rates. This impact cannot be ignored: a mere 1 per cent of accrued interest income spent on consumption would be worth 0.1 per cent of GDP. The maturing deposits are expected to have a major impact on tax revenues and on the Fiscal Investment and Loan Programme (FILP, see Chapter II) because tax liabilities on interest have been deferred to the time of maturity and because the postal savings system is a major source of funds to the FILP. The deferred tax payment means that the household savings rate on a national accounts basis has been biased upwards because tax payments are recorded on a cash basis and interest income on an accrual basis.

1. The figure is the sum of principal and interest, and yearly breakdowns are about 58 and 48 trillion yen in FY 2000 and 2001, respectively. Total liabilities of the postal savings system were 260 trillion yen as of March 2000, about 213 trillion yen of which was accounted for by the 10-year deposits. This was very popular in the early 1990s because of the (relatively) high fixed interest rate, about 6 per cent, and flexibility allowing depositors to withdraw their money after 6 months without penalty. This means that postal savings system effectively holds liabilities with put options.
2. According to the ministry, about 54 per cent (11.9 trillion yen) of the term-deposits maturing from April to October 2000 (22.1 trillion yen) have been re-deposited with the postal savings term-deposits.

The contribution of net exports to the recovery has been small

The contribution of net exports has not been large in the current recovery. Although the currency has appreciated since the summer of 1998 by more than 20 per cent in effective terms, export volumes have increased rapidly from the second half of 1998. Export growth has been underpinned by rapid market growth, especially in Asian countries with exports to the region expanding at an annual rate of some 20 per cent into this year (Table 3). IT-related exports are responsible for a third of the total growth (EPA, 2000*b*). Import volumes have also increased rapidly – and faster than domestic demand – leading to further market penetration. At the same time, trade with Asian countries has become more "horizontal" in nature, rather than "vertical".[16] The yen's appreciation has cut export prices, but its effects on import prices have been offset by the rise in oil-related import prices. As a result, the terms-of-trade deteriorated in the second half of 1999, but

Table 3. **External trade**

	1996	1997	1998	1999	Seasonally adjusted annual rates 1999 1st half	1999 2nd half	2000 1st half
	Trillion yen						
A. Balance of payments							
Trade	9.1	12.3	16.0	14.1	14.6	13.5	14.1
Exports	43.6	49.5	48.9	45.8	45.3	46.3	49.2
Imports	34.5	37.2	32.9	31.7	30.6	32.8	35.1
Services	–6.8	–6.5	–6.5	–6.2	–6.1	–6.3	–5.1
Investment income	5.8	6.7	7.4	5.7	6.0	5.4	6.2
Transfers	–1.0	–1.1	–1.1	–1.4	–1.7	–1.1	–1.0
Current account	7.2	11.4	15.8	12.2	12.9	11.5	14.3
Per cent of GDP	1.4	2.3	3.2	2.5	2.6	2.3	2.9
	Percentage change from previous year						
B. Trade in goods (customs basis), 1995 = 100							
Volume							
Exports	1.2	11.8	–1.3	2.1	–2.2	6.5	13.5
United States	–4.0	13.1	5.4	4.3	1.4	7.2	7.9
EU	–1.0	18.2	13.4	–1.4	–3.7	1.1	8.1
Asia	1.7	6.4	–15.3	9.7	1.4	18.1	22.2
Imports	5.6	1.7	–5.3	9.6	6.3	12.9	11.6
Manufactures	8.3	3.1	–5.9	13.1	8.0	18.3	17.5
Unit value							
Exports	6.4	1.9	0.7	–8.1	–6.9	–9.1	–4.1
Imports	14.0	6.0	–5.5	–12.4	–14.6	–9.9	2.0

Source: Bank of Japan, *Balance of Payments Monthly*; Japan Tariff Association, *Summary Report of Trade of Japan*, and OECD.

strengthened somewhat in the first half of this year (on a seasonally adjusted basis). The faster growth of import volumes than export volumes and the loss in the terms-of-trade reduced the current account surplus to 2¼ per cent of GDP in the second half of 1999. The invisibles balance has improved in the first half of this year, helping to lift the current account surplus to around 3 per cent (Table 3). As for capital transactions, both outward and inward direct investment increased substantially in FY 1999 (Table 4). A significant role for foreign capital in restructuring Japanese firms is reflected in a rapid rise in inward investment in recent years, though the level is still low relative to GDP (½ per cent) compared with other OECD Member countries. Inward investment has tended to take the form of friendly M&A in machinery, telecommunication and finance, and greenfield investments in retail, services and software (Takahashi and Ohyama, 2000).

Table 4. **Recent foreign direct investment flows**
Notifications, billion yen, fiscal years beginning 1 April

	1994	1995	1996	1997	1998	1999
Outward investment	4 281	4 957	5 409	6 623	5 217	7 439
of which to:						
United States	1 802	2 185	2 479	2 549	1 321	2 487
Cayman Islands, Panama	201	226	231	449	709	408
Asia	1 008	1 192	1 308	1 495	836	799
United Kingdom	226	333	387	505	1 252	1 307
Netherlands	110	144	124	404	271	1 156
France	44	156	57	213	67	126
Other Europe	273	195	263	253	204	200
Oceania	151	272	101	253	283	100
of which:						
Manufacturing	1 443	1 824	2 282	2 373	1 569	4 719
Finance and insurance	687	527	876	1 469	2 096	1 103
Real estate	539	581	700	679	360	236
Services	718	1 035	456	795	263	481
Inward investment	433	370	771	678	1 340	2 399
of which from:						
United States	160	177	239	152	808	249
Latin America	14	14	66	59	34	290
Asia	27	25	137	74	21	110
United Kingdom	12	11	41	49	37	90
Netherlands	52	54	80	146	128	471
France	7	11	11	9	17	746
Other Europe	80	52	88	108	120	107
Foreign-owned companies in Japan	31	23	100	84	173	162
of which:						
Manufacturing	197	141	311	267	313	980
Finance and insurance	67	100	27	162	457	512
Commerce and trade	109	68	166	100	176	349
Telecommunications	3	5	2	3	17	330
Real estate	3	2	27	48	42	17
Services	36	49	236	89	318	206

Source: Ministry of Finance.

Deflation tendencies have weakened

Price developments present a very mixed picture with deflation continuing, although there are no indications of a downward spiral developing. At the most general level, the domestic demand deflator declined by 1 per cent in the second half of 1999 but the decline picked up to 1½ per cent in the first half of 2000. Greater attention has often been given to the GDP deflator, which has continued to decline in the first half at 1.8 per cent (Figure 8). The rate of deflation

Figure 8. **Inflation indicators**

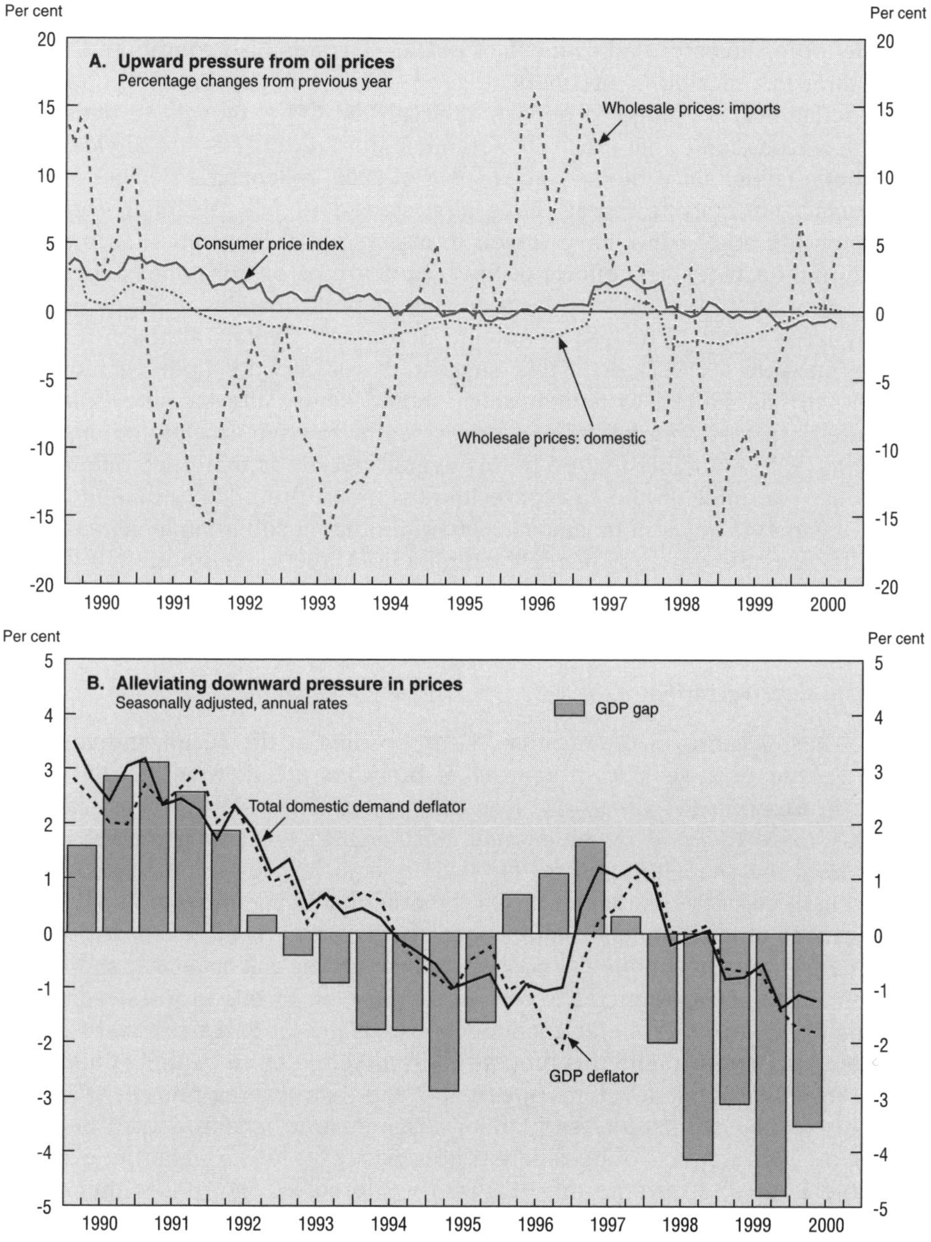

Source: OECD.

of domestic wholesale prices has moderated since the third quarter of 1999, and prices have even been rising since March 2000 for the first time in more than eight years if the effects of the consumption tax hike in April 1997 are excluded. The completion of inventory adjustment of producer goods also contributed to this trend through a pick-up in intermediate goods prices since spring 1999. Consumer price deflation has tended to persist, although the CPI is thought to understate price decreases somewhat (Box 1). A notable feature recently is that service prices have been falling since the second quarter of 2000, reflecting a decline of wage payments, and housing rentals have also started to fall. Declining consumer prices, on the other hand, have served to maintain real household incomes and consumption activity. The effects of the oil price hike on consumer prices have been rather limited, cushioned by a decline in profit margins of intermediaries and by large stocks of refined petroleum products.[17] Overall, although the GDP gap is sizeable – OECD estimates suggest it was around 4 per cent of GDP in 1999 – it has started to narrow which should slowly alleviate the downward pressure on prices. The fall in land prices seems to have accelerated since the spring of 1999. A notable feature in this overall decline is that price differentials have been widening. In the case of residential areas, the price decline in central Tokyo was only 3 per cent in January 2000, while that in suburban areas was much larger, for example nearly 15 per cent in Chiba (EPA, 2000*d*). This pattern is just the opposite to what was observed during the first half of the 1990s when there was a fairly even decline in land prices across geographical areas.

The state of restructuring

Restructuring of the economy is proceeding at the sector and company level. On the positive side, a number of branches are growing rapidly, based either on expanding IT demands or on the uses of IT, and in this sense Japan is certainly close to world developments. Mismatch in the labour market in part stems from the changing demand for skills due to this restructuring and is discussed in more detail in Chapter III. On the other hand, a number of firms are still in the throes of restructuring their balance sheets, and it is not even clear that in many cases they can continue to survive as their sectors will invariably shrink. The rising number of bankruptcies is only one indication of this process, which was temporarily delayed by credit guarantees, especially for SMEs (Figure 9). Larger firms are also involved and this process is discussed in more detail in Chapter III. At the macroeconomic level, it appears that the restructuring process still has a long way to run: profitability and labour costs, despite recent marked improvements, are still at levels quite different from past experience when the economy was able to grow at a rapid rate (Figure 10). Moreover, enterprises themselves report high levels of excess capital and labour which they judge will take some two to three years to correct – if, as they assume, the economy continues to grow only slowly.

Figure 9. **Credit guarantees delayed bankruptcies in 1999**

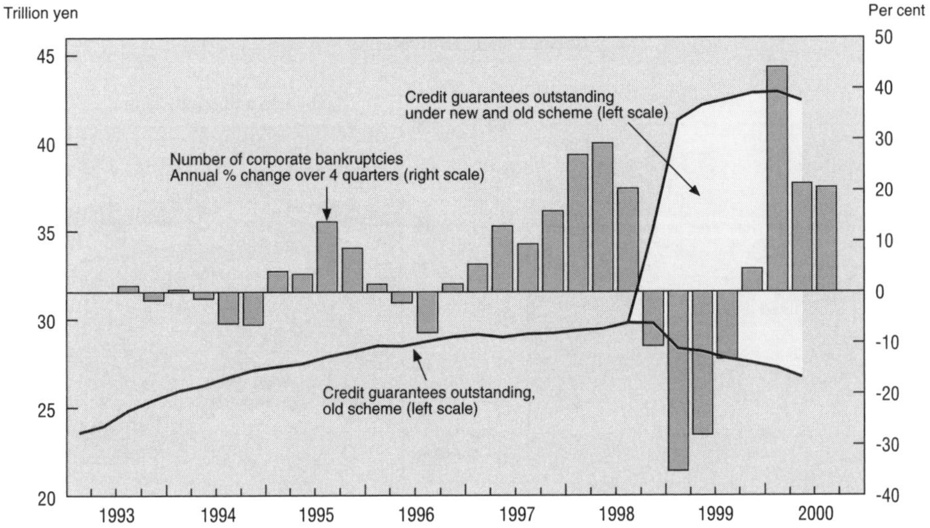

Source: Tokyo Shoko Research Ltd., Bank of Japan and Ministry of International Trade and Industry.

Prospects and risks

The projections for Japan presented here are those reported in the *Economic Outlook* 68 which was released in November 2000. Although world trade is projected to slow from 13.4 per cent in 2000 to 9.4 per cent and 7.9 per cent in 2001 and 2002, respectively, global activity would still constitute a favourable backdrop for continued moderate growth in Japan. The projections are based on the following assumptions:

– The supplementary budget passed in November 2000 will lift public works expenditures by some 2½ trillion yen with the bulk of the stimulus taking effect in the first half of 2001. This estimate is lower than in the fiscal package since local governments are assumed to continue to reduce their unsubsidised investment expenditures. Moreover, 1.4 trillion yen of expenditures in the supplementary budget are expected to be largely transfers and subsidies to other government institutions and so will not influence directly the overall fiscal stance. The initial FY 2001 budget is assumed to be almost comparable to the initial FY 2000 budget, following a guideline decided by the Cabinet in August. An increase in expenditure on social security by 750 billion yen is incorporated. For 2002, it is assumed that there will be no further fiscal stimulus packages and that local governments continue to reduce their own public works spending towards a level 5 trillion yen lower than in 1997, before the series of stimulus packages. The

Figure 10. **Corporate sector financial indicators**
Per cent, four-quarter moving averages, current prices

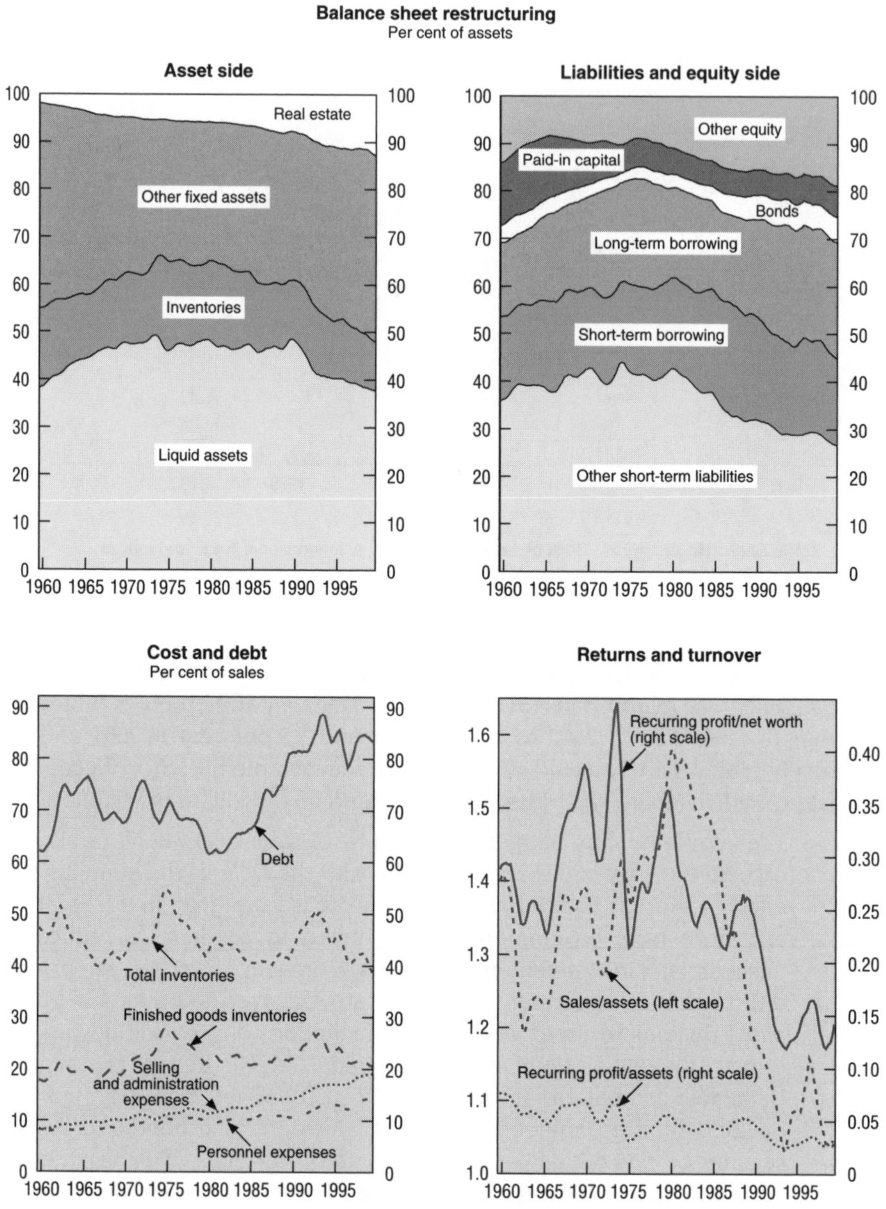

Source: Ministry of Finance.

underlying structural deficit is thus projected to tighten by 1 per cent of GDP in 2002, after broad neutrality in 2001.

- There will be no further change in monetary policy with the overnight rate remaining constant at 0.25 per cent. The three-month rate is assumed to drift upwards somewhat and the ten-year JGB to rise from 1.8 per cent to around 2¼ per cent in 2002.
- The yen rate is fixed at 108.80 yen per dollar (and the euro at 0.864 per dollar), while the oil price is assumed to be $30 per barrel up to mid-2001, thereafter declining gradually to $27 by the second half of 2002 (as in *Economic Outlook* 68).

GDP is expected to have increased by 2 per cent in CY 2000 and, after a temporary acceleration to around 2¼ per cent in 2001, growth is likely to slow thereafter to around 2 per cent.[18] Driving growth is an IT-led recovery of business investment as shown in machinery orders and surveys on business investment plans. Investment is expected to shift increasingly to IT-using sectors, supported by strong profits. However, to what extent the increase in investment will permeate into other industries is uncertain in view of over-capacity problems and stagnant orders in the construction sector. The recent rise in wage payments is likely to continue, following improvement of corporate profits, although the recovery of employment may be slow. Unemployment is projected to remain high, around 4¾ per cent, due to the weak recovery of employment and a rise in the labour force participation rate, which is currently well below its trend. With labour incomes rising and postal savings deposits maturing, private consumption is expected to continue to increase at a modest pace. On the other hand, residential investment should continue to decline as will public investment, although the latter will temporarily boost growth in the first half of 2001. The contribution from the external sector should remain limited even though the growth of exports is an important factor in the overall dynamism of the economy. The projected increase in export volumes may be offset by an increase in imports. High oil prices and the associated loss in the terms of trade will dampen growth prospects and raise prices, but with the dependence on oil much reduced, the effects should not be great. After declining to around 2½ per cent of GDP, the current account surplus is likely to recover to around 3 per cent of GDP at the end of the projection period. The domestic demand deflator should start to stabilise as the output gap declines and the one-off price reductions from deregulation normalise.

As noted above, uncertainty surrounding an assessment of the economy remains high. With regard to downside risks, structural adjustment issues remain paramount. The potential for disruptive bankruptcies cannot be excluded even though advances have been made in the legal framework, while banks remain vulnerable to both bad debts and to any marked declines in share prices. At the time of writing, the Nikkei 225 had fallen to 14 500 which, if maintained, would reduce the ability of the financial sector to deal with bad loans by squeezing the

Table 5. **Short-term outlook**[1]

	1999	2000	2001	2002	2000 1st half	2000 2nd half	2001 1st half	2001 2nd half	2002 1st half	2002 2nd half
Demand and output (volumes)										
Consumption										
Private	1.2	1.6	2.1	2.2	3.0	1.3	2.4	2.2	2.2	2.2
Government	1.3	0.2	0.5	0.6	0.1	0.2	0.7	0.5	0.6	0.6
Gross fixed investment										
Public[2]	7.8	–8.8	–1.3	–7.3	–5.6	–3.4	7.0	–14.6	–4.7	–4.7
Private residential	1.4	1.0	–4.3	–2.0	5.9	–6.8	–2.4	–5.6	–0.8	–0.8
Private non-residential	–5.9	5.4	6.3	5.5	9.4	5.2	7.3	5.5	5.5	5.5
Stockbuilding[3]	0.1	0.1	0.2	0.0	0.3	0.2	0.3	0.1	0.0	0.0
Total domestic demand	0.5	1.3	2.4	1.8	3.4	1.4	3.5	1.0	2.0	2.0
Exports of goods and services	1.9	13.6	5.5	5.3	17.0	8.0	4.5	5.0	5.1	6.0
Imports of goods and services	5.3	10.5	6.4	4.2	9.8	8.6	6.8	3.5	4.3	4.8
Net exports[3]	–0.3	0.7	0.0	0.3	1.2	0.1	–0.2	0.3	0.2	0.3
GDP	0.2	1.9	2.3	2.0	4.5	1.5	3.3	1.3	2.2	2.3
Inflation and capacity utilisation										
GDP deflator	–0.9	–1.5	–0.4	–0.2	–1.8	–0.8	–0.2	–0.4	–0.1	–0.1
Total domestic deflator	–0.9	–1.0	–0.2	–0.2	–1.5	–0.2	–0.2	–0.4	–0.1	–0.1
Private consumption deflator	–0.5	–0.5	0.0	–0.1	–0.6	–0.1	0.2	–0.1	–0.1	–0.1
Unemployment rate	4.7	4.7	4.6	4.6	4.8	4.7	4.7	4.6	4.6	4.6
Output gap	–3.8	–3.2	–2.2	–1.7	–3.3	–3.1	–2.1	–2.2	–1.9	–1.5
Memorandum items:										
Net government lending										
(per cent of GDP)	–7.0	–6.0	–6.0	–5.7						
Gross debt	105.3	112.3	118.6	124.7						
Net debt	37.8	43.6	48.8	53.6						
Short-term interest rate	0.2	0.2	0.6	0.9	0.1	0.3	0.5	0.8	0.9	0.9
Long-term interest rate	1.7	1.8	2.1	2.3	1.7	1.9	2.1	2.2	2.3	2.4
Current account (per cent of GDP)	2.5	2.8	2.7	3.0	2.9	2.7	2.6	2.8	3.0	3.1

1. Assuming an exchange rate of 108.8 to the dollar.
2. Including public corporations.
3. Contribution to GDP growth.

Source: OECD.

capital base of the banks. These factors may make the recovery fragile to various shocks, even if the shocks are insufficient in themselves to reverse the recovery trend. On the other hand, the economy is in the midst of a major restructuring so that business investment could easily accelerate. With many business expectations based on prospects for very low growth, any upward revision could result in a number of perceived barriers becoming less important.

II. Fiscal, monetary and financial-sector policies

Widely differing judgements about economic prospects and contradictory statistics have created a difficult environment for economic policy. In addition, fiscal policy has been subject to opposing considerations: a desire to support the economy, on the one hand, while wishing to hold down the build-up of debt on the other. At the same time, policy formation has been held back by the lack of timely fiscal data. The conduct of monetary policy under zero interest rates, exchange rate appreciation and balance sheet restructuring by the private sector has also been challenging. The monetary authorities now face the task of normalising monetary conditions while at the same time maintaining market expectations that monetary policy will remain accommodative. Cutting across both areas of macroeconomic policy has been the clear need to maintain long-term interest rates at a low level. Financial markets have also followed the development of structural and financial market policy quite closely reacting negatively when resolve to pursue reform has been perceived as weakening. This chapter first reviews the conduct of fiscal policy and the emerging issues of debt management and budget finance. The following section examines the evolution of monetary conditions and the conduct of monetary policy. Continuing measures to deal with problems in the financial sector are reviewed in the final section.

Fiscal policy

The government has intended to pursue a fiscal policy which would support the on-going economic recovery given uncertainties about its sustainability. The overall fiscal stimulus to the economy in CY 2000 may turn out broadly the same as CY 1999 on a general government basis, with the continuing decline in public works by local governments on their own funding mostly offset by stimulus packages. Similarly, the government has sought to maintain the fiscal stimulus with the latest supplementary budget in November 2000. Even though empirical studies are inconclusive about whether the effectiveness of fiscal policy in supporting economic activity has declined, the case for fiscal consolidation is growing as public debt is building up rapidly and conditions for its stabilisation are likely to become more difficult in the future. The reform of public finances currently under way can only reinforce the argument in favour of fiscal consolidation as the poor quality of public-sector balance sheets is made more transparent and the increased reliance on market-based financing leads to the greater likelihood of sanctions against irresponsible fiscal management. This section first reviews briefly the budgetary developments since autumn 1999 with some attention given to local governments' budgets. After assessing the overall stance of fiscal policy on a general government basis, as well as its likely impact on the economy, it ends with a discussion of difficulties in evaluating the quality of public sector balance sheets.

Continued expansionary policies

The November 1999 package and its budgetary measures

In order to ensure that the economy would stay on its recovery path, the government announced another fiscal package in November 1999 with 17 trillion yen in total expenditures (or 18 trillion yen, if those related to long-term care are taken into account) (Table 6). The package emphasised structural measures, in particular those related to SMEs. The special loan guarantee scheme, which started in October 1998, was also expanded by 10 trillion yen to 30 trillion yen, and its expiry date extended by one year to March 2001. As in the November 1998 package, the expenditure for infrastructure did not include local governments' own projects (Table 7). All these measures are reflected in the second FY 1999 supplementary budget, accounting for 6.5 out of the extra expenditure of 6.8 trillion yen (Tables 6 and 8). The difference between the two numbers, 18 trillion yen in the package

Table 6. **Fiscal measures in the November 1999 and October 2000 packages**
Trillion yen

	November 1999 package		October 2000 package	
	Amount of projects	Second FY 1999 supplementary budget allocation	Amount of projects	Expected budgetary costs
Social infrastructure investment	6.8	3.5	4.7	2.5
Measures for SMEs	7.4	0.8	4.5	0.8
Measures for promotion of residential investment	2.0	0.2	1.1 (residential investment and employment combined)	0.1
Measures for employment	1.0	0.2		
Stabilising financial system	–	0.9	–	–
IT-related measures	–	–	0.2	0.1
Disaster-related measures	–	–	0.5	0.4
Total	17.0	5.6	11.0	3.9
Memorandum item:				
Long-term care	0.9	0.9	–	–
Grand total	18.0	6.5	11.0	3.9

Source: Economic Planning Agency and Ministry of Finance.

Table 7. **Fiscal packages since 1992**

Billion yen, project cost base

	Total amount	Social infrastructure investment					Tax cuts	Others
		Public works		Building and equipment	Public works by local government	Sum of 2-5		
		General public works	Disaster relief					
	1	2	3	4	5			
28 August 1992	10 700	3 400	500	550	1 800	6 250	0	4 450
13 April 1993	13 200	3 640	530	1 150	2 300	7 620	150	5 430
16 September 1993	6 200	1 000	450	0	500	1950	0	4 200
8 February 1994	15 300	3 590	0	610	300	4 500	5 850	4 900
14 April 1995	4 600[1]	205[2]	718[2]	154[2]	0	1 077[2]	0	3 543[2]
20 September 1995	12 800	3 930	700	910	1 000	6 540	0	6 270
24 April 1998	16 700	4 500	200	1 500	1 500	7 700	4 600	4 350
16 November 1998	23 900	5 700	600	1 800	0	8 100	6 000	9 800
11 November 1999	18 000	4 486	700	1 614	0	6 800	0	11 200
19 October 2000	11 000	n.a.	500	n.a.	0	5 200	0	5 800
Cumulative	132 400	(30 451)[3]	4 898	(8 288)[3]	7 400	55 737	16 600	59 943

1. OECD estimate.
2. Budget figures, rather than project cost figures.
3. Excludes the cost of the October 2000 package.

Source: Economic Planning Agency, Ministry of Finance and OECD.

Table 8. **Central government budget**

Trillion yen

	FY 1998 Total budget	FY 1999				FY 2000 Initial budget
		Initial budget	First supplementary budget	Second supplementary budget[4]	Total budget	
Total expenditure	88.0	81.9	0.4	6.8	89.0	85.0
General spending	56.3	46.9	0.4	6.8	54.1	48.1
of which:						
Public works	16.9	9.9[5]	0.0	2.8	12.7	9.9[5]
Other	39.4	37.0	0.4	4.0	41.4	38.2
Debt servicing[1]	17.3	19.8	0.0	0.4	20.3	22.0
Transfers to local government	14.3	13.5	0.0	–0.4	13.1	14.9
Other spending	0.0	1.6	0.0	0.0	1.6	0.0
Total revenue	54.0	50.8	0.4	–0.8	50.4	52.4
Taxes	50.1	47.1	0.0	–1.5	45.6	48.7
Non-tax revenues	3.8	3.7	0.0	0.1	3.8	3.7
Surplus from previous year	0.0	0.0	0.4	0.6	1.0	0.0
Deficit[2]	34.0	31.1	0.0	7.6	38.6	32.7
Per cent of GDP	6.9	–	–	–	7.8	–
Financing:						
Construction bonds	17.1	9.3	0.0	3.8	13.1	9.2
Deficit bonds	17.0	21.7	0.0	3.7	25.4	23.5
Memorandum item:						
Net bond issuance[3]	36.8	–	–	–	32.4	–
Per cent of GDP	7.4	–	–	–	6.6	–

1. Including amortisation payments on existing debt.
2. The deficit is equal to the net issuance of government bonds (Financial Revenue Bonds).
3. Increase in outstanding stock of government bonds. Differs from footnote 2 by the change in cash balances.
4. The second supplementary budget provided only additional government guarantees to borrowing by the Deposit Insurance Corporation of 33 trillion yen.
5. Including special reserves for public works worth 0.5 trillion yen.

Source: Ministry of Finance and Bank of Japan.

and 6.5 in the supplementary budget, mainly came from the fact that the package included financing measures, 3 trillion yen of local government spending on infrastructure investment subsidised by the central government and some measures for which appropriations were made in the FY 2000 budget. Revenue estimates were revised down by 1.5 trillion yen from the initial budget (Table 8) although the revision was partially offset by other items. The resulting supplementary deficit worth 7.6 trillion yen was financed by new issuance of government bonds. The total new bond issuance in the fiscal year, 38.6 trillion yen, financed a record high level of 43.4 per cent of the total expenditures and exceeded effective tax revenues (*i.e.* excluding transfers to local governments). The Fiscal Investment and Loan Programme (FILP) was also revised to implement the fiscal package, by funding an additional 1.3 trillion yen to various organisations, notably local governments.

FY 2000 *budget*

The initial FY 2000 budget, together with the second supplementary FY 1999 budget, was also designed to support economic activity. Public works expenditures were set at the same level as in the previous initial budget,[19] hence smaller by the amount added in the supplementary budgets in FY 1999. However, taking account of implementation lags of the supplementary budget, actual public works were judged to have increased: indeed, in December 1999, the government officially estimated nominal public investment (including that of local governments) to increase by 0.7 per cent in FY 2000 on a national accounts basis. The estimate has been subsequently revised to a decline of 5½ per cent, which seems to have encouraged the government to announce another fiscal package (see below). Various efforts[20] were made to increase the efficiency of public works projects (see Chapter IV). The budgetary allocation for science and technology was boosted as FY 2000 is the final year of the five-year basic plan to strengthen basic R&D capacity. The start of long-term care raised expenditures related to social security, following on the previous year's supplementary increase. The budget also included employment-related expenditures[21] as part of the November 1999 fiscal package. Interest payments were not expected to pick up significantly[22] thanks to a decline in interest rates, but an increase in the costs of bailing-out financial institutions raised debt servicing. In fact, the provision of 4.5 trillion yen implies that the cumulative bailing-out costs are expected to exceed the initial funding of 7 trillion yen in the form of government bonds (JGBs) handed over to the Deposit Insurance Corporation (DIC).[23] Transfers to local governments were also pushed up by compensation for their revenue losses due to permanent tax cuts and other special aid to ease their financial situation, as well as by an automatic increase according to a formula to calculate the transfer, reflecting an increase in income tax revenues (mainly due to maturing postal savings).[24] Overall, total expenditure was greater in the initial FY 2000 budget than in the previous initial budget, but 4 trillion yen smaller than in the revised budget for FY 1999.

The budget foresaw a rise in tax revenues due to a special factor. A substantial amount of 10-year postal savings deposits are expected to mature in FY 2000 and 2001 (see Box 2 in Chapter I), and deferred payments of tax liabilities on interest incomes will be made. According to the official estimate, these payments may amount to 4.5 and 4.0 trillion yen in the respective fiscal years, three quarters of which is for the central government and the rest for local governments. Although corporate profits have improved, tax receipts were officially estimated to almost level-off because of investment-related tax deductions and the large volume of losses being carried forward. Revenue gains, together with reduced expenditures, are set to cut the deficit in FY 2000 by about 6 trillion yen, compared to the FY 1999 revised budget.

The expected withdrawal of postal savings has had a major impact on the FY 2000 FILP. The postal savings system, which accounted for about a fifth of the total funding of the FILP in FY 1999, will not increase its deposits with the Trust Fund Bureau (TFB) this year (Table 9). As a result, the size of the FILP will shrink by this amount, and TFB financial management is likely to be tightened. The TFB started to raise funds by selling JGBs under repurchase agreements with private agents and, when necessary, the BOJ and cut portfolio investment by a half to meet the liquidity needs. In particular, the TFB stopped rolling over its holdings of JGBs. However, the actual impact of an 8 per cent decline in available funds on general FILP (*i.e.* financing real activities of government institutions) could be minor since the funds actually utilised fell short of programmed amounts.[25]

The government announced another fiscal package in October 2000 with a more modest headline value of 11 trillion yen, compared with those of past packages (Table 7). Budgetary costs are expected to amount to 3.9 trillion yen (Table 6), which includes 2.5 trillion yen for social infrastructure and 0.8 trillion yen for financial measures for SMEs. This package is also intended to encourage structural reforms, paying special attention to IT, environment, ageing and infrastructure in urban areas. A proposal for distributing vouchers for IT training was replaced by lectures for IT beginners hosted by local governments. Perhaps more importantly, some initiatives have been promised for competition policy (see Chapter III). At the time of writing, insufficient details were available about the individual programmes to allow the OECD to form a judgement about the overall effectiveness of the package.

Local government

The mid-term estimates for FY 1999 budget outcomes (Table 10) suggest that local government expenditure is likely to have been slightly less in FY 1999 than in FY 1998, despite a slight increase envisaged in the Local Public Finance Plan (LPFP). Local governments' concern about their severe financial state is reflected in plummeting unsubsidised public works and increasing costs of debt servicing. In the absence of up-to-date information, it is unclear how the November 1999 package has been reflected in recent revisions to their budgets. Given the apparently limited effects of the November 1998 package on FY 1998 spending,[26] however, there may have been a decline in public works of some 2 trillion yen on a settlement basis in FY 1999. On the other hand, total revenues are likely to have grown, as expected, thanks to generous transfers from the central government more than offsetting a significant decline in local taxes. The deficit of local governments may have declined by some 1 trillion yen.

The FY 2000 LPFP projected total expenditure to increase slightly reflecting higher debt servicing and the introduction of long-term care, the cost of which is shared between the central and local governments. At the same time, according

Table 9. **Fiscal Investment and Loan Programme (FILP)**
Trillion yen

	FY 1998 Settlement	FY 1999		FY 2000 Initial
		Initial	Revised	
Disbursement				
Total	54.4	52.9	54.3	43.7
General FILP	37.1	39.3	40.7	37.5
Portfolio investment	17.3	13.6	13.6	6.2
of which:				
Housing Loan Corporation	6.2	10.1	10.1	10.4
Urban Infrastructure Development Corporation	1.1	1.0	1.0	1.0
Japan Policy Investment Bank[1]	3.2	2.9	3.0	2.0
National Life Finance Corporation[1]	3.6	4.2	4.2	4.2
Japan Finance Corporation for Small Businesses	1.7	2.2	2.2	2.2
Economic Co-operation Bank[1]	2.7	2.7	2.7	1.8
Japan Highway Public Corporation	2.3	2.1	2.2	2.1
Metropolitan Expressway Public Corporation	0.4	0.3	0.3	0.4
Hanshin Expressway Public Corporation	0.3	0.3	0.3	0.3
Honshu-Shikoku Bridge Authority	0.2	0.1	0.1	0.1
Local governments	10.0	7.7	8.7	7.7
Japan Finance Corporation for Municipal Businesses	1.9	1.7	1.8	1.6
Postal Savings Special Account	12.0	8.5	8.5	2.0
Pension Welfare Service Public Corporation	3.9	4.7	4.7	4.1
Postal Life Insurance Welfare Corporation	2.5	2.0	2.0	1.5
Others	2.4	2.3	2.3	2.3
Revenues				
Total	65.6	52.9	53.2	43.7
Industrial Investment Special Account	0.4	0.1	0.2	0.1
Trust Fund Bureau Fund	55.8	43.7	43.8	33.3
Postal Savings	12.2	11.5	n.a.	–
Employee/National Pension Fund	5.7	4.3	n.a.	2.7
Funds repaid and others	37.9	27.9	n.a.	30.6
Postal Life Insurance Fund	6.8	6.6	6.6	6.4
Government-guaranteed bonds and loans	2.6	2.5	2.6	3.9
Memorandum item:				
TFB's purchase of national government bonds (total)	15.2	2.8	2.8	0.0
Newly issued	11.0	0.0	0.0	0.0
Roll-over	4.2	2.8	2.8	0.0

1. The institutions were newly established in October 1999 through mergers. Figures for FY 1998 and FY 1999 are adjusted for these mergers.

Source: Ministry of Finance.

Table 10. **Local public-finance programmes (LPFP) and local budgets**[1]

Fiscal year, trillion yen

	1997			1998			1999		2000
	LPFP	After supplementary budgets (unconsolidated) (September)	Settlement (consolidated)	LPFP	After supplementary budgets (unconsolidated) (September)	Settlement (consolidated)	LPFP	After supplementary budgets (unconsolidated) (September)	LPFP
Total expenditures	87.1	109.8	97.7	87.1	112.9	100.2	88.5	112.7	88.9
of which:									
Public works	30.9	33.1	27.7	29.0	33.1	28.3	29.3	30.3	28.4
Unsubsidised	20.1	18.3	15.5	19.3	17.5	14.6	19.3	15.4	18.5
Debt servicing	9.6	10.4	10.3	10.5	11.0	10.9	11.4	11.7	12.1
Total revenues	74.9	95.0	85.8	76.1	97.8	87.7	77.2	99.1	77.8
General revenues	55.2	54.9	54.4	56.6	57.0	54.6	57.4	57.0	58.0
of which:									
Lump sum grants	17.1	16.3	17.1	17.5	17.2	18.0	21.5	20.2	22.3
Local taxes	37.0	36.3	36.2	38.5	37.2	35.9	35.3	34.3	35.1
Matching grants	13.3	15.3	14.3	13.0	15.8	15.7	13.2	16.5	13.0
Others	6.4	24.8	17.1	6.5	25.1	17.4	6.6	25.6	6.8
Deficit	12.1	14.8	11.9	11.0	15.0	12.5	11.3	13.5	11.1
Per cent of GDP		2.9	2.4		3.0	2.5		2.7	
Memorandum items:									
Debt increase (net)[2]			11			13		12	9
Per cent of GDP[2]			2.1			2.6		2.4	

1. Net figures and LPFP are adjusted for transfers among local governments while gross figures are not.
2. Actual figures up to FY1998. Figures for FY1999 and FY2000 are estimates of the Ministry of Home Affairs.

Source: Ministry of Home Affairs.

Figure 11. **Public works by local governments**

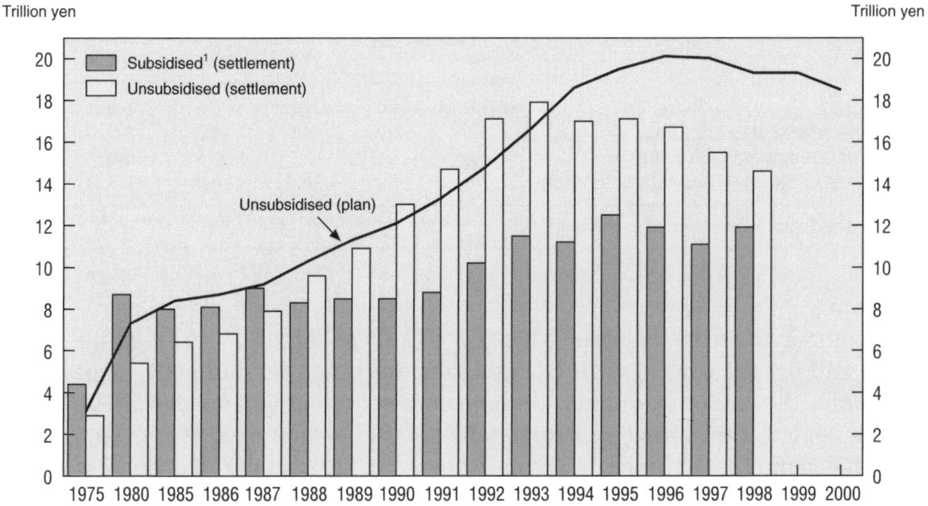

1. Subsidisation refers to cost-sharing with central government.
Source: Ministry of Home Affairs.

to the Ministry of Home Affairs (MHA), local government liabilities are expected to increase by some 9 trillion to 184 trillion yen at the end of FY 2000. One problem with the LPFP is how to make its planned public works spending more realistic. As Figure 11 shows, the actual amount of unsubsidised public works has always fallen short of the planned level since 1993 with the gap between the two widening over time, except in FY 1998. The latest LPFP reduced the planned level of this spending category by 0.8 trillion yen, which is small compared with the gap of 4 trillion yen in FY 1998. As in FY 1999, most of the increase in revenues is attributable to the lump-sum transfer from the central government. On balance, the deficit is programmed to edge down, though it may be underestimated for two reasons. First, half of the borrowing of the central government special account for transfers will have to be borne by local governments in the future. Second, local governments will have to pay some pre-determined portion of the liabilities of local public corporations.

Implications for general government balances

The OECD estimates that these developments increased the cyclically adjusted deficit of general government in relation to GDP by 1¾ percentage points in 1999 and cut it by ¾ point in 2000 (Table 11, Panel A). It should be noted that the

Table 11. **General government deficits and their international comparison**
A. General government deficits
Calendar year, per cent of GDP

	1997	1998	1999	2000	2001	2002
Net lending	–3.3	–5.0	–7.0	–6.0	–6.0	–5.7
Cyclically-adjusted net lending	–3.6	–4.2	–6.0	–5.2	–5.4	–5.3
Effects of taxes on postal savings				0.8	0.9	
Underlying cyclically-adjusted net lending	–3.6	–4.2	–6.0	–6.0	–6.3	–5.3

Source: OECD.

aforementioned effects of postal savings are likely to contribute to an improvement of 0.8 and 0.9 per cent of GDP in both calendar year 2000 and 2001, respectively. Therefore, the underlying cyclically adjusted deficit (structural deficit) would be almost neutral. The current structural deficit of 6.0 per cent of GDP in Japan is larger than that of the United States in the mid-1980s (5.2 per cent in 1986), but less than in three other episodes among G7 countries: the United Kingdom in the early 1990s (6.4 in both 1993 and 1994), Canada in the mid-1980s (7.5 in 1985) and Italy until 1996 (11.5 in 1985) Table 11, Panel B. The large current deficit may push up gross liabilities to above 120 per cent of GDP in 2002, exceeding that of Canada in the mid-1990s (101.4 per cent in 1995) and almost equal to that of Italy in the mid-1990s (124 per cent in 1994). However, financial assets held by social security funds may keep net debt and net interest payments at around 50 per cent and 1½ per cent of GDP, respectively, during the projection period, both about a half of the Italian counterparts.

Fiscal packages have stimulated aggregate demand…

Stagnation of the economy in the 1990s, despite a large number of fiscal packages (Table 7), has led many observers to doubt their effectiveness in stimulating activity. Fiscal policies have been expansionary, apart from a tightening in 1997. The OECD estimates expansionary policies as measured by the size of the deterioration in the structural deficit (8.5 per cent of GDP) could explain more than the total cumulative economic growth from 1991 to 1999 (7.9 per cent). But there seems to be no consensus about whether fiscal policy became less effective in the 1990s. Taking multiplier effects implied by various vintages of the EPA's (Keynesian type) macro-econometric models (Table 12) at face value (*i.e.* ignoring difference in specifications among models), it is possible to conclude that the effectiveness of fiscal policy declined significantly after the first oil crisis, and that underlying declining trends have continued in the 1990s (see Box 3). A more direct approach is to compare estimates based on the same model specifications between different periods. Hori *et al.* (1998) compared estimates of an EPA new version model between the two

Table 11. **General government deficits and their international comparison**

B. Comparison with other episodes of high indebtedness

	United States 1986	Japan[2] 2000	United Kingdom 1993/94	Canada 1985	Italy 1990	Italy 1985
Largest cyclically-adjusted net lending (a)						
Structural net lending (% of GDP)	–5.2	–6.0	–6.4	–7.5	–11.7	–11.5
Structural primary deficit (% of GDP)	–1.9	–4.5	–4.0	–3.5	–2.8	–4.3
Other economic indicators[1]						
Current account (% of GDP)	–3.2	2.8	–1.2	–1.7	–1.7	–0.5
Output gap (% of GDP)	–0.1	–2.9	–2.1	–0.4	1.1	–1.6
Long-term interest rates (%)	8.9	2.0	8.3	11.1	13.2	13.6
Sustainability[1]						
Imputed interest rate (b) (%)	8.1	3.5	5.9	9.8	9.2	9.9
Inflation rate of GDP deflator (c) (%)	2.8	–0.6	2.8	2.9	7.4	9.4
Potential output growth (d) (%)	3.3	1.4	2.2	2.6	2.5	2.3
Condition of sustainability ($e = b - c - d < 0$)	2.1	2.7	0.9	4.3	–0.8	–1.9
Debt outstanding in the year of largest structural deficit (f) (% of GDP)	62.6	112.8	56.2	66.4	103.7	81.9
Required primary surplus [$g = e*f/(1 + c + d)$] (% of GDP)	1.2	3.0	0.5	2.7	–	–
Required correction ($h = g - a$)[2] (% of GDP)	3.1	7.5	4.5	6.2	–	–
	1993	–	1995/97	1995	1994	1994
Peak of debt outstanding (% of GDP)	75.8	–	58.9	101.4	124.0	124.0

1. The values in the table are averages of those in the year of largest structural primary deficit and in the preceding and following years to eliminate idiosyncratic shocks in that year. As for the United Kingdom, the values are the average of those in 1992 to 1994.
2. Excluding the one-off effect of maturing postal savings (¾ per cent of GDP) and the effect of ageing on spending (3¼ per cent of GDP by 2010).

Source: OECD.

Table 12. **Fiscal multipliers[1] of EPA macro-econometric models**

	Estimation period	Year 1	Year 2	Year 3
Research Institute of EPA				
Pilot Model SP-18[2]	FY1965 to FY1975	1.27	1.83	1.85
World Economic Model version 1[2]	FY1967 to FY1977	1.19	1.99	2.51
World Economic Model version 2[2]	1966Q1 to 1982Q1	1.11	1.62	1.84
World Economic Model version 3[2]	1975Q1 to 1984Q4	1.16	1.56	1.65
World Economic Model version 4[2]	1979Q1 to 1988Q4	1.33	1.57	1.63
World Economic Model version 5	1983Q1 to 1992Q4	1.24	1.40	1.40
Short-run Macroeconomic Model of Japanese Economy	1977Q1 to 1989Q4	1.30	1.31	0.86
(Hori *et al.*, 1998)	1985Q1 to 1997Q4	1.21	1.31	1.24

1. The multipliers show the response of real GDP or real GNP to a permanent increase of real public investment equivalent to 1 per cent of real GDP or real GNP.
2. Refers to real GNP.

Source: Hori *et al.* (1998).

periods, and found that there was little change in the multipliers (where the monetary authority's reaction function was estimated in each period) (Table 12). Even if the interest rate elasticity of aggregate demand increased (see Box 3), there may be little crowding out through a rise in interest rates and an appreciation of the yen because fiscal packages were usually accompanied by monetary easing. Indeed, because the yen tends to appreciate *before* the announcement of fiscal packages, some studies such as EPA (1995) and Hori *et al.* (1998) doubt that there has been crowding-out through exchange rate appreciation.

Sceptics of the strong effect of fiscal policy usually adopt a neo-classical approach, often using reduced form estimation for empirical evidence. Even if Ricardian equivalence has been empirically rejected, it is not difficult to find models with adverse effects of expansionary fiscal policy on private demand. Government consumption may reduce private consumption through a substitution effect if one assumes that consumers maximise utility. A similar mechanism may work in the case of public investment, if (imputed) services of public infrastructure are included in consumers' utility function. In addition, their income could also be a function of public infrastructure, taking account of the effects on the supply side of the economy. In these models, low quality public works (in terms of low marginal utility or productivity) could discourage private consumption. There has been some evidence consistent with these views. The direct crowding-out effect of government consumption on private consumption has been detected and has turned out to be larger than found in similar studies for the United States (Homori and Asako, 1999). The larger effects in Japan may to some extent be attributable to the different composition of government consumption, in particular a low share of defence in Japan (see Chapter IV). VAR models[27] comprising public investment and some other macro variables usually show weaker effects of public investment

Box 3. Effects of public investment

A. What caused a decline in multiplier effects?

Surveying various models, Ban (1996) pointed out the following possible reasons for the decline in multipliers after the first oil crisis:

- weight of industries benefiting from public works, such as construction, civil engineering, cement, etc., decreased in final demand;
- aggregate demand became more interest-rate elastic (*i.e.* flatter IS curve);
- the exchange rate was floated and international capital mobility increased;
- price elasticity of import demand increased; and
- consumption became more sensitive to price developments, and investment less sensitive to short-term aggregate demand fluctuations.

Although all these reasons concern comparison between before and after the first oil crisis, the trends may have continued until now. There is also a possibility of increased income elasticity of imports due to a larger share of manufactured goods, although there has not been enough statistical evidence.

B. What do input-output tables tell?

Input-output tables provide some complementary information, although they are published with a long lag: the latest version just released is for 1995. A decline in the effect of public investment on production – not value added – is also observed. This tendency, which is also seen in other demand components (Table 13), resulted from a decline in the input ratio, itself brought about by two factors. First is technological progress, in particular in the manufacturing sector. Second, many industries increased inputs from the service sector requiring less physical input. Ohira (1994) argued that the decline in the effect of road construction reflected the fact that the construction industry started to use semi-finished goods, instead of raw materials, at construction sites in order to shorten the completion time.

Table 13. **Changing input-output structure in Japan**

Domestic production inducement coefficient by final domestic expenditures (real)

	Consumption expenditures			Gross domestic fixed capital formation		Increase in stock	Exports	Total, average
	Outside household	Private	General government	Public	Private			
MCA (1995)								
1980	1.657	1.596	1.391	2.075	2.082	2.320	2.368	1.785
1985	1.665	1.604	1.421	2.020	2.034	2.099	2.330	1.780
1990	1.673	1.595	1.438	1.965	1.971	1.961	2.245	1.756
MCA (2000)								
1985	1.613	1.576	1.452	1.969	2.007	2.174	2.312	1.745
1990	1.642	1.574	1.512	1.936	1.939	1.954	2.258	1.737
1995	1.674	1.535	1.544	1.904	1.910	1.703	2.164	1.690

Note: The comparisons between 1980, 1985 and 1995 and between 1985, 1990 and 1995 are based on 90-sector tables in MCA (1995) and 92-sector tables in MCA (2000), respectively.
Source: Management and Co-ordination Agency.

on GDP and private consumption in the post-oil crisis period (Matsuoka, 1999; Ihori *et al.*, 1999). Again, because these studies do not compare their estimates between the periods before and after 1990, it is difficult to assess whether the effectiveness of fiscal policy has declined in recent years.

While these arguments concern the effects of policies which are actually implemented, there have been uncertainties about whether the announced increases in public works have actually occurred. The calculated multiplier for *announced* measures is likely to have become smaller in recent years as financial conditions of local governments have deteriorated. A cumulative decrease in unsubsidised public works in the period FY 1993 to FY 1998, which amounted to about 3 trillion yen (0.6 per cent of GDP), has easily overwhelmed an increase in subsidised public works in the same period (Figure 11). There seems to have been no detailed empirical study on the implementation problem, partly because of insufficient information.

... but at the price of an unsustainable fiscal position

The expansionary fiscal stance in recent years has played an important role in supporting the economic recovery but the current fiscal position is unsustainable since the potential growth rate is lower than the real interest rate. As illustrated in last year's *Survey*, merely stabilising the debt-GDP ratio at a rather high level requires substantial spending cuts and/or revenue increases. Excluding "windfall gains" from tax revenues due to maturing postal savings, the underlying structural primary deficit may be 4½ per cent of GDP in 2000. Considering that the pension reform has been implemented as projected in the last *Survey* and that there has been no visible progress in health care reform, the gist of the analysis in the last *Survey* (see Table 27, page 114) remains unchanged. Necessary fiscal consolidation by 2010 only to eliminate the structural primary deficit would be 7¾ per cent of GDP, which is the sum of structural primary deficits of 4½ per cent of GDP and pressure on spending due to ageing worth 3¼ per cent of GDP. A surplus of around 3 per cent of GDP is, however, required to prevent "snowballing" interest payments, given that potential output growth (1½ per cent according to the OECD) is likely to be lower than the real interest rate on government liabilities during the period to 2010. In Japan, the effective average interest rate which is imputed from national accounts (3½ per cent in 2000) is greater than the long-term interest rate because a high proportion of the debt is 10-year bonds so that the effect of the decline in the market rate in recent years has been lagged. Therefore, the imputed interest rate may continue to decline, easing the sustainability condition to some extent, although such an effect should be balanced against recent changes in the market structure for government bonds, which makes it more sensitive to market sentiment (see below). Although the condition of sustainability may not be strongly violated in Japan, there is a much higher level of debt-to-GDP and a larger structural primary deficit prior to fiscal consolidation than in other countries. The required fiscal correction may therefore be larger in Japan than in other countries during their fiscal consolidation episodes (Table 11, Panel B). The need for fiscal consolidation efforts would be even greater were liabilities to be assessed on an accrual basis and if the poor quality of public sector assets was taken into account.

Government balance sheets

According to the official figures, Japan's general government gross debt at the end of March 1999 was roughly 119 per cent of GDP – OECD figures exclude the liabilities held by government non-financial institutions (about 15 per cent of GDP)[28] and consolidate further (about 2 per cent of GDP).[29] Either set of figures indicates that gross debt rose by more than one hundred trillion yen in the two years to March 1999, over 20 percentage points of GDP. It is sometimes argued that while gross debt is very large, net debt is still small and hence should not be a matter of concern. The substantial difference between the gross and net debt figures (more than 60 per cent of GDP in 1998) is mostly due to financial assets owned by social security funds (some 50 per cent of GDP that year). However, net debt is likely to be under-estimated for at least the following two reasons:

- The definition of social security fund is so broad that corporate pension funds are included, whose financial assets amount to about 50 trillion yen (10 per cent of GDP). This problem should disappear when Japan adopts the 93SNA system in October 2000.
- The economic value of financial assets in public corporations is partly supported by future payment of subsidies[30] by the government, which need to be registered as liabilities and offset against assets. Estimates covering all such subsidies are not available, but those required to support future operations of 14 FILP institutions are estimated to be 6.4 trillion yen (Table 14), or 1.3 per cent of GDP, which provides a lower bound for the magnitude of such adjustment.

A further caveat is that both gross and net debt become larger if implicit and contingent liabilities are included. Some large implicit liabilities include the following. First, implicit gross liabilities of the Welfare Pension System (Tier I and II for employees) may be of the order of 720 trillion yen or 145 per cent of GDP as of March 2000 (see Table 24 in Chapter III).[31] Second, liabilities for retirement allowances for government officials, for which the central and local governments have no reserves, would be likely to amount to more than 20 trillion yen if all government officials retired tomorrow (Washimi *et al.*, 1999). Taking most of the implicit liabilities on board would raise both gross and net debt by at least some 150 per cent of GDP. As for contingent liabilities, the examples given below illustrate both the possible magnitude and the difficulties involved in obtaining estimates. Central government guarantees for external financing of government institutions amounted to 52 trillion yen in March 2000. In the absence of default

Table 14. **Policy costs analysis for selected FILP institutions**

Billion yen

	Policy costs (a)	Subsidies in initial FY 2000 budget (b)	Ratio (a/b)	Reference: Loans outstanding from FILP (March 2000)	Reference: Share in total FILP loans outstanding Per cent
Housing Loan Corporation	782.2	447.5	1.7	74 695.7	18.0
National Life Financial Corporation	127.7	43.8	2.9	11 130.3	2.7
Japan Finance Corporation for Small Business	98.2	28.2	3.5	7 890.7	1.9
Agriculture, Forestry and Fisheries Finance Corporation of Japan	479.2	84.8	5.7	3 832.1	0.9
Japan Finance Corporation for Municipal Enterprises	11.2	1.4	8.0	15 849.8	3.8
The Okinawa Development Bank of Japan	95.1	11.9	8.0	1 760.9	0.4
Development Bank of Japan	138.4	84.0	1.6	18 828.2	4.5
Japan Bank for International Co-operation					
International Financial Account	148.7	0.0	n.a.	10 074.1	2.4
Overseas Economic Co-operation Account	660.5	306.3	2.2	4 866.2	1.2
Teito Rapid Transit Services	–4.3	12.8	–0.3	476.6	0.1
Social Welfare and Medical Service Corporation	84.6	12.1	7.0	2 492.4	0.6
Japan Scholarship Foundation	108.2	14.3	7.6	499.0	0.1
Japan Highway Pubic Corporation	4 296.5	307.0	14.0	21 686.8	5.2
Honshu-Shikoku Bridge Authority	31.4	53.3	0.6	2 165.3	0.5
Central Japan International Airport Corporation Ltd.	–12.5	24.8	–0.5	50.3	0.0
Total	7 045.1	1 432.2	4.9	176 298.4	42.6

Source: Ministry of Finance and OECD.

information, however, it is not possible to quantify contingent liabilities associated with such guarantees. Another contingent liability accrues from (special) loan guarantees for SMEs. On the basis of comparison of actual and assumed default rates, the provisions for defaults budgeted in the past appear to be adequate.[32] Finally, it is not excluded that the financial burdens of support to public corporations by (central or local) government could become unacceptably large, as has been observed in the past.[33] In that event, the government may either have to cut them back and/or to stop the support entirely and take over the liabilities. Part of loans and investment in these corporations could, therefore, be regarded as a kind of contingent liability.

The OECD's conventional analysis of balance sheets should be expanded further to include real assets and (financial and non-financial) public corporations, in order to evaluate the situation fully. For this purpose, Table 15 taken from EPA's *Annual Report on National Accounts* provides comprehensive information. An interesting finding about tangible assets is that general government was the only net purchaser of land in the 1990s (Box 4). In the period from 1991 to 1998, it suffered from capital losses worth 71 trillion yen and purchased new land amounting to 44 trillion yen, resulting in a net decline of holdings by 27 trillion yen to 103 trillion yen. Net purchase of land mainly reflects the surge in public investment in this period. However, an obvious weakness of this *Report* is the lack of information about the breakdown of net fixed assets, *i.e.* more than three-quarters of tangible assets is a black box. As in the case of non-reproducible tangible assets, however, local governments are likely to account for a large share of total tangible assets, given the current intra-government transfer system. In other words, a likely sizeable holding of tangible assets by local governments is a counterpart to high indebtedness of the central government, which could be an indicator of "fiscal illusion". Detailed analysis is not feasible because of the aforementioned data problem. More disclosure is clearly needed to judge the healthiness of government balance sheets. Overall, however, the public sector held tangible assets worth 660 trillion yen, while its net worth was 390 trillion yen, implying that future generations will have to bear some 40 per cent of the bills for building up the current level of infrastructure.

The actual situation is likely to be much worse. As discussed above, because the financial asset figure is likely to be heavily biased downwards, net worth could easily be negative: the current generation is free riding on the burden of their descendants. In addition, because depreciation of social infrastructure is not provided (or infrastructure is assumed to be maintained in good condition free of charge during its life specified by the MOF),[34] the value of net fixed assets may be overestimated.[35] According to Washimi *et al.* (1999), depreciation of general (*i.e.* non-toll) roads alone could amount to 35 to 50 trillion yen (*i.e.* 7 to 10 per cent of GDP), depending on ways of calculating depreciation. This bias should disappear as 93SNA is introduced. However, EPA has announced that it will

Table 15. **Closing stock of assets and liabilities**

Trillion yen, end of 1998

	National total	Private sector[1]	Public sector[1] (a + b)	Public corporations (a)	General government[2] (b)			
					Total	Central government	Local government	Social security fund
1. **Tangible assets**	3 072.8	2 413.7	**659.2**	133.1	**526.1**	(17.2)	(93.8)	(0.8)
Stocks	77.3	74.1	3.2	3.2	0.0	0.0	0.0	0.0
Net fixed assets	1 307.9	799.8	508.2	93.9	414.3	n.a.	n.a.	n.a.
Residential buildings	263.8	n.a.	n.a.	n.a.	n.a.	n.a.	n.a.	n.a.
Non-residential buildings	325.5	n.a.	n.a.	n.a.	n.a.	n.a.	n.a.	n.a.
Other structures	521.8	n.a.	n.a.	n.a.	n.a.	n.a.	n.a.	n.a.
Transport equipment	27.3	n.a.	n.a.	n.a.	n.a.	n.a.	n.a.	n.a.
Machinery, equipment and etc.	191.6	n.a.	n.a.	n.a.	n.a.	n.a.	n.a.	n.a.
Less: Consumption taxes refunded	22.2	n.a.	n.a.	n.a.	n.a.	n.a.	n.a.	n.a.
Non-reproducible tangible assets	1 687.6	1 539.8	147.8	36.0	111.8	17.2	93.8	0.8
Land	1 616.5	1 482.5	133.9	30.8	103.2	17.1	85.3	0.8
Others	71.1	57.3	13.8	5.2	8.6	0.1	8.5	0.0
2. **Financial assets**	4 334.2	3 268.8	**1 070.0**	653.3	**416.7**	153.0	38.2	239.3
Currency	52.5	58.6	1.4[3]	0.0	0.0	0.0	0.0	0.0
Transferable deposits	186.0	180.4	7.0	0.0	0.0	0.0	0.0	0.0
Other deposits	893.9	784.4	110.0	5.4	104.6	47.2	19.6	37.7
Short-term government securities	32.2	0.6	31.6[3]	25.2	6.5	6.5	0.0	0.0
Bonds, long term	556.6	310.7	245.9[3]	221.0	24.9	8.3	0.0	16.6
Corporate shares	301.6	298.6	3.0	2.3	0.7	0.5	0.1	0.1
Loans by The Bank of Japan	1.9	0.0	1.9	1.9	0.0	0.0	0.0	0.0
Call loans and bills bought	69.9	63.8	6.1	6.1	0.0	0.0	0.0	0.0
Commercial papers	18.1	10.3	0.1	0.1	0.0	0.0	0.0	0.0
Loans by private sector	709.7	709.7	0.0	0.0	0.0	0.0	0.0	0.0
Loans by public sector	366.3	0.0	368.8[3]	337.3	31.5	17.9	9.0	7.2
Life insurance	310.5	289.5	21.0	0.0	21.0	3.5	0.0	17.5
Transfers from general government	4.7	0.0	4.7[3]	0.0	4.7	4.7	0.0	0.0
Trade credit and advances	248.5	237.2	11.3	11.3	0.0	0.0	0.0	0.0
Other financial assets	582.0	325.1	257.2	37.9	219.3	64.2	6.3	159.9
Total assets (1 + 2)	7 407.0	5 682.4	**1 729.2**	786.4	**942.8**	(170.2)	(132.0)	(240.1)

Table 15. **Closing stock of assets and liabilities** *(cont.)*

Trillion yen, end of 1998

	National total	Private sector[1]	Public sector[1] (a + b)	Public corporations (a)	General government[2] (b)			
					Total	Central government	Local government	Social security fund
3. Liabilities (except corporate shares)	3 864.1	2 536.6	**1 339.8**	770.7	**569.1**	441.2	140.2	1.5
Currency	52.5	0.0	60.0	60.0	0.0	0.0	0.0	0.0
Transferable deposits	186.0	181.7	5.6	5.6	0.0	0.0	0.0	0.0
Other deposits	895.4	644.0	251.9	251.9	0.0	0.0	0.0	0.0
Short-term government securities	33.1	0.0	33.1	1.0	32.1	32.1	0.0	0.0
Bonds, long term	595.1	179.0	416.2	74.1	342.0	296.9	45.1	0.0
Loans by The Bank of Japan	1.9	1.9	0.0	0.0	0.0	0.0	0.0	0.0
Call money and bills sold	69.9	50.3	19.6	19.6	0.0	0.0	0.0	0.0
Commercial papers	18.1	18.1	0.0	0.0	0.0	0.0	0.0	0.0
Loans by private sector	709.7	679.7	29.9	13.4	16.6	4.0	12.6	0.0
Loans by public sector	366.3	158.2	210.7	39.3	171.4	90.2	82.3	1.5
Life insurance	310.5	199.7	110.8	110.8	0.0	0.0	0.0	0.0
Transfers from general government	4.7	0.0	4.7	4.7	0.0	0.0	0.0	0.0
Trade credit and advances	248.5	248.3	0.2	0.0	0.2	0.0	0.2	0.0
Other liabilities	372.6	175.8	197.0	190.2	6.8	18.0	0.0	0.0
Total net worth (1 + 2 – 3)	3 542.8	3 145.8	**389.4**	15.7	**373.7**	(–271.0)	(–8.2)	(238.6)
Corporate shares	336.8	336.8	0.0	0.0	0.0	0.0	0.0	0.0
Net worth	3 206.1	2 809.0	389.4	15.7	373.7	(–271.0)	(–8.2)	(238.6)
Net financial liabilities (3 – 2)	–470.0	–732.1	269.8	117.4	152.4	288.2	102.0	–237.8

1. Gross debt and financial assets. Debtor/creditor relationships within a sector have not been netted against each other with respect to financial assets and liabilities in this table.
2. As breakdowns of net fixed assets are not available, some numbers, shown in parenthesis, are calculated as if net fixed assets were zero.
3. Number needs to be consolidated to get liabilities for the public sector.

Source: Economic Planning Agency.

Box 4. Land development corporations

Government is an important factor in land markets. This is because the Land Development Public Corporations, which were set up by local governments and are included in public corporations in Table 15, are engaged in prior purchase of land for infrastructure development, which was encouraged by the fiscal packages in the 1990s in order to stimulate land markets. Some of their holdings are intended to be sold to the private sector (as in the case of land development projects for industrial use). However, because EPA's annual report does not provide a revaluation of land held by public corporations, the capital losses incurred are unclear. According to the Ministry of Home Affairs (MHA), some 44 and 12 per cent of their holdings have been owned for more than 5 and 10 years, respectively, indicating capital losses could be substantial and would constitute another problem for local governments. This delayed disposal is often caused by the severe financial condition of local governments which are committed to eventually taking the land at cost-based prices. As for land for industrial use, the delay is mainy due to lack of demand caused by economic stagnation.

not provide full consolidated public sector accounts because of the lack of necessary information, despite the United Nation's recommendation. The official gross figure in the table (1 340 trillion yen) is severely bloated because of insufficient consolidation within the sector.[36] Crude adjustments reduce the gross debt to some 845 trillion yen (some 170 per cent of GDP), *i.e.* larger than the official gross debt of general government by more than 50 percentage points.[37] A final remark is that net liabilities of public financial institutions are *assumed* to be zero, but the direction of bias this would impart is unclear.

Monetary policy: maintaining easy monetary conditions

From February 1999 until August 2000, the Bank of Japan maintained its policy of keeping the uncollateralised overnight rate close to zero (the "zero interest rate policy") by providing as much liquidity as the market demanded. Notwithstanding this policy, indicators of monetary conditions give conflicting signals. On the one hand, the nominal effective exchange rate has appreciated, and bank credit to the non-financial sector has declined. Deflation has continued and real interest rates have tended to rise. Those who put much weight on these indicators have continued to call for further easing, even through unconventional methods. On the other hand, base money has grown quite rapidly, sometimes exceeding 10 per cent from the previous year and the real and nominal money supply (M2 + CD) has expanded by some 2 to 3 per cent. While real interest rates have risen, they remain at historically low levels. The BOJ itself had always talked about the need to move away eventually from the policy it regarded as only a temporary measure until deflationary concerns had been dispelled. In the course of the year, they prepared markets for an eventual change in policy, although markets only incorporated expectations of an increase of some ¼ percentage point. On 11 August, the BOJ indeed raised overnight rates by a quarter of a point. This section first reviews recent monetary developments with respect to money and credit aggregates and the central bank's policies in terms of operational measures. This is followed by a discussion of interest rates and exchange rate developments. The section concludes with an assessment of monetary conditions and turns to the more difficult challenges which will arise during the coming year.

Money and credit aggregates and operational measures

After growing by some 7 per cent in 1999, the growth rate of base money accelerated in the first half of 2000 to some 11 per cent which is more characteristic of the average growth rate prior to 1999 (Figure 12).[38] Excess liquidity held by banks at the BOJ has averaged some 1 trillion yen and at times it has gone as high as nearly 20 trillion yen as banks hedged against such events as a leap year effect, Y2K and a seasonal tightening at the end of the financial year (Figure 13). A side effect of this monetary policy has been a halving of the call money market with the

Figure 12. **Monetary aggregates**
Per cent change over 12 months

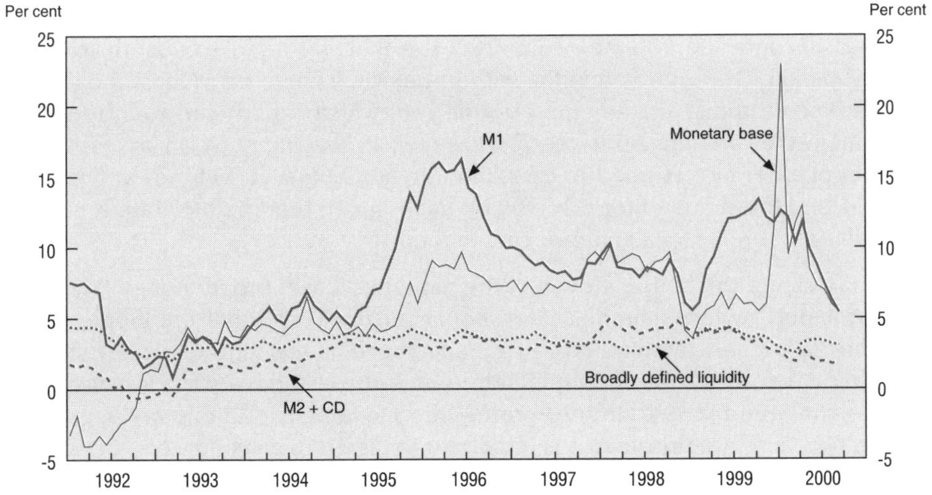

Source: Bank of Japan.

Figure 13. **Balance of current deposits of financial institutions at the Bank of Japan**

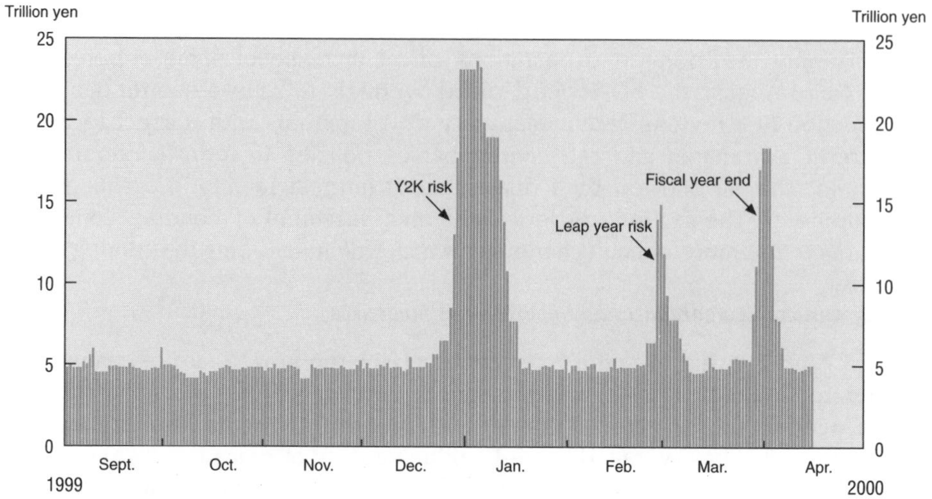

Source: K. Okina and N. Oda, "Further monetary easing policies under non-negativity constraints of nominal interest rates", Ninth International Conference, Bank of Japan, Tokyo, July, 2000.

level of outstanding transactions falling from around 36 trillion yen before the zero rate policy was announced to some 20 trillion at the start of this year. In the days following the rate increase, the volume of transactions rose to 25 trillion yen. With the raising of the overnight rate to around ¼ per cent from 11 August, a key question has become the volume of liquidity the BOJ will need to absorb from the money market. One view is that the withdrawal will have to be at least the level of excess bank liquidity (*i.e.* around 1 trillion yen) which would lead to a decline in base money of around 2 per cent.[39] However, in making such an assessment a number of other factors need to be taken into account, such as funds at the *Tanshi* dealers, and the demand for reserves by banks given that the new rate is still low and will not represent a significant cost to them.

Despite the ample growth of the monetary base, broad money (M2 + CD) has expanded by less than half this amount (Figure 12) so that the money multiplier has fallen. Indicators of money demand such as the ratio of money stock to GDP (the latter might well be understated) and the real money stock have nevertheless continued to rise. In interpreting the movement of monetary aggregates during 1999 and into this year, it is important to take into consideration the special nature of the period. First, one study suggests that in 1998 there was a substantial build-up in precautionary money balances leading to a temporary increase in both the money multiplier and velocity (Hayakawa and Maeda, 2000). With the bank crisis essentially resolved at the end of 1998 and the zero interest rate policy in force from February 1999, the precautionary balances have been run down in the course of the year and into 2000, contributing to slow money growth even as the economy has recovered. Second, it is difficult to define the quantity of money under the condition of zero overnight interest rates and near zero rates on short-term financial instruments since money and short-term assets are increasingly close substitutes. Taking into account such substitution by a divisia index, which weights various elements of the "money supply" by relative rates of return, indicates a dramatic rise in "quasi money" following the introduction of the zero rate policy in March 1999 (Figure 14).

An important reason for the diverging behaviour of base money and broad money has been the decline in bank lending as well as the fact that excess bank reserves have been essentially costless to hold. Bank lending to the economy has declined 2.1 per cent (4.7 per cent including debt write-offs) in the year to June 2000 (Figure 15) and the composition has also changed: lending by public sector financial institutions has risen and now accounts for a fifth of total lending to the non-financial corporate sector. Moreover, some 12 per cent of outstanding loans now carry a government guarantee of some form. Taken together, the decline in bank lending to the non-financial sector of the economy has reduced the money supply growth by some 1 to 2 per cent over the past year (Figure 16). On the other

Figure 14. **Development of the divisia money index in Japan**

Per cent change over 12 months

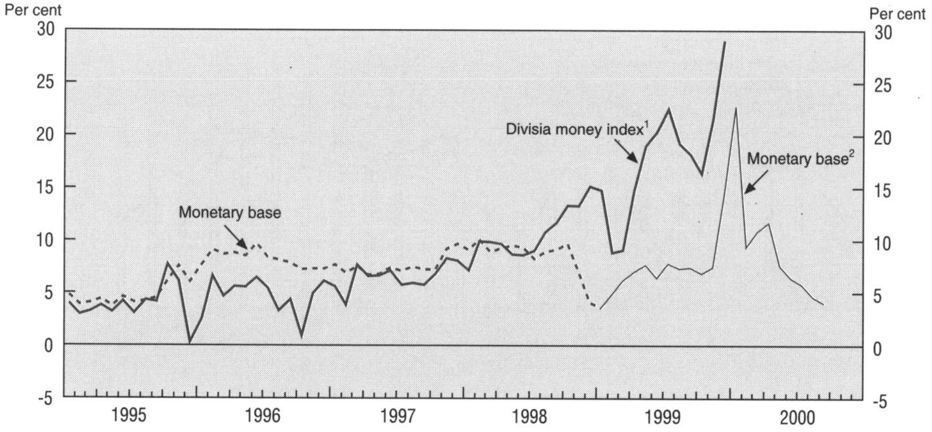

1. Monetary base, short-term government bonds (financial bills + treasury bills) and Bank of Japan bills sold.
2. Since 1997, includes deposits of money market brokers (Tanshi).

Source: K. Okina and N. Oda, "Further monetary easing policies under non-negativity constraints of nominal interest rates", Ninth International Conference, Bank of Japan, Tokyo, July, 2000.

Figure 15. **Loans and discounts of financial institutions**
Per cent change over 12 months

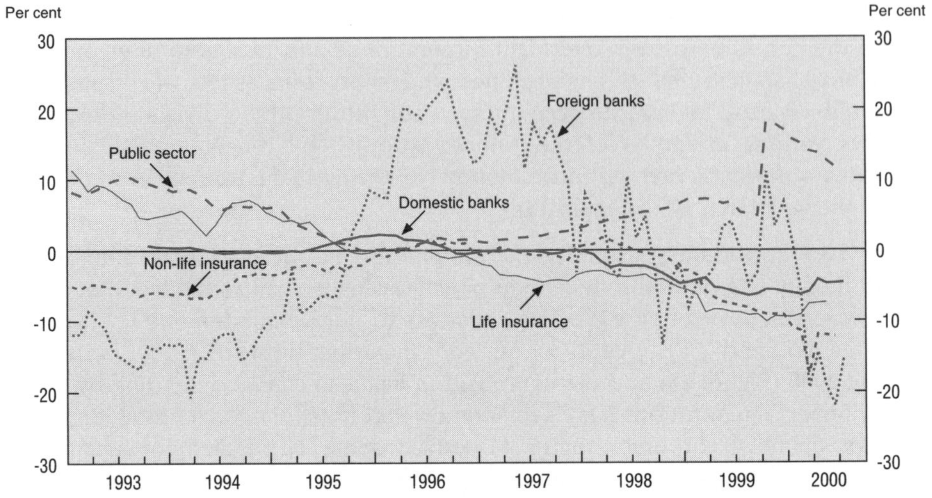

Source: Bank of Japan and OECD.

Figure 16. **Contributions to change in the money stock**
Contribution to change from a year ago, end of period

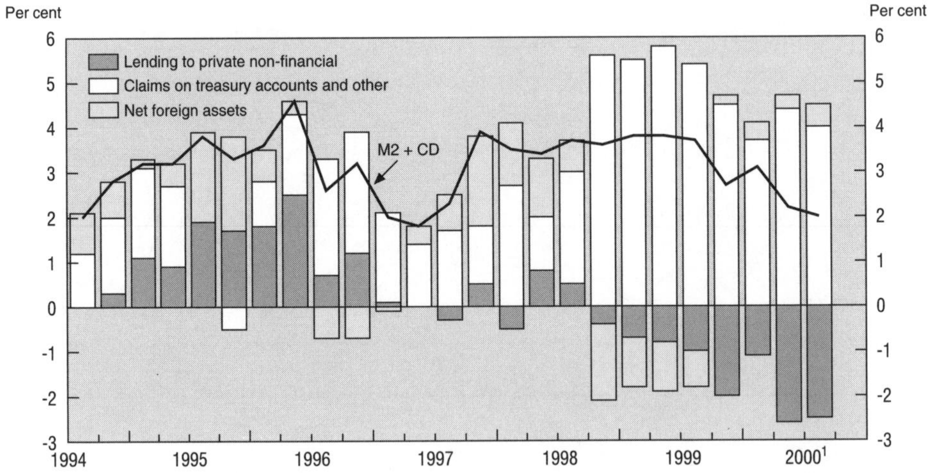

1. Data for third quarter 2000 are end-August.
Source: Bank of Japan and OECD.

hand, lending to the budget has raised the growth of the money supply by some 5 per cent, and the banking sector now accounts for some 15 per cent of the government bond market.

Interest rates and the exchange rate

The maintenance of the policy-controlled overnight rate at close to zero during the past year has been reflected in the yield curve which has remained flat for maturities up to one year. Although upward sloping at longer maturities, the yield gap (ten year yields less 3-month yields) has remained constant at around 1½ percentage points (Figure 17). Underlying these developments has been the commitment of the BOJ not to change the zero interest rate policy until the danger of deflation had passed. Over the past year, the criteria for such a development has been continually refined by the BOJ in its public announcements and by mid-2000 they were indicating that a change in policy could be close. These developments have been reflected in the implied forward interest rates (Figure 18). Whereas in mid-1999 there appears to have been some expectation that the zero rate policy would be lifted within six months to a year, by August the zero rate policy appeared to have become more entrenched. However, from February 2000 expectations shifted once again, indicating an expected policy change in three to six months. The shift in expectations can be attributed to increased comments by the BOJ that the policy should only be viewed as a temporary measure and could change with stronger economic data. However, the rise in rates following an ending of the zero rate policy was expected by the market to be only small (*i.e.* in the order of 25 basis points) – an expectation which proved to be correct.

The ending of the zero interest rate policy from 11 August was preceded by a month in which the BOJ announced that it would monitor financial market developments in response to the unexpected bankruptcy of a department store chain on July 12, one of the largest non-bank bankruptcies to date in Japan. Interest rates on the lowest rated corporate bonds moved up somewhat and share prices of firms known to be seeking debt forgiveness fell, but otherwise reaction to the announcement was muted. Share prices, on the other hand, continued a fall which began in May losing around an additional 5 per cent over the month before the decision to raise overnight rates. It is not at all clear that the impending change in policy rates or the bankruptcy were the major factors driving the stock market in this period. Also significant was the uncertainty about government policy with respect to the sale of one of the large city banks (see below) and the disagreement between the government and the BOJ concerning the lifting of the zero-rate policy, which soured the atmosphere. Foreigners became net sellers of shares in this period.[40]

A remarkable feature of the monetary situation has been the relative stability of long term interest rates (Figure 17). As noted above, banks have been major purchasers of bonds supported by easy access to funds from the central

Figure 17. **Interest rates and the yield curve**

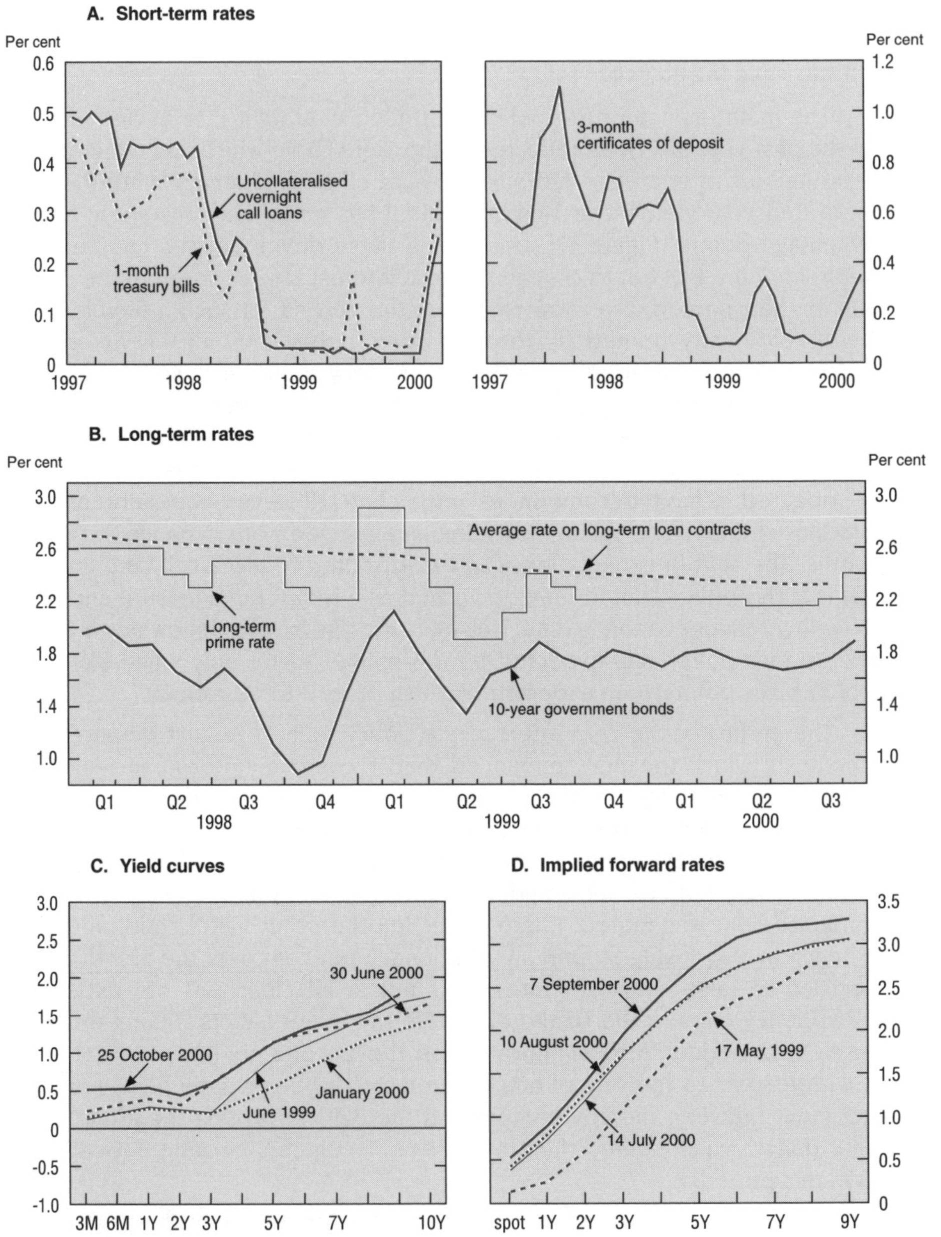

Source: Bank of Japan and Bloomberg.

Figure 18. **Implied forward interest rates**

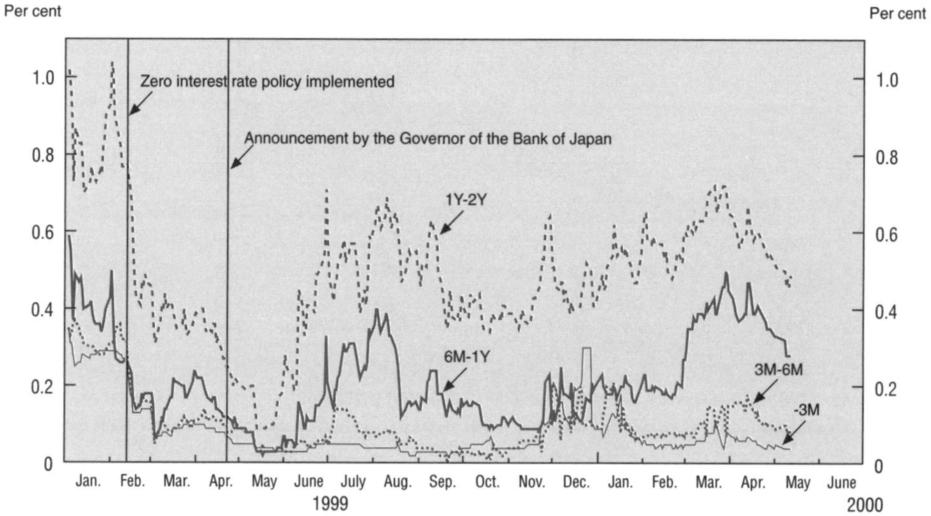

Source: K. Okina and N. Oda, "Further monetary easing policies under non-negativity constraints of nominal interest rates", Ninth International Conference, Bank of Japan, Tokyo, July, 2000.

bank and by the low demand for loans. Even so, as noted above, there has been an increasing demand by banks for shorter maturities which is being met by a change in issuance by the government. Other measures have served to support the bond market, even though that was not the express intention of the authorities. In particular, the BOJ entered into a repurchase agreement with the Trust Fund Bureau (TFB) in November 1999 so as to avoid the TFB having to sell large quantities of bonds to meet withdrawals from the postal savings system as 110 trillion yen of deposits mature between April 2000 and March 2002.[41] In addition, the BOJ has continued to purchase around 5 trillion yen of bonds outright per year, lifting their holdings to around 40 trillion yen.

The nominal effective exchange rate has appreciated by some 12 per cent over the review period, despite repeated interventions, exerting deflationary pressures (Figure 19). Driving the appreciation of the exchange rate has been the low level of capital outflow on the part of domestic financial institutions (especially insurance companies) despite the large and widening interest rate differential. It is as though their expectation of exchange rate appreciation has remained strong. On the other hand, during the first half of this year issues of samurai bonds by large foreign companies have increased in response to the interest rate differential. Contributing to upward pressure on the yen during much of the past year

Figure 19. **Interest differentials and the effective exchange rate of the Yen**

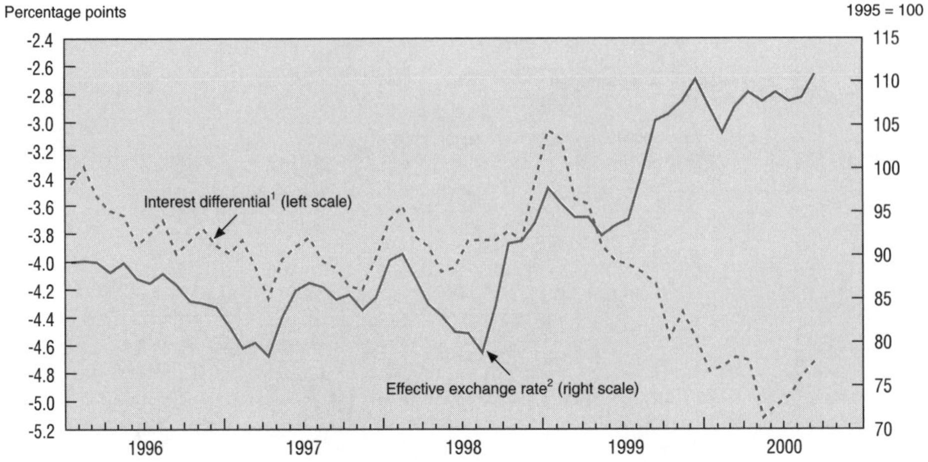

1. Weighted average of short- and long-term differentials against the United States and Germany with equal weights on the terms and twice the weight for the United States as for Germany.
2. Against 40 trading partners.

Source: Bank of Japan and OECD.

has been a rapid rise in inflows of both direct foreign investment and portfolio investment with non-resident holdings of equities rising from 15 per cent in September 1999 to 17.6 per cent in March 2000. In response, the MOF has intervened unilaterally on a number of occasions when the yen/dollar rate has threatened to strengthen from the 100 to 105 yen/dollar zone. On several occasions there has been criticism that the BOJ has sterilised such interventions thereby reducing their effectiveness.[42] The BOJ has stated that they were not concerned to sterilise interventions *per se* but to maintain zero overnight rates which has implied excess liquidity in the money market of some 1 trillion yen. Presumably, if they had left excess liquidity in the banking system after intervention, the funds would have been simply transferred to the money market brokers (*tanshi*). There is, however, some evidence that when banks placed excess reserves in this manner, the three-month rate was brought under downward pressure (Fukao, 2000).

With respect to capital markets more generally, there is some evidence of improved efficiency in pricing for risk.[43] Corporate bond spreads (over 10-year government bonds) have declined to levels at or below those prevailing before the financial crisis began in late 1997 (Figure 20). Indeed, those bonds with the poorest credit ratings (*i.e.* Baa) are now trading at a premium of around 50 basis points, well below the level in 1997. Moreover, this decline has occurred even as

Figure 20. **Yield spreads of corporate over government bonds**

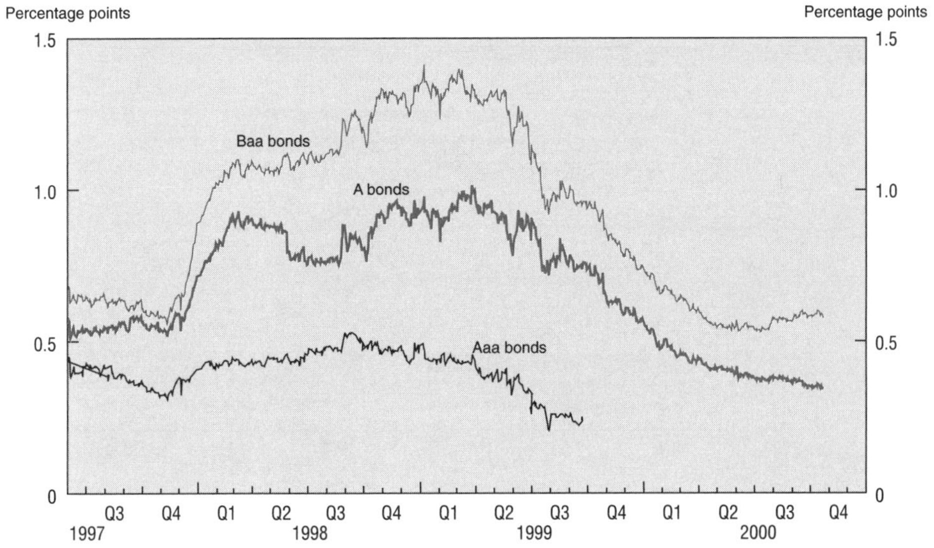

Source: Japanese Securities Dealers Association, "Over-the-Counter Standard Bond Quotations".

the rate of bankruptcies rose at the start of 2000. Taken together, the evidence might suggest that capital market efficiency has not improved but this conclusion is premature. Credit guarantees have artificially shifted the wave of bankruptcies from early 1999 to 2000, while the new corporate restructuring law, which came into effect in April, has also resulted in a surge of bankruptcy petitions in the April/June period. Closer analysis of premiums and corporate credit ratings suggest that markets are pricing risk more carefully than in the past and that rating agencies are more closely looking at indicators of default (Packer, 2000). One study (Nikko Salomon Smith Barney, 2000*a*) has shown that although median spreads are down, the mean spread is still above that of late 1997. More companies are now rated in the -BBB category or below (10 per cent of companies as opposed to 3.7 per cent in October 1997), and for those at the riskiest rating levels spreads are higher than before the crisis. Moreover, the role of a Keiretsu affiliation in reducing spreads appears to have declined as group companies and, following some cases where they have not aided ailing companies, banks are now perceived to be less able or less inclined to support them.

It is much more difficult to form a judgement about whether banks are now pricing for risk since they have substantial bad debts from the past to deal with. The spread between short-term prime rate and short-term lending rate on

Figure 21. **Bank lending margins**
Percentage points

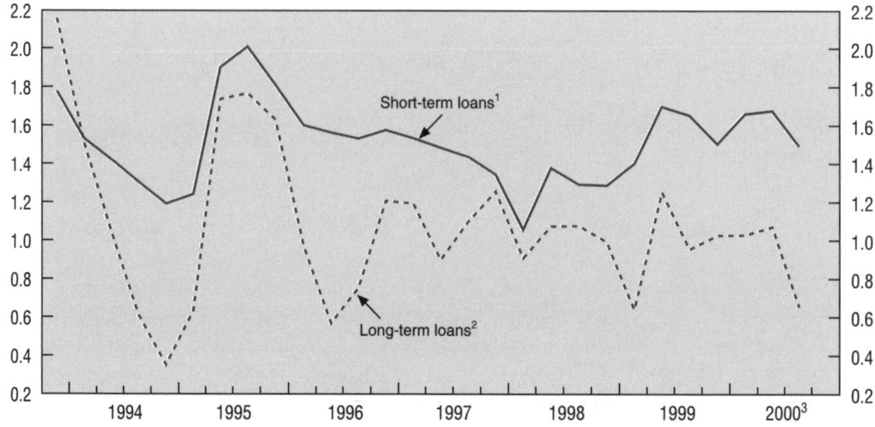

1. Excess of average rate on short-term loans and discounts less 90-179 day CD new issue rate.
2. Excess of average rate on long-term loans and discounts less five-year bank debenture rate.
3. Third quarter 2000 is the average of July and August.

Source: Bank of Japan and OECD.

new loans has widened somewhat showing some pricing for risk although the evidence is not compelling and spreads on long-term rates have declined (Figure 21). More important will be to see how they choose to handle old bad and doubtful debts.

Significant changes are also taking place in the markets for government bonds. A high share of public sector holding – the highest among G7 countries – and long maturity are current features of the JGB market, accounting for a low level and a modest growth of (net) interest payments. However, as shown in the reduced subscription by the TFB in FY 1999 and 2000, the situation has started to change gradually. In contrast to developments up to FY 1998,[44] the increase in holdings by private banks (26.4 trillion yen) exceeded that of the total increase of JGB outstanding (24.3 trillion yen), since the public sector's holdings decreased (except postal life insurance), reflecting a tight financial situation of the FILP. The private sector's holdings are expected to increase further because: 1) the potential supply of JGBs remains substantial due to a likely continuation of a large fiscal deficit; and 2) the financial assets held by the public sector are likely to decrease because of the aforementioned large-scale withdrawal of postal savings as well as changes in public institutions' investment behaviour in the wake of the FILP reforms starting in FY 2001. All these suggest that further improvement is necessary in JGB markets. As OECD (1999*b*) summarised, there were several signs of insufficient liquidity (*e.g.* the largest bid-ask spreads in G7 countries) in the JGB markets, which could be rectified by more diversified issuance of bonds along the yield curve and a review of transaction and withholding taxes. Indeed, reforms are advancing in the desirable direction. Exclusive reliance on 10-year bonds has been reduced, *e.g.* 5-year bonds were introduced in February 2000. Tax treatment has changed,[45] although it appears to have had little effect on the share of foreign investors' holdings, which is still lower than both in the past and in other countries. Further improvement could alleviate the private sector's reluctance to hold JGBs due to stricter implementation of mark-to-the-market accounting rules (see Chapter III), thereby helping to moderate a likely pick-up in long-term interest rates. More diversified maturity structure, on balance, may result in shorter average maturity, making interests payments more sensitive to future interest developments. The shortening of average maturity has often been observed in countries with a large debt-to-GDP ratio, but the case in Japan may reflect the elimination of market distortions (such as lax accounting rules, large holdings by the public sector, absence of medium-term bonds, etc.) rather than concerns about future inflation as Missale and Blanchard (1994) argued.

The changes in the public sector's investment behaviour and in accounting rules may also exert a large impact on markets for the so-called local bonds (which comprise local government bonds and bonds issued by local public enterprises). This is because about 60 per cent of the issuance of local bonds is accepted by public sector financial institutions (TFB,[46] Postal Life Insurance, Finance Corporation of Local Public Enterprise) and 30 per cent by private banks (mainly regional banks) through bilateral negotiations, leaving only 10 per cent to market disciplines.[47] In terms of institutional arrangement, local bonds are quasi-JGBs because: 1) issuance of local bonds is planned based on the LPFP (decided by the Cabinet) and needs permission[48] by the Ministry of Home Affairs (MHA); 2) costs of debt servicing are supported by lump-sum transfers from the central government; 3) if local governments' financial situation were to deteriorate, their financial management would come under the control of the MHA. As a result, conditions for the issuance of local bonds are virtually the same as those for JGBs and uniform across local issuing bodies. However, price differences do emerge in the secondary markets, implying capital losses for some banks. To sum up, although the coming FILP reform should, in principle, lead to a major change in the current practice, the effects could be minimal if the postal savings system would continue to purchase local bonds as in the past. Reforms may nevertheless be a response to demand for more liquidity in the markets. In this case, more information (such as consolidated balance sheet of local governments and local public corporations) should be disclosed, and more seasonally stable issuance could be implemented. They should, however, be accompanied by a more comprehensive overhaul of local finances (see Chapter IV).

Assessment of monetary policy: toward a new operational framework

Was monetary policy easy enough?

Looking back over the past year, the question naturally arises not only whether monetary policy was easy but if it realistically could have done more to support growth and an unwinding of deflationary pressures. The conflicting short-term macroeconomic statistics reviewed in Chapter I make a clear-cut judgement difficult. The monetary conditions index indicates a tightening of conditions due to the appreciation of the yen (in part to the weakness of the euro) (Figure 22, Panel A). However, with interest rates already low, and in the absence of a multilateral agreement to depreciate the yen, it is hard to see what the policy implications could have been apart from a large and sustained intervention which did not take place. In the event, Japanese industry has adapted to the exchange rate through lower wages and other cost cutting measures which have prolonged deflation but have not necessarily lowered the level of activity. Calculations of both the Taylor rule for interest rates and the Macallum rule for the monetary base also show that policy was not easy enough. However, such calculations are very sensitive to the accuracy of the GDP measures for 1999/2000 and the associated output gap. If activity in fact recovered in the second half of 1999 (as argued in Chapter I), the monetary policy stance would have been broadly appropriate. Base money also grew rapidly, and lending attitudes improved, especially for the larger firms (Figure 22, Panel B). Moreover, it has to be kept in mind that the significant easing of policy in 1998 and in 1999 could only be expected to have a lagged effect on prices and on output at the best of times. The instability of the money multiplier could hardly be attributed to monetary policy, although it does point to widespread balance sheet adjustment as a major problem in implementing policy both in the past and in the immediate future.

Why was the policy changed?

The decision in August to raise the overnight rate was hardly a surprise. Nevertheless, the government was firmly opposed to the decision and in the days leading up to it emphasised the dangers to the recovery, which was portrayed as fragile. Although the BOJ stated that the policy was lifted since deflationary concerns had been dispelled, several additional reasons have also been put forward. First, the zero rate policy, although extended, was essentially an emergency measure and with the threat of a deflationary spiral past, the bank needed to re-establish room for manoeuvre. In the year leading up to the change, the criteria for determining when the deflationary threat had subsided was refined; by mid-2000 the criteria included a firm business recovery and a rise in household incomes, though not necessarily a rise in consumption. Moreover, the bank came to regard not all declines in price indices as reflecting deflation but rather the welcome effects of deregulation which stimulates activity. Second, the policy led

Figure 22. **Monetary conditions**

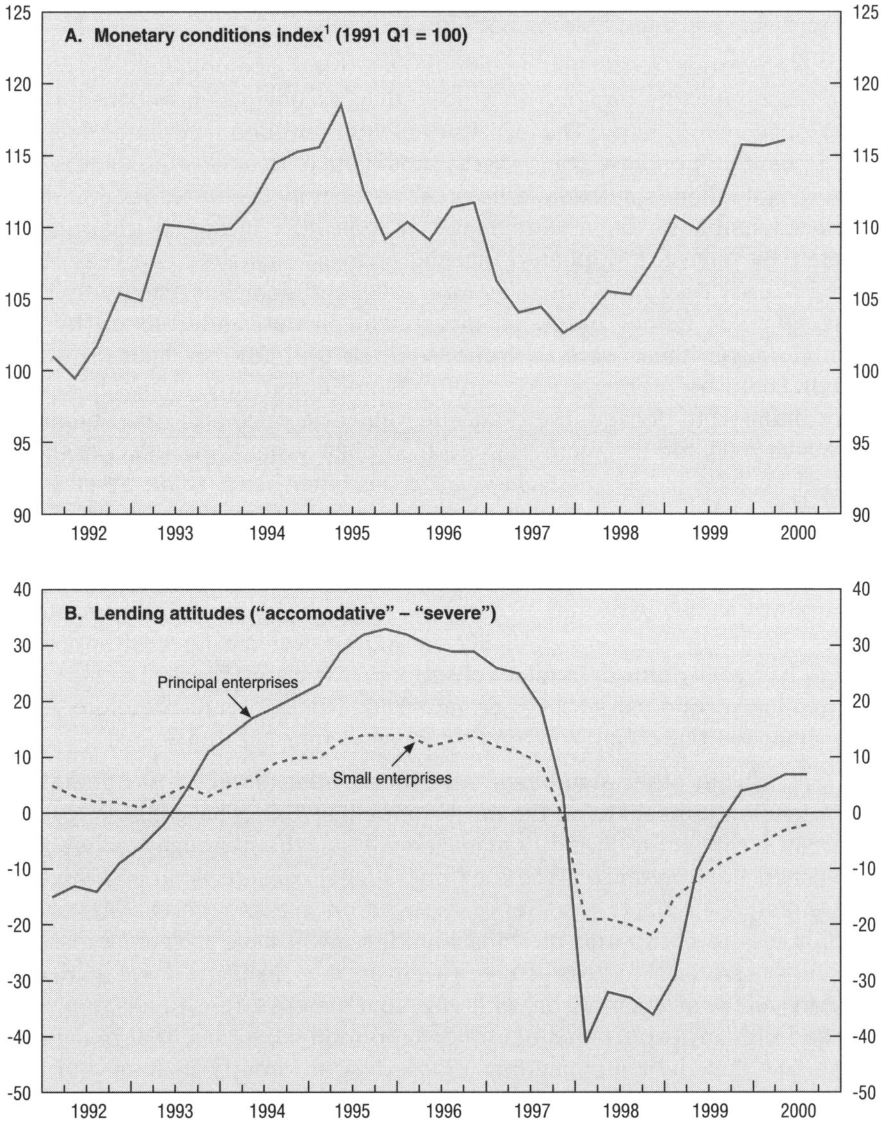

1. Defined as the level change in the three-month deposit rate deflated by the four-quarter percentage change in the GDP deflator (adjusted for the 1989 and 1997 tax hikes) plus one-quarter of the percentage change in the real effective exchange rate of the yen (unit labour cost definition) against 29 OECD and 12 non-OECD trading partners. The weight (one quarter) was derived from INTERLINK model simulation properties.

Source : Bank of Japan and OECD.

to moral hazard on the part of banks and discouraged restructuring on the part of enterprises. Third, continuation of the policy could delay needed fiscal adjustment. In addition, some members of the policy board argued that the low rate of return to savers has been holding back the economy.

With respect to the first argument – the threat of a deflationary spiral had passed – contradictory data led to a more than usually active debate for only a quarter point rise in rates. The BOJ has recently reiterated the importance of a forward-oriented monetary policy so that it is difficult to assess the decision without knowing the bank's inflation forecast. In its monthly economic assessment, the BOJ placed emphasis on a wide range of indicators including quarterly GDP estimates. By August, it appeared that the recovery was already a year old (the EPA had already dated the trough as April 1999) and domestic activity seemed to be strengthening further based on investment, in turn underpinned by strong profits. Moreover, there were indications, albeit contradictory, that private consumption could be picking up (Chapter I). More importantly, although consumer prices continued to decline, the domestic wholesale price index had been rising since March 2000, the first time in more than eight years if the effect of the consumption tax hike in 1997 is excluded. On the other hand, some other analysts argued that a slowdown in activity was imminent, especially with fiscal policy tightening in the second half of this year.[49] On balance, it was increasingly difficult for the BOJ to continue to justify the policy at a time when the economy was recovering and was widely expected to continue to grow. The projection presented in Chapter I points to deflation gradually unwinding over the forecast horizon but, although half-yearly growth is relatively strong, it is also projected to slow somewhat from the second half of 2001 and into 2002. The key issue, therefore, was not simply lifting the policy but in setting a framework for what comes next.

As for the other arguments, a technical adjustment to the operation of monetary policy appears to be the most compelling. Banks have certainly not had to give much thought to liquidity management and the overnight money market has declined in importance. This is an operational consideration and might well have warranted a greater cost being imposed on excess reserves. As for moral hazard, access to cheap and plentiful liquidity might have lowered pressure by banks on enterprises to restructure. However, it is likely to have had only a secondary effect in comparison with the government's re-capitalisation of the banks and with any expectation of further support in the future. That being said, it is important that debt restructuring proceed in an orderly manner and ample provision of market liquidity and easy monetary conditions in the future will be an important aspect of this process.[50] Fiscal policy is not normally a direct concern of the monetary authorities although its stance clearly needs to be taken into account. With the level of public debt an important concern, it will be important in the future that overall economic policy is able to maintain long term rates at a low level.[51]

What path in the future?

Looking ahead to the coming review year and beyond, with financial institutions weak (see following section), balance sheet restructuring underway and the economy subject to headwinds, it would seem necessary for monetary policy to remain expansionary for a while. The key policy issue is what this will mean in practice and how it can be credibly implemented and explained to the public. Calls on the bank to be "responsible irresponsibly", to create inflation so as to reduce public debt (*chosei* inflation) and to bring about negative real interest rates are not helpful in this respect. Such proposals are implicitly based on a judgement that the economy is and will remain in deep recession and that it is skirting on the edge of a dangerous deflationary spiral. It is therefore best to consider two aspects: a policy framework under "normal" conditions (*i.e.* an economy steadily recovering) and potential policy options if the economy were to be subjected to further deflationary shocks before it has fully recovered.

A distinction is often misleadingly drawn between "classical" monetary policy on the one hand and inflation targeting on the other. However, the conduct of any monetary policy requires the authorities to have a clear idea of the level of inflation – or deflation – they would regard as acceptable and an idea about tradeoffs with other policy objectives. Moreover, as the BOJ has noted, such an understanding needs to be formed in a future-oriented manner. Whether to publish the price objective is the key issue, a secondary consideration being whether projected inflation is to be targeted with a probability distribution around it, as in the United Kingdom and over what time period, as in Australia which specifies an average rate over the cycle.[52] Under the conditions which Japan is likely to experience in the immediate future, it may be useful to specify a medium-term inflation target since it would facilitate the explanation of sustained easy monetary policy. To some extent this was the case during the past year when the goal was specified "until the deflationary concerns have been dispelled". Given the complex transformation through which the economy is passing, targeting a specific rate of projected inflation would not seem practical. Above all, it is crucial as Okina points out whether "... the central bank and the broad public can share an understanding that inflation targeting is not a measure for bringing intentional inflation from the back door, but a framework for assuring flexible policy operations" (Okina and Oda, 2000).

What level of inflation could the authorities choose as a medium-term target and what instruments/indicators might be used? A marked feature of the international monetary scene for quite some time has been the instability of the yen exchange rate combined with pressure to establish a strong yen for commercial policy purposes. Some observers have argued that the latter objective has often led to deflationary monetary policy in Japan (McKinnon and Ohno, 1997). From the perspective of the trilateral system, dollar, euro and yen, it might be useful to choose a target reflecting "targets" in effect in the other two areas, broadly 1 to 2 per cent per annum in the medium term. An objective of zero inflation in the future might also be considered since, with high wage and price flexibility, deflationary shocks could be associated with lower real output costs than in other economies.[53] However, the expectation of a continually appreciating exchange rate and difficulties with implementing monetary policy at low levels of interest rates might lend some instability to the economy. As noted in last year's *Survey*, an objective without policy instruments to achieve it is hardly a credible policy, leading to arguments that, with interest rates close to zero, there is no point in setting a price objective, even for the medium term. Operational questions are indeed important. Experience in Japan as well as ongoing research would appear to indicate that the closer interest rates are to the lower bound, the more important it is to monitor monetary aggregates. Moreover, there may have to be a mix of instruments such as purchasing bonds, writing options on bonds, purchasing foreign exchange and buying private securities since not all asset prices may be fully adjusted to the low policy rate.[54]

At the Monetary Policy Meeting on 13 October 2000 the Bank took important steps to promote the public understanding of its evaluation of economic and financial developments and the conduct of monetary policy. The Bank issued a policy report, *On Price Stability*, and announced its decision to publish regularly (in April and October) the *Outlook and Risk Assessment of the Economy and Prices* (*Assessment*, hereafter) which will form a part of its *Monthly Report of Recent Economic and Financial Developments*. *On Price Stability* clarified many of the issues raised above, thereby facilitating the public understanding of the Bank's thinking on what its goal ought to be in both the short and long term. In a nutshell, the Policy Board members concluded that "while it is not appropriate at present to express a definition of price stability by some numerical values which can be used as a guidepost in the conduct of monetary policy, it is possible and useful for the central bank to disclose viewpoints when judging price stability". *Assessment* is a new attempt at such disclosure. It focuses on risks of events which, even if associated with a low probability, could have a large impact on the economy. This complements the Bank's view on most likely developments a few months ahead, which the Policy Board has already been making public through the *Monthly Report*. *Assessment* includes as reference material forecasts for the current fiscal year of real GDP growth, domestic WPI and CPI excluding perishables by individual Policy Board members.[55] The first *Assessment* was published at the end of October.

What if downside risks materialise?

With interest rates likely to be low for quite some time and the money multiplier unstable for the time being, the question arises how monetary policy should respond if the deflationary risks noted in Chapter I were to materialise. Under such conditions and with wages and prices flexible, monetary policy would have to assume the role of the nominal anchor by, *inter alia*, expanding the money supply.

The instruments which could be used have by now been widely discussed and are associated with specific costs and benefits.[56] Summarising a large literature:

- Purchasing government bonds: the problem with such a policy, apart from moral hazard questions related to public sector activity, is that it would have to be on an enormous scale to be effective since risk aversion by the private sector would mean that bond purchases would only lead to a much lower increase in private loans. Any losses by the BOJ would have to be assumed by the government as a public good, although there is no legal provision for this at the moment.
- Purchasing foreign exchange: it is probably an effective policy although it would depend on the exchange rate constellation ruling at the time of the shock. Such a policy would have to be initiated by the MOF but then supported by the BOJ. The major drawback is that it would need a multilateral agreement to be effective.
- Purchasing goods and services: this amounts to directly monetising a budget deficit. This policy might be politically unacceptable unless the expenditure system of the public sector is regarded as delivering value for money (see Chapter IV).

Financial-sector policy: stabilising the transmission mechanism

The financial condition of the banking sector, which is still burdened with non-performing loans, has complicated the conduct of monetary policy and has served to destabilise the money multiplier. Balance sheet adjustments on the part of the non-financial sector have also been important. Some companies have been actively cutting liabilities and financing investment with improved cash flows while others have been seeking debt forgiveness and debt restructuring from the banks (see Chapter I). This section looks at policy developments over the past year which seek both to reform the prudential framework as well as to guide the development of a sounder, more efficient, banking sector.

Completing the regulatory framework

The regulatory system is changing with the amalgamation of the Financial Supervisory Agency (FSA) with the Financial System Planning Bureau of the Ministry of Finance in July 2000 to form the Financial Services Agency (FSA). At the end of the year it will be merged with the Financial Reconstruction Commission (FRC). The new Financial Services Agency will have a powerful role being responsible not only for financial policy but also for bank inspection and for the supervision of banks under pubic control, together with the oversight of the bank restructuring agreements set up at the time of their recapitalisation. Being responsible for policy, inspection and ownership raises dangers of a conflict of interest.

The Financial Services Agency will therefore be divided into three bureaux with various firewalls.[57] The financial policy bureau (Planning and Co-ordination) will be overseen by an advisory council with members from outside the FSA, while firewalls between the two other divisions comprise mission statements for each bureau.

Since April 2000, the FSA has assumed regulatory power over an additional 279 credit co-operatives (with the exception of those in agriculture) and intensive inspections began in July. Inspections are underway and although there are clear signs of financial problems, the size of the sector needs to be kept in perspective: total loans and deposits amount to some 20 trillion yen or some 3 per cent of total financial institutions. Using public funds, should it prove necessary, for re-capitalisation will be harder in this sector. However, new legislation is to be enacted to allow co-operatives to issue their own preferred subscription certificates which will be equivalent to preferred stock used in the re-capitalisation of the banks. In order to support SMEs, there have been arguments in Japan that the criteria for granting co-operatives/unions public funds should be easier than for the banks, and as a result the law was amended in May 2000 to allow capital injections into financial institutions which are important for a region. Granting further preferential treatment to a small weak sector would go in the opposite direction to broader financial sector reform.

The FSA has also been active in tightening and clarifying regulatory standards. The rules covering debt waivers and other forms of support to faltering group companies by banks have been clarified: the new rules require city banks, regional banks and credit unions/co-operatives to show that a debt cancellation will keep final losses smaller than a liquidation. Previous rules were too vague so that decisions about affiliates had been put off. In a regulatory tightening, the FSA has ruled that most regional banks will not be able to count unrealised portfolio profits as part of their capital ratios of 4 per cent. It will also apply to secondary regional banks and to credit unions and co-operatives. The banks with international operations will still be able to set 45 per cent of such profits against their capital ratio of 8 per cent. Moreover, pending full mark-to-market in FY 2001, from September banks will have to book portfolio losses if values fall by 30 per cent from the book value. In January 2000 it was set at 50 per cent but different treatment for this sector provoked widespread criticism.

Bank mergers and debt restructuring have also raised some regulatory issues with respect to shareholdings. Banks are now permitted to exceed 5 per cent limit on equity holdings in a non-financial firm in the event of a debt-for-equity swap or in the event of a full bank merger. Nevertheless, the regulation (and the mark-to-market rule) is forcing banks to reduce their industrial holdings. However, where a bank merger is in the form of a holding company, which is the case for some proposed large mergers, the competition law allows 15 per cent of a company to be held.

A potentially important development has been the application by a number of non-financial companies for banking licenses, which could serve to invigorate competition and efficiency in the sector. This has raised a number of regulatory issues including the effective separation of the owning company's finances from the bank, the need for more closely defining related-lending regulation and the extent to which owning companies would be subject to inspection. Although the regulatory framework is still evolving, the first case is already underway with the sale of Nippon Credit Bank to a domestically-led consortium.

A new deposit insurance law is now in force, but although there are many welcome features, the full guarantee – introduced as a temporary measure in 1996 – has been extended from April 2001 to April 2002 for fixed deposits and until 2003 for current account deposits. The new framework adopts as a basic principle that large creditors should accept responsibility for their decisions and so caps the deposit guarantee at 10 million yen. The law also facilitates faster resolution of bank crises from April 2001 by allowing good assets and deposits to be transferred, ideally over a weekend, to a bridge bank allowing normal transactions the next working day or as soon as possible. In the case of a large failure which could involve systemic risk, a crisis management committee chaired by the Prime Minister is foreseen which can either decide to fully protect all deposits or to inject funds into the system. The law also extended the deadline for the lifting of full deposit guarantees on the grounds that some small and medium financial institutions, including credit co-operatives needed more time to adjust since detailed audits will only be finished this year. However, while this consideration might well be justified, there was a concern about extending this delay to all other banks, especially as an exemption in cases of systemic risk is now in place. Some interpreted the move as backing away from a pre-announced reform intended to force the pace of bank restructuring, but the authorities have denied this intention. Another weak point of the new deposit protection law is that risk-based insurance premiums for banks have not been introduced.[58]

A new law has come into force aimed at expediting the liquidation and reorganisation of failed insurance companies (see also Chapter III). It will also make it easier for financially troubled life insurers to restructure before liabilities exceed assets. Insurers will be required to report to the FSA if they find it difficult to remain in business, even though they still have a positive net worth. The new law also makes it clear that even though policy holders have been granted a seniority status, high promised returns on insurance policies can be reduced but only once the company has entered bankruptcy procedures and a reorganisation plan is in place. Such cuts are also permitted for policies issued by a liquidated company which have been acquired by another company. In addition, budgetary measures have been also incorporated in the legislation (see Chapter II). The law also makes it easier for mutual companies to incorporate, which would make restructuring easier to organise. The policy holder insurance fund, which is financed by the sector, has been increased to 960 billion yen but remains relatively small in comparison with the public funds available to the banking sector.[59]

Dealing with financial institutions in crisis

Although the most pressing problems of the financial sector were effectively dealt with in March 1999 when the major banks were re-capitalised, the authorities have still had to deal with insolvent financial institutions. A total of five second tier regional banks were taken under state control in 1999: four of them had negative net worth of some 1.4 trillion yen as of March 2000, 30 per cent more than the sum six months earlier. More than 8 trillion yen will be put into these banks but their assets are expected to continue to lose value. The Financial Supervisory Agency suspended the operations of a life insurance company in June following a corrective order it issued in February after it revised down the solvency ratio from 305 to 175 per cent – much below the 200 per cent threshold. By the end of March, the ratio had fallen to -190 per cent. The action represented the third failure in the industry, which is under stress due to negative yield gaps and due to falling numbers of new insurance policies and a change in them away from savings plans to death benefits. Insurance companies have been aggressively cutting costs and realising reserves on stock holdings but most observers judge that wider restructuring might be necessary: estimated losses of life insurance companies from the negative spread in fiscal 1999 amounted to 1.5 trillion yen and is retarding consolidation and de-mutualisation. Negative spreads may widen further. Finally, the authorities have already liquidated some 80 credit co-operatives since 1993.

With respect to the insolvent banks which have been taken into state ownership or public control, two large and five small banks have now been, or are in the process of being, sold – one large bank (LTCB) to a foreign consortium. Sale of the two large banks has raised a number of issues. Bad debts have been taken off their balance sheets and will remain with the government.[60] However the liability of the state does not stop there. Thus the LTCB (now called *Shinsei*) and the Nippon Credit Bank (to be called *Aozora*) can sell back loans to the government at face value less specific provisions if the value declines by more than 20 per cent during the next three years.[61] If the bank forgives any part of the debt they must bear the cost of the loan themselves. While this avoids the possibility that the bank might be too generous with debt forgiveness, it does leave the public purse open for greater costs in the future and for making difficult decisions about company restructuring which should otherwise be left to market institutions. The clause has become particularly contentious for the two large banks. One option would have been to sell the banks as they were for a lower price (as indeed happened with the five regional banks) but the authorities maintain that this was not possible for such large banks.[62] Another option would have been a loss sharing arrangement but there were legal obstacles preventing this course of action. This constraint has been lifted from April 2001.

The major banks: bad debts and restructuring

Despite the important re-capitalisation by the authorities in March 1999, the major banks remain burdened by non-performing loans. They returned to profit in the fiscal year ending March 2000 earning 3.4 trillion yen. However, a great part of this profit was accounted for by sales of cross held shares when the stock market was still quite strong, sales to March 2000 accounting for profits of 2½ trillion yen. Although a number of banks plan to reduce their holdings of shares continuously as part of the move to full mark to market accounting in 2001, they also had to meet the net profit goals necessary to qualify for public funds issued in March 1999. On the other hand, they wrote off 4.5 trillion yen in bad debts, three times what they had forecast in September 1999, although half the write-off in FY 1998. The major banks forecast to write off a further 1.6 trillion yen this year but this could be conservative, especially in light of requests for debt forgiveness which have been made and the new bankruptcy law which gives debtors greater protection from creditors. Japan's main city banks still had 17.8 trillion yen bad and doubtful loans on their books on 31 March 2000 against specific provisions of some 10 trillion yen (Table 16). In view of the losses coming to light in the non-financial sector following tighter accountancy standards, many observers still feel that the banks will be burdened by loan losses for a while despite cumulative write-offs of some 50 trillion yen since FY 1992.[63] With regard to the disposal of bad loans, banks have already written off 52 trillion yen (face value) against which reserves of 24 trillion had been provided. Moreover. recent estimates suggest that some 10 trillion yen of bad loans have been sold off at a fraction of face value.[64] While this represents a major clean-up of assets, there are still some 30 trillion of non-performing loans suggesting that banks are still hoping that real estate prices will recover. An obstacle to the more rapid disposal has been the small market for asset-backed securities and the lengthy and inefficient legal bankruptcy procedures which many banks have wanted to avoid. Until recently the rent laws have also made the establishment of real estate values difficult (see Chapter III).

The balance sheet of the major banks remains weak despite re-capitalisation, and income prospects are modest. The major banks have owned traditionally a large volume of cross-held shares and have been able to use a proportion of the unrealised reserves to meet their capital requirements. However, with continuous stock revaluations in recent years it appears that the unrealised reserves are now much smaller than before: one recent estimate is that hidden reserves now disappear when the Nikkei 225 falls below 17 000, compared with half this level ten years ago (Fitch, 2000). Given their large holdings (Table 17) this makes them vulnerable to stock market swings. The large banks must also repay at some stage public money held as preferred shares and they also include as Tier I capital deferred tax reserves which depend on the projected value of future earnings: these two assets together account for 42 per cent of Tier I capital

Table 16. **Loss on disposal of bad loans**[1]

Billion yen, financial years

	1992	1993	1994	1995	1996	1997	1998	1999
Loss on disposal of bad loans	1 640	3 872	5 232	13 369	7 763	13 258	13 631	6 944
				(11 067)	(6 210)	(10 819)	(10 440)	(5 398)
Net transfer to allowance for loan loss	945	1 146	1 402	7 087	3 447	8 403	8 118	2 531
				(5 576)	(2 534)	(6 552)	(5 490)	(1 339)
Direct write-offs	424	2 090	2 809	5 980	4 316	3 993	4 709	3 865
				(5 490)	(3 676)	(3 501)	(4 268)	(3 609)
of which:								
Write-offs of loans	204	235	706	1 721	973	851	2 377	1 881
				(1 568)	(850)	(791)	(2 255)	(1 734)
Loss on sales to the CCPC	219	1 855	2 103	2 526	1 133	1 043	359	278
				(2 132)	(971)	(921)	(339)	(272)
Summing up from FY 1992	1 640	5 512	10 744	24 113	31 877	45 135	58 766	65 710
				(21 811)	(28 021)	(38 840)	(49 280)	(54 678)
Summing up of direct write-offs	424	2 514	5 322	11 602	15 918	19 911	24 620	28 185
				(10 812)	(14 488)	(17 988)	(22 256)	(25 865)
Risk management loans	12 775	13 576	12 546	28 504	21 789	29 758	29 627	30 366
				(21 868)	(16 441)	(21978)	(20 250)	(19 772)
Outstanding amount of allowance for loan loss	3 698	4 547	5 536	13 293	12 334	17 815	14 797	12 230
				(10 345)	(9 388)	(13 601)	(9 258)	(7 678)

1. Before FY 1994, data are composed of city banks, long-term credit banks and trust banks. Figures in parenthesis refer to the amount of city banks, long-term credit banks and trust banks.
2. Hokkaido Takusyoku, Tokuyo City, Kyoto Kyoci, Naniwa, Fukutoku, and Midori Bank are excluded from FY 1997 onward. Long-term Credit Bank of Japan, Nippon Credit Bank, Kokumin, Kofuku and Tokyo Sowa Bank are excluded from FY 1998. Namihaya Bank and Niigata Chuo Bank are excluded from FY 1999.
3. Net transfer to allowance for loan loss refers to the total amount of net transfer to the specific reserve for loan loss and net transfer to the general reserve for loan loss.
4. Direct write-offs refer to the total amount of write-offs of loans, loss on sales of loans, loss on supports to other financial institutions, etc. However, before FY 1994, it was composed of write-offs of loans and loss on sales to the CCPC.
5. Risk management loans comprise loans to borrowers in legal bankruptcy (LBB), past due loans (PDL), and restructured loans. Before FY 1994, disclosed bad loans were composed of LBB and PDL.

Source: Financial Services Agency.

Table 17. **Balance sheet of city banks**
Trillion yen, March 2000

Capital		**Assets**	
Equity	7.1	Premises	4.4
Retained earnings	2.0	Securities	59.9
Reserves	6.9	*of which:* Shares	28.2
Current profits	1.2		
Total capital	**17.2**	Loans and discounts	210.8
		Reserves for non-performing loans	–4.8
Liabilities		Cash and deposits	15.7
Deposits	20.9		
Certificates of deposit	33.6	Other	34.8
Debentures	4.5		
Call liabilities	16.7		
Other	256.1		
Total	**349.0**	**Total**	**349.0**

Source: Bank of Japan and OECD.

of the internationally active banks. As noted above, loans have fallen as major clients have restructured their own balance sheets, and loan margins remain low (Figure 21) with some 13 per cent earning less than 1 per cent (Table 18) which is below the prime rate. Offsetting the decrease in loans, the banking sector has built up a large position in government bonds (64.8 trillion yen) which now account for 10 per cent of their assets and for 15 per cent of the bond market. With interest rates at historical lows, they could be exposed to significant losses under mark-to-market rules if rates were to rise, although some risks have apparently been hedged in the financial markets.

Recognising the urgent need to improve both earnings and balance sheets, the major banks have embarked on an unprecedented wave of merger proposals which, if concluded, would radically change the face of the banking sector. Eleven of the largest banks have announced plans to combine into four new banking corporations. Ranked by assets, three of these would be in the world top five and the biggest would be the world's largest. However, the mergers are moving very slowly and actions to significantly improve profitability appear to be some way off, attracting considerable criticism by market observers (Iimura, 1999). The restructuring plans that banks had to produce at the time of the injection of state funds will now have to be re-negotiated in line with the bank mergers. It will be important for the authorities to set stringent conditions for effective restructuring both with respect to large banks – and elsewhere in the financial sector (Box 5). At the end of the day there is also the question of the early return of public funds which is in the form of preferred shares.

Table 18. **Loans and discounts by interest rate**[1]

End of year shares in per cent

	1994	1995	1996	1997	1998	July 1999
Interest rate						
Less than 1 per cent	1.3	7.0	9.7	6.9	6.5	13.4
1 to 2 per cent	0.8	24.4	25.5	32.0	33.6	29.3
2 to 3 per cent	6.7	30.9	33.5	38.2	40.9	39.7
3 to 4 per cent	45.0	18.7	18.3	13.5	12.4	12.1
4 to 5 per cent	27.9	9.4	6.5	4.9	3.5	3.0
5 to 6 per cent	9.0	3.9	2.7	1.9	1.1	1.0
6 to 7 per cent	4.4	2.5	1.6	1.0	0.7	0.5
7 to 8 per cent	2.6	1.5	0.9	0.6	0.4	0.4
8 to 9 per cent	1.3	0.9	0.6	0.5	0.4	0.3
9 to 10 per cent	0.4	0.3	0.2	0.2	0.2	0.1
More than 10 per cent	0.6	0.5	0.4	0.3	0.3	0.3

1. Banking accounts only.

Source: OECD and Bank of Japan.

Box 5. Restructuring other sections of the financial sector

Regional banks have been under pressure to deal with their non-performing loans and to keep their capital ratios above the official level of 4 per cent. In FY 1999, 16 regional banks (25 per cent of the total) and 27 regional banks Tier II (49 per cent of the total) have boosted their capital, including six which have received an injection of public money. The capital ratio of regional banks has thus risen from 9.32 per cent to 10.2 per cent in March 2000, while for Tier II banks the ratio has risen from 6.76 per cent to 8.09 per cent. Moreover, it is planned to sell two regional banks to a foreign investor.

Reorganisation of agricultural credit coops, which account for 14 per cent of lending to individuals, is lagging. In 1996 it was decided to reduce the number of primary co-operatives from approximately 2 000 to 530 by March 2001. As for the new national structure, there are four options one of which includes reducing the middle tier (the prefectural federations of agricultural credit co-operatives), leaving only the national Norinchukin Bank and the individual coops. This initiative followed the clean-up of the *jusen* housing loan corporations to which the co-operatives were heavy lenders. However, by April 2000, 1 411 co-operatives remained, and prefectural federations are officially estimated to have around ½ trillion yen of non-performing loans, 9 per cent of their loan portfolio.

III. Structural policies to enhance growth and secure recovery: a review of progress

Recent *Surveys* have recommended a broad range of specific structural measures designed both to help Japan rapidly overcome balance sheet problems and resource misallocation inherited from the bubble economy as well as to strengthen growth potential in the future when more rapid total factor productivity growth will have to offset the effects of declining population. This assessment was shared by last year's OECD *Review of Regulatory Reform*, which concluded that the regulatory system had become increasingly outmoded so that a sharp break with past practices was needed. The *Review* went on to note that "the challenge today is to deepen and speed up the regulatory transition already underway, managing its effects on economic and social life so as to sustain and expand political capacities for reform". Although a number of measures have been implemented during the past year, the government has had difficulty in dispelling a sentiment both in Japan and overseas that reform remains half-hearted and partial. This chapter reviews the recent policy measures against the background of previous recommendations and identifies the priority areas which need to be addressed. The first section reviews the measures which have been taken with a view to facilitating corporate restructuring. The impact of these and other measures on the corporate system is also discussed. The second section discusses developments in labour market policy and how these address the evolving patterns of unemployment, worker mobility and labour utilisation. The third section examines regulatory and other measures which have been taken to improve the framework conditions for fostering competitive markets. The last section discusses options for reform of pensions and healthcare systems. A summary of recommendations from both previous *Surveys* and the *Regulatory Review* and an assessment of progress is provided in Table 19.

Table 19. **Recommendations for structural reform and assessment of progress**
Based on previous and current Surveys and the Review of Regulatory Reform

Previous Survey's recommendations	Action taken since 1999 Survey	Survey assessment/ recommendations
I. Reform the financial sector (see chapter II)		
i) Recapitalise the banking system	Two nationalised banks now sold. Recapitalisation now extending to regional banks and eventually to credit coops and unions.	Pressure needs to be maintained on banks to restructure. Re-negotiation of restructuring agreements with newly merging banks needs to maintain strict conditions.
ii) Shore up the life insurance sector	Inspections underway and prompt corrective action (PCA) procedures in force. Several companies have been forced to stop operations. Reform of safety net in place with possibility to cut promised rates of return to policy holders.	Premiums of the Policy Protection Corporation paid by companies should be differentiated according to risk of the company. Support de-mutualisation.
iii) Tighten regulatory oversight and boost transparency and disclosure	New Financial Service Agency established combining policy and regulatory functions. Consolidated accounting being implemented. Universal deposit protection extended beyond March 2001.	Universal deposit protection should not be further postponed.
iv) Complete the "Big Bang" liberalisation by March 2001	Entry of banks into insurance business through subsidiaries permitted from October 2000. Sales of certain insurance services by banks permitted from April 2000.	Remove unnecessary compartmentalisation and restrictions on issuance and purchasing of securities.
II. Enhance product market competition		
i) Accelerate deregulation	Deregulation programme expanded in March 1999.	Implement the 917 measures as early as possible. Extend the work of the Regulatory Reform Committee. Examine regulatory issues in the legal sector.
ii) Further strengthen competition policy. Allow victims of unfair trade practices to go directly to court	Consumer Contract Law implemented. Competition law extended to electricity and gas. Injunction relief introduced and damage action system improved.	Ensure independence of Fair Trade Commission in the new ministerial system. Immunity from prosecution for co-operation with FTC could be introduced.

Table 19. **Recommendations for structural reform and assessment of progress** *(cont.)*

Based on previous and current Surveys and the Review of Regulatory Reform

Previous Survey's recommendations	Action taken since 1999 Survey	Survey assessment/ recommendations
iii) Take steps to encourage competition in utilities. Lift fare controls in transport sector.	Tariffs can be set freely except for price caps in some areas. Airline prices deregulated. Agreement to lower interconnection charges in telecommunications. Electricity liberalisation introduced.	Establish independent regulatory bodies in electricity and in telecommunications with role to establish and promote competition. Consider restructuring the dominant telecommunications company. Establish effective network access in electricity, telecommunications and gas.
iv) Eliminate use of supply/demand adjustment mechanisms	Abolished in the transport sector from February/March 2000.	Progress needs to be consolidated through implementation. Market excess clause for taxis should be applied with prudence.
III. Promote industrial restructuring and boost technology and innovation		
i) Update the Commercial Code and ease restructuring	Update of commercial code in progress and committee now examining broader reforms. Mergers based on stock swaps permitted and laws passed easing corporate splits and transfer of assets and employment. Industrial Revitalisation Law legislated.	Ensure true outsiders on boards and cut functions of auditing committee. Recognise corporate officer systems. Ease share issue regulations. Avoid need for government approval of business restructuring plans for cases under the Revitalisation Law.
ii) Revise the patent law	Researchers accorded intellectual property rights on government-sponsored research.	Monitor new system.
iii) Increase emphasis on basic research and improve efficiency of public technology spending	On-going efforts to make the system more flexible, competitive and open.	Continue these efforts and evaluate the achievement of the Basic Plan after 2000.
iv) Encourage more start-ups and venture business	Numerous tax and lending programmes since the November 1998 Emergency Economic Measures.	Programmes lacking focus. Venture finance less of a problem than before but venture firms not effective.
v) Streamline bankruptcy procedures	New reorganisation law in force since April 2000 and a large number of firms have made filings.	Monitor implementation of new law and especially how courts are implementing it. Complete reform of other bankruptcy laws.

Table 19. **Recommendations for structural reform and assessment of progress** *(cont.)*

Based on previous and current Surveys and the Review of Regulatory Reform

Previous Survey's recommendations	Action taken since 1999 Survey	Survey assessment/ recommendations
IV. Liberalise the agricultural sector	A new Basic Law enacted in July 1999. Little progress in reducing producer support although a move away from price support is underway.	Reduce producer support. Extend the range of products for which support shifts from prices to direct income aid. Encourage farm consolidation through changes in land and tax policies. Remove any direct support for the agricultural co-operatives. Improve efficiency of public works in rural areas.[1]
V. Use market-based instruments to improve environmental outcomes	Automobile Acquisition Tax already based on fuel efficiency and other automobile-related taxes may be similarly changed. Fees being considered for household garbage disposal.	As in previous survey: make greater use of the tax system and market pricing more generally to achieve official objectives.
VI. Boost public sector efficiency (see Chapter IV)		
VII. Reform the pension system		
i) Overhaul the public component to put it on a sustainable basis	Pension Reform Law passed in 1999.	Source of government financing from 2004 needs to be settled.
ii) Ensure the corporate pension system is adequately funded	Disclosure required in FY 2000; shortages to be funded by FY 2015. Employers allowed to contribute cross-held shares, along with their voting rights.	
iii) Propose basic framework law for corporate pensions	No action.	Same as in previous Surveys.
iv)	Pension Fund Association has adopted guidelines requiring fund managers to exercise voting rights to increase returns.	Monitor operation of system
VIII. Reform the health care system		
i) Institute a long-term care insurance scheme	In operation since April 2000.	Do more to even out regional disparities in premia. Provide modest subsidies to family-based care.

Table 19. **Recommendations for structural reform and assessment of progress** *(cont.)*

Based on previous and current Surveys and the Review of Regulatory Reform

Previous Survey's recommendations	Action taken since 1999 Survey	Survey assessment/ recommendations
ii) Modify the basic health insurance system.	Still under discussion.	Reduce pharmaceutical consumption; encourage move away from fee-for-service payments.
Broaden contribution base.	No action.	Same as previous Survey.
Avoid longer-term oversupply of physicians	No action.	Same as previous Survey.
Avoid incentives for over-prescription of medicines and excessive numbers of "acts"	DRG-type system being considered for hospital financing.	Stop direct dispensing of drugs by doctors. Doctors' incomes could be supported by raising average fee levels in exchange for constraints on the number of acts.
IX. Increase the flexibility of employment and improve active labour market policies		
i) Allow temporary employment agencies to play a larger role	Market now liberalised apart from a small negative list. One year time limit on contracts.	Consider extending the one-year limit on contracts to include temporary to permanent possibility.
ii) Make corporate pensions portable	Defined contribution pension plans being considered.	Such a move would deepen the mid-career labour market.
iii) Permit private job placement firms to play a more important role	Done.	As in previous survey: the exclusion of port and construction workers needs justification.
iv) Evaluate the effectiveness of all active labour market policies	Number and size of programmes increased.	The importance of this recommendation has grown with the increase in spending on such programmes.
v)	Comprehensive Plan for Employment Activation.	Ensure that the government jobs are indeed only temporary. Justify regional differentiation of subsidies or remove it.
	Unemployment benefits shortened for older workers in retirement but lengthened for older workers who lose their jobs.	Consider making benefits paid to older workers degressive over time so as to encourage reservation wage to decline.

Table 19. **Recommendations for structural reform and assessment of progress** (*cont.*)

Based on previous and current Surveys and the Review of Regulatory Reform

Previous Survey's recommendations	Action taken since 1999 Survey	Survey assessment/ recommendations
X. Increase labour force skills		
i) Improve the quality and availability of training outside of firms	Training subsidies increased.	Consider wider provision for younger workers who are finding it hard to get employment with firms which offer associated training possibilities.
ii) Improve the education system	Minor higher education changes since April 2000.	Same as previous Survey.

1. See also OECD, *Agricultural Policies in* OECD *Countries*, Paris, 2000

Source: OECD.

Enhancing corporate performance

Facilitating enterprise restructuring

In recent years, a policy priority has been to encourage and to facilitate enterprise restructuring by changing the legal framework (Table 20). Among the most important changes is a radical overhaul of the accounting system which makes more apparent than ever before the urgent need for restructuring in a large number of enterprises. The first step, which has been in effect for firms as of the financial year ending on 31 March 2000, reinforces consolidated accounting through a more effective definition of subsidiary companies (*i.e.* effective control rather than just the level of share ownership). The new code makes it difficult to

Table 20. **Selected institutional changes to facilitate corporate restructuring in recent years**

A. Major legal changes

Year	Laws	Contents
1997	Commercial codes	Procedures for corporate mergers were rationalised
	Anti-monopoly law	Holding companies were allowed (effective in December)
1998	Financial holding company law	Financial holding companies were allowed (effective in March)
1999	Commercial codes	Share swaps were introduced; procedures related to parent and subsidiary companies were rationalised
2000	Private rehabilitation law	A new reorganisation law replacing the Composition Law (effective in April)
	Commercial codes	Procedures for corporate splits introduced

B. Accounting rules

Effective since	Contents
March 2000	Consolidated accounting was reinforced; cash flow statements were introduced; consistency with tax treatment was ensured
March 2001	Securities held for transaction purposes are to be marked to market; real estate held for sale is to be revalued if the market value is 50 per cent lower than the book value;[1] net retirement payment liabilities are to be disclosed, together with measures to eliminate them
March 2002	Shares for cross holding purposes are to be marked to market

1. Even if the decline is less than 50 per cent, the amount of capital losses may be requested to be disclosed when it is sizeable

Source: OECD.

conceal losses and liabilities by transferring them to unconsolidated firms and has resulted in a 12 per cent increase in the total number of parent and consolidated companies. For some listed companies, the results have apparently come as quite a shock to members of the board. Cash flow statements have also been introduced which, together with business line disclosure in force since March 1991, should help stakeholders to make more informed decisions. The mark-to-market principle is to be strengthened step by step over the next two years. In particular, the principle is to be applied to cross share holdings from March 2002, and this is serving to force a review of portfolios.[65] Where real estate loses more than 50 per cent of its balance sheet value a revaluation must be made which will make clear to both insiders and outside observers the true net worth of the company. However, some construction and real estate companies seem to have started to window dress their balance sheets by shifting inventories of real estate for sale to the companies' fixed assets.[66] Since net retirement liabilities are also scheduled to be disclosed from March 2001, some companies have started to provide necessary reserves by contributing share holdings to trusts.[67] The overall impact of recognising unfunded pension liabilities remains unclear since there are widely differing estimates of the required provision.

To support enterprise reorganisation, a new law was passed in May which eased both the transfer of assets and of employees. In either spinning-off a division into a separate company or integrating a division with another existing company firms will no longer require the approval of individual creditors or have their assets assessed by a court. Restructuring through mergers and holding companies is also made easier (Table 20). For example, a holding company can now be more easily established through share swaps (as a result of the 1999 revisions), and subsidiary companies might then be reorganised under the holding company according to each business line through mergers (the 1999 revisions) and corporate spin-offs (the 2000 revisions). There have been some signs of progress in restructuring, facilitated by the expected availability of these new tools, most notably in the finance sector. Three major banks (Industrial Bank of Japan, Dai-ichi Kangyo and Fuji banks) plan to reorganise their business through jointly setting up a holding company, while Sumitomo and Sakura and other banks plan to use mergers.[68] Taxation issues nevertheless remain to be clarified. They include whether realised gains from company splits should be taxed as well as how to handle losses being transferred to another subsidiary to avoid tax payments. Screening measures should be developed. Tax rules covering corporate splits are due to be announced in December 2000 while consolidated taxation is under review.

New legislation passed in May clarified the ambiguity as to whether the consent of employees is required before transferring them to newly formed companies. It specifies cases where consent is not needed (*e.g.* where the operations are equivalent). The changes also make it clear that employment contracts and labour agreements would, in principle, be carried over to a new company resulting from corporate splits.[69] Related ordinances still need to be issued, which will have an important influence on the applicability of the law. New corporate structures such as holding companies may nevertheless lead to a change in traditional employment practices (Tachibanaki *et al.*, 1998) since wage bargaining and contract conditions can in principle be handled at the subsidiary company level.

Corporate restructuring is also likely to be facilitated by a new corporate reorganisation law [Private Rehabilitation Law (*Minji Saisei-ho*)] which has been in force since April 2000. The new law aims to provide a more efficient reorganisation scheme (for SMEs in particular) by easing requirements for filing and setting up a debtor-in-possession procedure (see Box 6 for details of Japanese schemes). It rectifies defects of the existing laws and also incorporates several new streamlined procedures for a more effective restructuring.[70] The courts can approve a restructuring plan more quickly than under the other laws. The plan requires approval of half the creditors as opposed to two-thirds under the old laws, and vital assets can be protected even against a creditor secured by the asset in question. In the Japanese case this is usually land, and the priority claim can be extinguished by paying the appraisal value of the collateral to the court. In the first three months of implementation, 146 companies filed for the procedures including one company on the first

Box 6. Japanese corporate bankruptcy framework in an international perspective

The Japanese legal structure is a mixed one, initially under German influence (as liquidation and composition procedures were created after Germany in the 1920s) but was supplemented with a US-type reorganisation law after World War II. The Japanese bankruptcy system consists of two liquidation procedures, Liquidation (*Hasan*) and Special Liquidation (*Tokubetsu Seisan*), and three reorganisation procedures, Corporate Restructuring (*Kaisha Kosei*), Private Rehabilitation (*Minji Saisei*) and Corporate Reorganisation (*Kaisha Seiri*). Special Liquidation and Corporate Reorganisation are based on the commercial code, while the rest are on their own special laws. The balance between liquidation and reorganisation varies across countries. Priority on the former increases transparency for creditors but increases the probability of closing a firm which would be viable, whereas emphasis on the latter increases the probability of saving a firm which would be non-viable. Among G7 countries, Germany and the United Kingdom are likely to be the most pro-liquidation, while the United States the most pro-reorganisation, according to Rajan and Zingales (1995); Franks and Torous, 1993; White, 1996. Germany started to implement a new reorganisation procedure in April 1999, but its effects remain to be seen in view of the fact that the United Kingdom's introduction of such a procedure in the late 1980s did not change the basic nature of its system.

list of the Tokyo Stock Exchange, and 22 other companies switched to the new procedure. Up till now, companies have tended to prefer out-of-court procedures: according to a private information service company (Teikoku Data Bank), only about an eighth of bankrupt firms utilised legal procedures in the 1990s. However, because a high level of support from so-called main banks is now expected to be less widely available, the legal framework which the new law provides might be even more important in the future.[71] It is too early to evaluate the new scheme, especially since implementation is left to the courts where capacity to deal with bankruptcy cases appears to be limited.[72] Predictability about how the new law will function might take a while to be established. The new law is the first stage of an overall reform of the system and will be followed by revisions to a scheme for personal bankruptcies. A change to the law covering bankruptcy for companies with overseas assets is also under deliberation.

A number of temporary measures, which will remain in effect until March 2003, were introduced by the Industry Revitalisation Law in October 1999, but in its first year of operation the impact on restructuring is not clear.[73] MITI and other related ministries granted 45 approvals by the end of July for corporate restructuring plans, mainly for large firms. However, although this scheme facilitates corporate restructuring, some of the plans might have been forthcoming without the additional incentives. Prefecture governors have granted only 70 approvals for financial aid to venture firms and existing SMEs starting new business lines. Another scheme seeks to encourage R&D through granting 100 per cent patent rights to private companies for projects sponsored by the government. MITI has applied this principle to all the projects it has granted since the implementation of the law (1 111 cases in FY 1999 covering expenditures of 256 billion yen).

Changing corporate governance

Many of the recent legal and regulatory reforms that are intended to help enterprises restructure and to deal with their balance sheet problems have implications for the corporate governance system. Thus accounting reform not only fosters restructuring but also increases information disclosure to outsiders, thereby increasing the potential for market-based monitoring. New prudential regulations for banks and changes in their organisation are a response to financial market developments but they also change the incentives and the capacity for banks to play a key role in monitoring corporate performance. The new bankruptcy law will help firms to restructure but it also shifts the balance of negotiating power from creditors to debtors, which is in line with the reduced power of the banks to act as a key force in corporate restructuring.

Pressures to change the system of corporate governance are coming from a number of directions, one of which is the significant change in the share ownership structure of listed companies. Banks and insurance companies have been selling their share holdings to compensate for losses from non-performing loans, and this has accelerated in recent years (Figure 23). These sales have been partially absorbed by non-financial companies and trusts. Mergers and acquisitions climbed by 27 per cent in 1999 and by 36 per cent year on year in the first half of 2000. Nearly all such cases were negotiated rather than hostile. Foreign investors have been major buyers holding a larger share than individuals by the end of FY 1999. Indeed, foreign investors held more than 33 per cent of the total shares in 30 companies in the first section of the Tokyo Stock Exchange in FY 1998, up from 12 companies in FY 1990, according to Nissei Research Institute.

Although foreign shareholding has increased and FDI has risen strongly in recent years, the overall pattern of shareholding is proving much more durable so that the impact on corporate governance might be more limited. In particular, the tradition of cross shareholding has survived to date: the Nissei Research Institute found that for 2 426 companies there were cross shareholdings in 95.2 per cent of them as of March 1999. These holdings corresponded to around 16 per cent of the stock market value of the companies concerned, down by about 5 per cent during the last 10 years although with a tendency for the decline to accelerate in the recent years.[74] At the same time, stable or "friendly" stock holdings, although falling in recent years, nevertheless still accounted for 40 per cent of shareholdings in listed companies (Figure 24). Some authors have argued that it is these

Figure 23. **Changing share ownership structure**
Listed companies, fiscal year, end of period

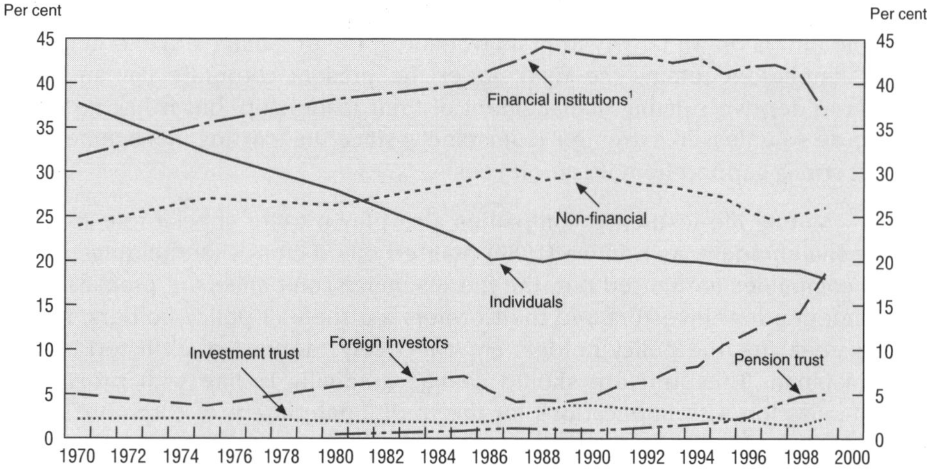

1. Excludes investment and pensions funds.
Source : Tokyo Stock Exchange.

Figure 24. **Friendly and cross shareholdings**
Fiscal year, end of period

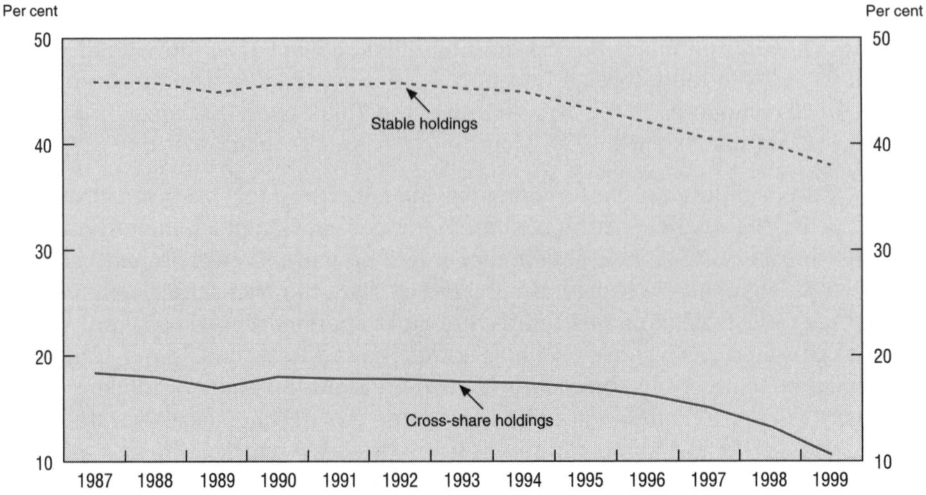

Source: NRI Research Institute.

holdings which are crucial in maintaining what some term "labour-managed firms".[75] The large friendly shareholders support the management of the firm which in turn is drawn largely from its workforce, the dominant stakeholder.[76] The large shareholder retains the right under the present corporate law and legal system to deprive existing management of their leadership, but it has no incentive to do so unless in extreme circumstances since the existing management can expect strong support from its employees.

Mutual life insurance companies also play a quite special role in being stable shareholders. As Komiya (1989) pointed out, if cross shareholdings among listed companies are netted out, the life insurance companies are practically the only independent investors and their owners are then all policy holders, that is, legally speaking, the policy holders are effectively "owners" of all listed companies in Japan. This structure should change gradually in line with progress in demutualisation with implications for the traditional pattern of corporate governance. As noted in Chapter II, major progress has been made this year to facilitate restructuring of life insurance companies, which are suffering from major losses due to negative spreads, but are slow to restructure themselves because of their peculiar organisational structures as mutual companies. The revised Insurance

Industry Law could make demutualisation of these companies less difficult by allowing the cashing of resulting fractional lot stocks. The demutualisation could allow these companies to raise funds from the market to strengthen their capital base and to utilise a holding company scheme more easily.[77] However, it seems unlikely to bring about substantial windfalls for policy holders and have effects on the economy, unlike earlier examples in Australia and the United Kingdom.[78]

Though employees' pension funds have the power to instruct trust banks and insurance companies who manage their assets as to how to exercise their voting rights, they have tended to refrain from taking a position. This is changing in response to the 1998 decision by the Pension Fund Association to formulate a policy regarding the exercise of these rights. These guidelines were revised in October 1999 by inserting a clause that called for investment managers to exercise voting rights with the aim of increasing the returns to their investment. These changes are said to be leading fund managers to take their fiduciary responsibilities more seriously.

A key element of the corporate governance system is the commercial code, which is being fundamentally reviewed by a committee of the Ministry of Justice over the next two years. There are a number of issues in this area. Formalising the structure of group companies is a key issue with the law lagging behind practice, *e.g.* the Securities and Exchange Law has consolidated accounting rules, but the commercial code and tax laws do not treat group companies as such. Consolidated accounting has to be provided for as well as dividends based on group earnings. Lower quorum levels and less detailed approvals at stockholder meetings are also sought by companies. Proposals have also been made to change the code so as to better support dynamic new start-ups (see the following section). Japanese companies have not fully separated management decision-making power from responsibility for overseeing the implementation of decisions. Under the commercial code both are defined as board of director functions. Many companies intend to simplify their boards, whose members are mainly appointed from inside the firm, and set up a corporate officer system.[79] By the end of 1999, 226 companies had introduced a corporate officer system which was hardly known in 1997. Such changes alter the governance system in subtle ways, weakening the incentive effect of internal promotion under the practice of lifetime employment. Compensating for such changes *via* increased performance-related pay would appear to be a logical development and indeed more than 50 listed companies have announced plans to adopt stock options this fiscal year; around 10 per cent of listed companies had introduced stock option schemes by the end of March 2000.

Other key issues in corporate law reform concern the role of the "statutory auditors" (*kansayaku*) and the procedures for shareholder law suits.[80] The "statutory auditors" originated as a temporary institution which has become permanent.

They are observers in board meetings and their role was redefined in 1974 to include monitoring and policing of management decisions. The corporate law revision in 1993 further specified that for large corporations (defined to be companies with paid-up capital of at least 500 million yen or total debt of at least 20 billion yen) the audit board should comprise three persons with a minimum of one from outside the firm.[81] They are charged with overseeing directors including the chairman of the board who are usually insiders in the sense that they have been promoted internally. Some of the audit board members are also insiders and they are appointed by the stockholders on the proposal by the chairman and board of directors. The system thus suffers from insufficient outside monitoring. Some have suggested the need to convert statutory auditors into outside directors and to introduce a law requiring half the board directors to come from outside the company. The fee for filing shareholder derivative law suits declined in 1993, following the legal clarification given to its determination, which dispensed with the extra fee for such actions. The number of suits has more than tripled since then. The rise in law suits has been one of the reasons for companies reducing the size of their corporate boards recently and for establishing executive officers.[82] There are now proposals to cap directors' liability to the company for their business judgement in the case of successful suits. An opposing position is that the threat of suits has made for more efficient management.

Overall, the authorities have made significant headway in facilitating corporate restructuring while at the same time supporting the tendency already underway for external monitoring to play a greater role in the system of corporate governance. With respect to restructuring, what remains is for the government to maintain consistent pressure on the banks to both improve their risk assessment and to deal efficiently with the balance sheet problems of their clients (Chapter II). In this respect, it will be necessary for the government to support and to use the market-based instrument which it has introduced such as the new reorganisation procedures. The setting of accounting standards could also be devolved to a non-governmental body, which would clarify the independence of standards from more general economic policy considerations. However, the key issues concern the development of the system of corporate governance and the need to maintain coherency of the system (Heinrich, 1999; Hoshi, 1998). With the system spontaneously moving toward greater external monitoring it will be important to act quickly to fill in the gaps. To this end the Commercial Code needs to be reformed with a greater emphasis placed on external directors. Such a reform would make the statutory auditors superfluous. The role of capital markets is also likely to increase, which will in turn require a tightening of insider trading rules and explicit limits to the role of large shareholders. Germany, which has had a somewhat similar system of corporate governance, has also had to adopt new arrangements (*e.g.* insider trading laws and take-over codes which limits the actions of large shareholders) to reflect the greater role of capital markets.

Stimulating entrepreneurial activity

Policy has continued to be strongly supportive of SMEs with loan guarantees and financial support through public financial institutions. In addition, as part of their restructuring plans for receiving re-capitalisation (Chapter II), the banks have had to raise their lending to SMEs. This resulted in a surge of lending in March this year. The new framework law for policy, which was passed in December 1999, has raised the average capital size defining SMEs, thereby giving them access to financial support programmes. The new law also emphasises a key role for start-ups which have become a concern of the government: the rate of business start-ups is 2.7 per cent, the lowest in the post-war era and down from around 6 per cent in the period 1975-78.[83] At the same time, as noted in Chapter I, the rate of bankruptcy has risen to high levels. The government has set an objective to increase the number of start-ups from 140 000 at present to 240 000 mainly by creating an appropriate environment including easier financing from public financial institutions. SMEs also benefit from favourable treatment in bidding for public contracts but, as noted in Chapter IV, the associated costs would appear to be unacceptably high.

A key barrier for sophisticated start-ups is often not finance *per se* but access to overall support facilities and getting experienced directors in quickly. The idea of venture finance has been imported from the United States but it is not working in the same manner. One aspect of this is that venture funds invest in too many companies – the average number of enterprises invested in by a US fund is six whereas in Japan it is around thirty – and they tend to be later-stage companies in more traditional activities. Moreover, a US fund will normally sift through hundreds of business plans to find a potential candidate and will stay with the company for a long period. The Japanese funds are said to lack staff for this and they tend to quit the firm at the time of its IPO. Until recently, stock options were not allowed for non-employees including support groups, but now that this barrier has been removed, the way is set for the development of more mature forms of venture support.

Going beyond the area of new start-ups, MITI set up a 17 member study group in April to help companies that plan to go public speed up their decision making and enhance the efficiency of their management. Among the ideas the Committee is considering are changes to the Commercial Code increasing the number of shares companies can issue without changing their charter. The goal is to promote flexible fund procurement and capital tie-ups. The ministry is also proposing to introduce new preferred stock that will entitle its holders to exclusive voting rights on important management decisions such as mergers and board appointments. This would pave the way for speedy decision making. At the moment they may only be entitled to preferred dividends and have no right to vote.

Financial markets able to support entrepreneurial high growth firms have been developing rapidly, with three now in competition with each other. In December 1999, the Tokyo Stock Exchange launched its MOTHERS market and on 9 June this year the NASDAQ Japan market in the Osaka Securities Exchange started operations. In addition, there is JASDAQ, an OTC run by the Japan Securities Dealers Association in Tokyo. Analysts estimated that 150-200 companies will go public this year, more than double the 75 last year, but by the middle of the year prices had fallen and a number of plans were being reviewed. The JASDAQ has seen 39 IPOs in the first half of this year compared with 20 during the same period last year. The markets are in competition with each other although each is striving to find a market niche. JASDAQ is trying to expand a market-maker scheme and each trading house is to carry some float. The market also intends to facilitate de-listing for shares with low trading volumes. MOTHERS lists firms within one year of foundation and they can be making losses as long as they are judged to have growth potential. Prices of some stocks have fallen below their IPO value as investors have become more selective. More generally, there is a problem of market liquidity since there is not a market maker akin to the successful Neue Markt in Frankfurt (OECD, 1999*c*).

Direct and indirect support for SMEs is now widespread and, with so many programmes now available, there is the danger of a lack of focus and the potential for rising dead weight costs. Policies have been driven by the need to boost the economy in the short run which under the conditions was understandable. However, there is a growing need to rationalise the programmes and to focus resources in key areas where there might be an institutional failure. In general, reduced regulatory barriers (such as those being investigated by a MITI study group) and lower corporate taxes/social contributions would be preferable to direct support targeted at industries, which are in any case expected to grow.

Supporting the evolution of labour markets

Although the labour market is showing some signs of improvement this year, the overall situation is still worrisome. Involuntary unemployment has surged to around 1 million from only 320 000 in 1992, and a growing share of the unemployed can be regarded as structural. According to the EPA, structural unemployment in FY 1999 averaged 3.6 per cent, up from around 2.2 per cent in the early part of the decade. The share of unemployed out of work for more than 12 months is now around 22 per cent and the participation rate has slid from 63.3 per cent in 1990 to 62.9 per cent in 1999 (Table 21). Discouraged workers as a percentage of the labour force have gone up from 1 per cent to 2.2 per cent over the same period. Moreover, the nature of work relations is now more diverse: part-time, temporary and contract workers account for 27.5 per cent of employees according to a Ministry of Labour (MOL) survey, up 4.7 percentage points from September 1994 with part-time workers accounting for 20.3 per cent. On the other hand, there is a substantial churning of labour and resource reallocation is underway. Service sector employment accounts for nearly 55 per cent of the labour

Table 21. **Some structural labour market indicators**

	1986	1987	1988	1989	1990	1991	1992	1993	1994	1995	1996	1997	1998	1999
Discouraged workers (per cent of labour force)	1.4	1.5	1.3	1.1	1.0	0.9	0.9	1.0	1.3	1.4	1.5	1.7	1.9	2.2
Share of unemployed out of work (per cent)														
– More than 6 months	39.0	38.7	40.5	37.1	38.0	36.0	35.0	33.8	35.1	38.2	40.2	40.9	39.0	44.4
– More than 12months	17.1	18.8	20.2	18.5	19.0	17.6	15.3	15.3	16.5	18.1	19.6	20.9	20.7	22.4
Total job separations in past years (per cent of employment)	7.9	9.1	9.3	9.0	7.3	8.7	8.8	8.8	9.3	10.1	10.1	10.5	10.9	12.0
Share of separations resulting in unemployment (per cent)	18.4	19.9	16.0	13.9	12.9	12.5	13.7	16.2	18.5	18.8	20.6	19.1	20.7	23.9
of which: Share involuntary	47.3	n.a.	43.4	36.5	31.3	34.8	32.6	40.2	43.4	42.5	40.7	40.3	46.1	47.2
Separations resulting in new job (per cent of employment)														
Total	3.1	3.1	4.1	4.2	3.5	4.2	4.4	4.1	4.0	4.2	4.3	4.7	4.9	4.9
Aged 25-34	4.0	3.7	5.4	5.3	4.9	5.4	6.2	5.9	5.5	5.6	6.1	6.7	6.6	6.9
New job in past year (per cent)														
Share through public job placement service	n.a.	n.a.	n.a.	7.8	6.7	6.3	5.8	7.4	9.1	8.5	9.7	8.7	9.1	10.8
Share through media advertising	n.a.	n.a.	n.a.	25.0	24.2	26.3	26.9	27.3	28.6	31.5	32.1	34.3	34.9	35.3

Source: Management and Coordination Agency, *Report on the Special Survey of the Labour Force Survey*, February (annual).

force, up 5 percentage points since 1990, although still much lower than in other countries. However, with the vacancy to unemployed ratio rising, there is some concern about rising job mismatch.

Background to the evolving structural problems in the labour market

The organisation of the labour market is related to the system of corporate governance in Japan, being characterised by the practice of lifetime employment and an age dependent wage structure. These labour market characteristics underpin the system of corporate governance dominated by insiders (*i.e.* the long-term employees). The system is, however, under pressure for change. The rapid ageing of the population is reflected in a shift in the age composition of enterprises towards older workers and to a rise in the average tenure (Figure 25). Combined with the seniority-based wage system, ageing is leading to underlying wage cost increases of 2 per cent per annum (Hattori and Maeda, 2000). Although there has been some flattening of the wage profile, especially for university graduates, it has not been enough to offset the tendency for wages to rise. Faced with high wage costs in the past and with cyclical downturns, large firms have been able to adjust by reducing employment of young workers and by transferring existing workers to related SMEs which have been traditionally almost always short of labour. This is no longer the case (Figure 26). Employment of school/university leavers has fallen and greater resort has been made of part-time and temporary workers to lower labour costs, and to overtime on the part of existing lifetime employees.

The traditional labour system is faced with three sets of issues concerning older workers, youth and part-timers. First, there has been an increasing number of layoffs of older workers (above 55 years) often associated with the bankruptcy of a firm. With the average duration of unemployment of this ex-insider group high, the layoffs have contributed to the rapid rise in the overall rate of unemployment. Job offers often specify an upper age limit which excludes them and they are in any case expensive, being used to their old seniority related pay. They are more likely to become discouraged workers which, if taken into account, would lift the rate of unemployment of older workers from 6½ per cent to around 9½ per cent.

Second, there is a serious youth unemployment problem developing since new workers are being squeezed out of employment by incumbents and for some, this is leading to a more precarious attachment to the labour market. In addition, there is a mismatch between job applicants by young workers and job offers, and voluntary youth unemployment is increasing. Within Japan there is often a tendency to consider youth unemployment as a luxury since it is in part due to a high voluntary quit rate.[84] However, one study shows that the youth quit rate is related to the state of the economy (Ohta, 2000). The share of never-been-employed in youth unemployment is now 22 per cent and steadily increasing since 1990 when it was 16 per cent. The percentage of young (15-34) reluctant or unable to obtain

Figure 25. **Age composition of male workers by firm size**

Per cent of total

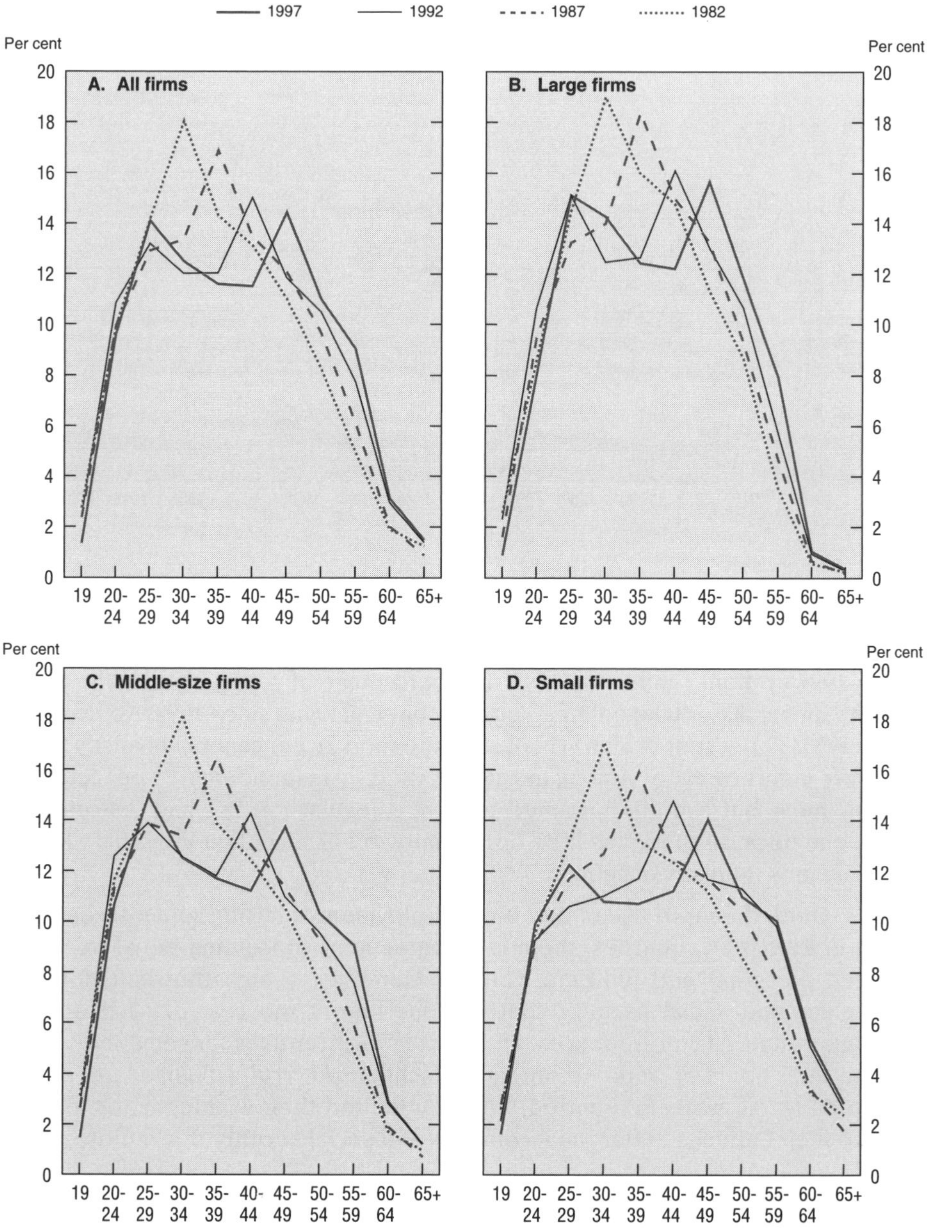

Source: Hattori and Maeda (2000) and the Ministry of Labour.

Figure 26. **Judgement on the excessiveness of employees**
Diffusion index

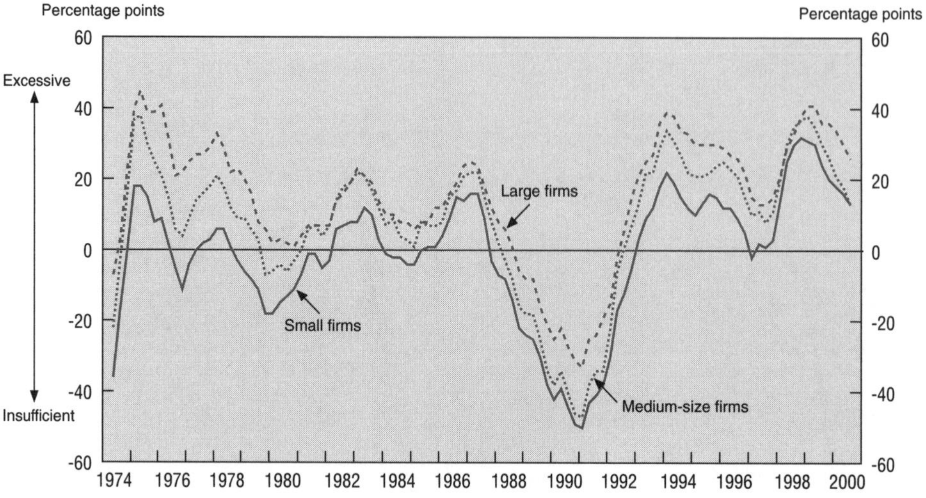

Source: Bank of Japan.

permanent employment or who are on part-time jobs has reached 1.5 million at the end of 1997 up from 1 million in 1992. The percentage of young people who do not go on to university or take full time jobs has been growing since 1992. At the end of March 1999, 32 per cent of high school graduates and 23 per cent of university graduates were in this category. Among the causes cited by respondents, 25 per cent seek self fulfilment but two-thirds wanted to have a regular job but had difficulties to obtain one because there was little opportunity to enhance their job skills while on part-time jobs (Ministry of Labour, 2000).

Third, the rapid rise of part time employment is raising some issues since, unlike in European countries, there is no agreement concerning equal treatment between part-time and full-time workers. Moreover, a high threshold for both income tax and social security contributions lowers the cost of such workers, although with fiscal consequences, and creates disincentives for some individuals to raise their hours of work. According to Tachibanaki *et al.* (2000), 40 per cent of female part-time workers reported that they limited their working hours in order to keep their earnings under the income tax and social security thresholds.

Policy response and outstanding issues

Against the background of these labour market problems the government has introduced a number of measures over the past year which have been described as moving from employment preservation to new job creation and reducing job mismatch.[85] Following a package of measures taken in June 1999 costing 0.5 trillion yen and designed to create 700 000 jobs (see *Survey* 1999, p. 205 for details), the November 1999 stimulus package (Chapter II) announced 1 trillion yen for employment policy measures: 274 billion yen for FY 1999 and 722 billion for FY 2000. The focus will be on business start-ups and support for employment in SMEs subject to adjustment. Subsidies will be granted to business firms which employ full-time workers who have lost their jobs at subcontractors and firms which come under pressure to reduce their workforce when large enterprises (designated enterprises) which they supply carry out restructuring through, for example, plant closures.[86] The subsidy will also cover those who have lost their jobs in the designated local area. Business firms which employ such workers will be subsidised for six months by flat payments of 100 000 yen per worker. 32 billion yen was earmarked for this latter programme.

Faced with the unemployment rate rising to 4.9 per cent in March 2000, the government introduced a new package of measures in May, which also included a proviso for additional actions to be introduced automatically should unemployment exceed 5 per cent.[87] The aim was to create 350 000 jobs in a year but the new package added no new funds to those allocated to labour market measures last year since the take-up rate by enterprises was exceedingly low: only 1 per cent of the funds had been allocated by April 2000. Like the previous measures from June 1999, employment subsidies are only available for enterprises in one of 15 business categories (including IT, health services, and long-term care) designated as new or growth sectors, but they are not available if a firm has dismissed workers in the preceding six months. New workers must also be hired through a government-authorised employment agency. The original scheme was only available for employers who hired involuntary unemployed workers between the age of 30 and 59. The new scheme has expanded the eligibility criteria to those under 30 years of age, school graduates who have not found jobs, and those under 60 years of age who have joined vocational training. There will be a fixed payment regardless of age (700 000 yen per employee).

Despite the announcements during the past year of a number of labour market measures, it is very difficult to establish the size of these programmes. As noted above, the June 1999 measures appear so far to have brought a very limited response, although several of them have achieved results exceeding initial objectives. Moreover, up till 1999 labour market measures appear to have been very modest indeed (Table 22).

The high and rising level of unemployment has brought the unemployment benefits scheme into financial difficulties, forcing a greater differentiation between recipients and an increase of premiums from April 2001. Since FY 1994, the system has run a deficit reaching over 1 trillion yen in FY 1999. With no policy

Table 22. **Public expenditures in labour market programmes**
Fiscal years starting April 1

	Public expenditure as a percentage of GDP			
	1995-96	1996-97	1997-98	1998-99
1. Public employment services and administration	**0.03**	**0.03**	**0.03**	**0.03**
2. Labour market training	**0.03**	**0.03**	**0.03**	**0.03**
Training for unemployed adults and those at risk	0.03	0.03	0.03	0.03
Training for employed adults	–	–	–	–
3. Youth measures	–	–	–	–
Measures for unemployed and disadvantaged youth	–	–	–	–
Support of apprenticeship and related forms of general youth training	–	–	–	–
4. Subsidised employment	**0.06**	**0.04**	**0.02**	**0.02**
Subsidies to regular employment in the private sector	0.06	0.04	0.02	0.02
Support of unemployed persons starting enterprises	–	–	–	–
Direct job creation (public or non-profit)	–	–	–	–
5. Measures for the disabled	–	–	–	–
Vocational rehabilitation	–	–	–	–
Work for the disabled	–	–	–	–
6. Unemployment compensation	**0.39**	**0.40**	**0.43**	**0.52**
7. Early retirement for labour market reasons	–	–	–	–
Total	**0.52**	**0.50**	**0.52**	**0.61**
Active measures (1-5)	0.13	0.10	0.09	0.09
Passive measures (6 and 7)	0.39	0.40	0.43	0.52
Reference:				
GDP (national currency, at current prices, 10^9)	489 289	504 660	507 552	497 205
Labour force (thousands)	66 720	67 370	67 940	67 890

Source: OECD, *Employment Outlook*, June 2000.

changes, reserves were projected to run out this financial year. As part of the revisions to the system, premiums are set to rise from 0.8 per cent of the total wage bill to 1.2 per cent. The minimum annual salary required to join the system will be abolished to encourage part-time and temporary workers to participate although it is uncertain how this move could affect the overall financial position of the system. The key policy change, however, is a greater differentiation among recipients concerning the duration of benefits according to the reasons for giving up a job. A frequent criticism of the system is that it has allowed people in their early 60s who have retired at the statutory retirement age to enjoy generous unemployment benefits.[88] From April 2001 the duration of benefits will be reduced to 90-180 days for those who have left their job through retirement and have not arranged another post. Benefits for those who have lost their jobs through bankruptcy or dismissal will on the other hand be increased to 90-330 days. This latter provision will raise the benefit period for the group 45-59 years who have become involuntarily unemployed. Incentives are also to be provided to encourage the unemployed to find a new job quickly. They include changing the methods for calculating re-employment allowances to those who have found a job quickly and raising the subsidies for educational training.

The past year has been very active from the point of view of labour market policy with two policy packages and a reform of the unemployment insurance system. Active labour market measures have been increased although the poor take-up rate overall (there are exceptions with some individual programmes) does raise questions about the design and balance of some of the programmes and about their focus. Greater emphasis on active labour market measures such as employment subsidies (or new job creation) raises the issue of dead weight cost (whether these people would have been employed anyway) and substitution (all that alters is who is employed rather than total employment). On this latter point, care will have to be taken that the young will not end up being displaced by older workers who have been one of the policy priorities. Follow-up research to assess the effectiveness of programmes appears not to be well developed although this could change next year with the reorganisation of government and a greater focus on policy analysis (Chapter IV).

Generally speaking, the programmes have continued to support older workers and those considered to be insiders, and the extension of the retirement age also goes in the same direction. Changes to the unemployment insurance system, although addressing the problem of retired workers claiming unemployment benefits, has in fact increased support for middle-aged workers and encourages them to continue to expect work at wage levels which are acknowledged to be too high.[89] Consideration needs to be given to adopting measures which would encourage the reservation wage to fall. A key labour market problem – the steep age profile of wages which makes older workers expensive – is an issue about which the government can do little. However, it should not seek to underpin the system but let it evolve in the direction social partners agree.[90]

Employment mismatch is a key area for concern although specific policy measures are not always easy to identify since causes may be connected to labour market institutions such as permanent employment. However, one area where policy does have a role is in youth training. With many young people finding it difficult to secure permanent employment and the associated human capital formation there is a role for policy in promoting training. Experience in other countries suggests that this form of active labour market measures might be the most useful and least distortionary. Public programmes could be *via* vouchers allowing youth to select from private institutions.

Improving the framework conditions for competitive markets

Since 1995, the goal of regulatory reform has been to shift the structure of the economy to one which relies much more on market forces. To this end, last year's *Survey* noted that sustained efforts had begun to reduce economic intervention in many sectors, among them large retail stores, gasoline imports, telecommunications and financial services. Recent estimates suggest that important benefits have already accrued to consumers (Table 23).[91] The *Survey* also noted that the deregulation plan for 1998-2000 had been revised, lifting the number of proposals from 624 to 917, and that the need for promoting reform to improve economic outcomes had been stressed once again. There has been uneven progress over the past year in achieving these goals, while the need to solve a number of issues concerning market access and regulatory powers has become more pressing. Reflecting these concerns, the Regulatory Reform Committee is now considering a further 97 items for review by late this year covering, *inter alia*, securing competition in the telecommunications industry.

A key condition for well functioning markets is competition law and enforcement strong enough to prevent and remedy misconduct, and in these areas several important changes are underway. The coverage of competition law has been widened by lifting the exemption for railways, electricity and gas.

Table 23. **The benefits of liberalisation**

Billion yen

Sector	Increase in consumer surplus up to FY 1998	Difference		Major measures taken
		1996-> 97	1997-> 98	
Telecom (domestic)	3 855	853	822	Privatisation of NTT, easing regulations of entry and charges, deregulation of mobile phone sales
Telecom (international)	262	16	14	Privatisation of KDD, easing regulations of entry and charges
Air transport	357	99	73	Deregulation of entry into routes and discount fare setting
Car inspection	612	100	42	Simplifying car inspection
Power generation	1 713	125	681	Introducing yardstick competition
Oil products	1 449	212	218	Liberalising imports of oil products
Gas	13	–	5	Introducing yardstick competition
Share transaction	318	118	50	Liberalising stock brokerage
Total	8 532	1 526	1908	

Source: EPA, January 2000.

Injunctive relief through civil litigation against violations of the Anti-Monopoly Act has been introduced in those areas where it is easiest to prove, and the existing damage action system against such violations has been improved.[92] The FTC is not empowered to offer firms immunity in exchange for co-operating with investigations, which would be a powerful instrument for enforcement in difficult cases involving cartels and bid rigging. The bidding procedures for public works have become an increasingly important issue for competition policy and this topic is taken up in Chapter IV. As part of the general reform of governmental institutions, the Fair Trade Commission is due to become a department of the Ministry of Public Management, Home Affairs, Posts and Telecommunications from the beginning of 2001 with the Ministry also covering the functions of the current Ministry of Posts and Telecommunications. The regulatory powers wielded by both the current MPT and MITI will remain with the ministries and there are no plans to establish independent regulators as in many other OECD countries. This section first considers the progress which has been made and the outstanding issues in the area of market access. It then examines progress in improving market mechanisms in the real estate sector.

Improving market access in the network industries...

Telecommunications

While welcoming progress towards competitive markets in telecommunications and lower prices for consumers, the OECD *Review of Regulatory Reform*, whose conclusions were echoed in last year's *Survey*, pointed out that there were a number of outstanding regulatory issues which prevented fair and transparent competition in the market place. These included:

- the lack of clear information to applicants on the minimum requirements to receive licenses;
- fragmented regulations on rights of way and facility sharing preventing new entrants from constructing new networks relatively cheaply and rapidly;
- the lack of a fair and transparent interconnection framework and interconnection charges which are high by international standards;
- the lack of legal provision on how to allocate spectrum in particular for mobile licenses;
- the lack of regulatory safeguards such as number portability and carrier pre-selection which gives an advantage to the incumbent;
- the lack of an explicit funding mechanism for universal services.

Above all, the two reports criticised the dual role of the Ministry of Posts and Telecommunications as both regulator and policy maker in the communications field and the limited role of the Fair Trade Commission. Experience over the last year has reinforced the validity of these conclusions, and the fear expressed in last year's *Survey* that the regional reorganisation of NTT (the former monopolist) would not lead to increased competition has been confirmed.

Although carrier pre-selection and number portability will be established at the end of 2000, the opportunity to develop further a competitive telecommunications market, including appropriate price regulation, has not been fully exploited during the past year.[93] Debate has centred on the precise type of costing formula which should govern NTT's interconnection charges in the future: which form of Long Run Incremental Cost (LRIC) to introduce, which data base, and over what time period. However, underlying the debate and influencing it in important directions has been what appears to be excessive concern with the finances and employment of the NTT group and with the desire to avoid any increase in the basic rate (*i.e.* re-balancing) for local telephony. Indeed, a bill which passed the Parliament in May, which authorises the regulator to lower interconnection charges, includes non-binding parliamentary advice that care should be taken that cuts do not adversely affect the management of the two local NTT's or subscriber charges. Moreover, the universal access principle was reaffirmed in the advice, which specifies the same basic rate all over the country, without developing an explicit source of finance apart from cross subsidisation by NTT. The debate only changed in tone after the two regional subsidiaries of NTT announced greater than expected profits in FY 1999.

Unfortunately, rather than the government seizing the opportunity to carry out competition-oriented reforms for the benefit of Japanese consumers and in line with its own deregulation programme, the matter became the subject of international dialogue with the United States. As a result of intensive discussions, a deal was struck in July 2000 with the following key points:

- NTT will cut its interconnection charges (FY 1998 is the base) by 60 per cent at the regional level and by 22½ per cent at the local level over the next three years, FY 2000 to FY 2002. The cuts will be front loaded with 80 per cent of the regional cuts and 70 per cent of the local cuts coming in the first two years using FY 1990 traffic data, with rates retroactive to April 2000.
- A study will be launched to examine the methodology and the data base which will be used to set interconnection charges for NTT in the future. The study is to be completed by the end of 2002.[94]
- NTT will be required to open new points of access to its networks and publish conditions of access.
- Regulations that hamper the construction of networks will be eased and the government will promote measures to improve access to underground tunnels for cables, which are controlled by NTT and the electric utilities.

- The government has undertaken that the Fair Trade Commission will act independently and enforce competition in all sectors including telecommunications.

A great deal will depend on exactly how these undertakings will be implemented, and it is important that they should not be on an *ad hoc* basis.

Electricity

Following the opening of the generating market to new entrants (see 1999 *Survey*) retail sales of electricity of more than 2000 kW have been liberalised since March 2000 breaking down the monopolies of the ten integrated regional utilities. The liberalisation accounts for 30 per cent of the market. At the same time, the competition law has been modified removing the exemption of gas and electricity, but as in the case of telecommunications there will be joint oversight by both the regulator (in this case MITI) and the Fair Trade Commission. While the anti-monopoly law does not explicitly include powers to prevent abuse of dominant market position it nevertheless does include powers to deal with a refusal to sell. The FTC and MITI have jointly issued guidelines listing what are regarded as desirable and undesirable actions by market participants.

As in all network industries with vertically-integrated incumbents, access to the grid on competitive conditions will be essential. The transmission fee is derived according to rules set by MITI and prices range from 0.91 yen to 2.61 yen per kilowatt hour, but higher if special charges are taken into account. Line fees are higher than in other countries. MITI will review the current framework by 2003 and, with transmission prices high by international standards and regional discrepancies large, there is a need to examine the system from the perspective of creating and protecting competition both in and between the existing regional franchises. Since the positive effects of lower access charges could be reduced by a lack of interconnection capacity, MITI's review ought to include considering mandated measures to improve the links among the ten vertically-integrated electricity companies. The review should also go beyond the issue of interconnection fees to re-examine the more basic issues of whether generating and transmission should be under separate ownership, and whether ownership of the generating capacity should be spread among a larger number of companies.

... and in other sectors

Some of the most contentious deregulation and trade issues over the last decade have involved conditions of entry for large surface area stores. A new law covering the operations of large retailers (Law concerning the measures by large-scale retail stores for preservation of the living environment) is in force since June. The surge in construction activity in the retail sector during the first quarter may reflect concern about how the law will be applied by the municipalities. Unlike in the past, this law will be implemented at local level subject to guidelines issued by the central government. This is because the law is intended to address local environmental issues about the operation of large stores and it does not directly address the issue of opening, which in the past involved agreement with small local traders. The new law is also part of the efforts to promote decentralisation in Japan. A number of localities have moved reportedly to establish tighter restrictions on opening hours than set in the guidelines, ostensibly due to environmental considerations. This tendency could become more pronounced unless local governments have a greater participation in the tax revenues which development may bring.

In the transport sector, prices have been liberalised for domestic airlines from 1 February this year and two new entrants have started operations.[95] Price competition between the three established airlines and the new entrants has been marked. However, airlines are precluded from selling air and hotel packages directly to customers who must purchase such products from a licensed tourist agency. This is contrary to the practice in most other countries. The lack of airport landing slots retards competition, and landing fees and other costs are the highest in the world, suggesting inefficiency in airport utilisation. The Ministry of Transport has introduced a point system for allocating new slots at Haneda in Tokyo.[96] Some slots were reserved for new airlines but the rest were allocated by assigning points based *inter alia* on financial health, density of air routes and safety record. Although a point system is more transparent than many alternative slot allocation systems, care must be taken to ensure that incumbent airlines are not favoured in the allocation process perhaps because they are more clearly able to exhibit financial health or have a more extensive route system. Experience shows that new entrant airlines are often at a significant competitive disadvantage to incumbents. Ideally, the slot allocation process would specifically have the objective of fostering both route-by-route and network-by-network competition. In the road transport sector, regulations covering taxis have also been liberalised, including long-term supply-demand balancing. The new law, however, includes emergency adjustment measures to temporarily restrict new entries and fleet expansions for areas where there is conspicuous over-supply. The application of such measures should be restricted to extreme cases and carried out with due attention to consumer interests.

In sum, there have been advances in the competition policy framework and in establishing greater market access in the network industries (*i.e.* electricity and telecommunications) and in other sectors. However, a number of general and specific problems need to be dealt with. At the most general level, there is a need to ensure the independence of the Fair Trade Commission with respect to investigations and staffing once it becomes a part of the Ministry of Public Management, Home Affairs, Posts and Telecommunications next year.[97] This is all the more important in view of the conclusions of the *Review of Regulatory Reform* that although the substantive legal basis for competition policy is sound, competition enforcement was not yet strong enough to take a leading role in energising the process of regulatory reform. In the telecommunications sector, it has been difficult to separate the government's macroeconomic and ownership interests from its other objectives to establish a competitive and efficient market. Consideration should be given to establishing independent regulatory bodies in this sector and in electricity, underpinned by strengthened competition enforcement, charged with maximising benefits to consumers.[98]

With respect to telecommunications there is a pressing need to undertake a number of regulatory reforms and a good case for changing the market structure. A start has been made with an agreement to lower interconnection charges for the NTT regional companies although some could remain high by international standards. Moreover, it will be difficult to lower them quickly unless the responsibility for universal access is paid directly by the government rather than by cross subsidies as at present. The mobile arm of NTT is also in a dominant market position and charges a high interconnection fee. The development of competition has been retarded by very real barriers to competitors building their own networks due to unresolved questions about rights of way.[99] These issues need to be settled quickly. Going beyond regulatory measures, it has become evident that the restructuring of the dominant company NTT – splitting it into two regional carriers, a long distance carrier and a mobile arm all under a holding company – did not lead to a more competitive sector. Rather, the difficulties of setting both regulatory and competition policy have been increased by the need to deal with a group of companies able to undertake non arms-length transaction with each other. Consideration needs to be given to a radical restructuring of the group perhaps along the lines of the AT&T break-up which restricted entry by the new firms into new markets until they proved that effective competition had been established in the local loop. In their present form, the two regional operators should not be allowed to enter new markets while enjoying dominance in the provision of the local loop.

Establishing a more efficient housing and real estate market

Real estate has an enormous importance in Japan and in the past has played a major role in the monetary transmission mechanism, the supply of credit being closely related to the value of real estate as collateral. It has also had a significant impact on resource allocation so that an efficiently functioning real estate market is important. Advances have been made in establishing a market for commercial mortgage-backed securities and there were seven issues in the first half of this year for 375 billion yen, twice that of all 1999. A law to expand the scope of permitted assets for investment companies to include real estate itself will come into effect in November 2000;[100] it has been possible to hold real estate-backed securities since September 1999. Nevertheless, progress has been made in establishing a number of preconditions for more efficient real estate markets.

Fixed-term rental contracts for houses, a long-awaited reform, came into force in March 2000. The new law marks a break with past practice in that it specifies quite clearly what the legislator is seeking. In the past, laws have often been rather vague leaving it up to the courts to interpret. A significant distortion in the rental housing market has been evident for some time with only a small supply of family houses (50 to 100 square meters) coming onto the market in contrast to a strong supply of apartments for students and singles, smaller than 50 square meters. This distortion has been caused by the protection of tenants' rights, which has evolved in line with case law concerning the clause "due cause": an owner has to prove that their demand for vacating a house is justified. This interpretation by the courts has reduced the incentive for owners to rent housing accommodation. On the other hand, there is a supply of small houses and apartments for singles and students since they are expected to leave after a short period. Although the introduction of the new fixed-term contract is expected to alleviate this anomaly, it will take some time because the law is applied to new but not existing contracts. The new form of contract should encourage issuance of asset-backed securities by enhancing predictability of future returns on the assets.

Protection of tenants in its current form and malfunctioning of the judicial system have delayed the disposal of collateral real estate backing non-performing loans.[101] Banks have tended to avoid court-managed forced auctions until recently, using them only as a last resort because they wished to avoid giving the impression of an aggressive collector to third parties. However, they are coming to use them more frequently these days. The auctions, however, suffer from several deficiencies, although procedures have been improved in various ways by successive measures to encourage the disposal of non-performing loans.[102] The most fundamental problem is not the procedure itself, but protection of short-term rental contracts (Abe and Ohara, 1999; Kume and Fukui, 1999; Fukui and Kume, 1999). According to the civil code, a contract with a duration of less than three years has to be respected even if it was established after the collateral right had been granted to a creditor. In fact, successful bidders in an auction frequently find someone (legally or illegally) occupying the property and insisting on tenant rights, and they find it difficult and costly to evict them.[103] Unless they pay "tenants" for their "rights", the successful bidders would have to launch a lawsuit to evict them, another costly procedure. This problem is also aggravated by other procedural defects. The information disclosed by the courts to potential buyers is insufficient.[104] Although the minimum price set by the court in consultation with real estate evaluation experts should be lower than otherwise to compensate for the expected costs of eviction, in practice this is not the case.[105] Moreover, the long period required for the appraisal has tended to make the minimum price higher than the market price because the latter has been on a declining trend since the early 1990s. The lengthy period has resulted from the very small number of experts with whom the court consulted, even though there are many experts available. As a result, there has been an accumulation of unsold collateral cases. More recently, however, sales of collateral have increased in line with the number of experts engaged by the courts and the minimum price is now more in ine with the market price.

The problems in the real estate market are only one example pointing to the need for reform in the legal sector (including the way courts work) and in business services more generally. Other examples include bankruptcy and corporate reorganisations, all of which are bringing pressure on the highly restricted legal profession. These examples also point to the need for clear laws rather than vague statements of principle, which must be then interpreted by the courts. In this regard, the new fixed-term rent law represents an important break with the past. With respect to the real-estate sector, a serious problem arises from the ability of owners to frustrate or to devalue the rights of creditors with respect to collateral property. In such cases, court procedures should be simplified by only requiring an execution order rather than a judgement and consideration should be given to abolishing such "tenant" rights as opposed to the normal rights of tenants.[106] If the system functions well, the properties with rental contracts should enjoy premiums because they involve no cost of searching for tenants and no opportunity costs due to vacancies.

Reforms of pension and health care systems

Pension reform

A bill to reform the pension system,[107] which was drafted in July 1999 and therefore called the 1999 reform plan, was finally enacted in March 2000 after a long period of consultation among the political parties in power and deliberations at the Diet. The bill aims to cut benefit payments by 20 per cent once planned measures are fully effective, thereby alleviating burdens on current and future working-age generations. Major points of the reform are:

- Tier II (income-related) benefits are to be reduced by 5 per cent;
- Tier I (lump-sum) and II benefits for those aged 65 or above are to be indexed only to an inflation rate, *i.e.* totally separated from wage growth;
- age eligibility for Tier II benefits is to be raised step by step from 60 to 65; and
- working elderly aged 65 to 70 will be required to pay contributions, while their benefits are partially cut according to their earned incomes.

In addition, the government decided to "try to find a stable financial source and raise the share of state payments of Tier I benefit payments from a third to a half by 2004". However, even with this reform the contribution rate would still have to rise from 13.5 per cent of total compensation to around 20 per cent in 2025. Even if cost savings from this reform are taken into account, the current pension scheme for employees (Employees' Pension Insurance) is officially estimated to have 2 140 trillion yen of gross liabilities on a present value basis (or 4.3 times as large as GDP) as of March 2000 (Table 24, Panel A). Furthermore, the current PAYG nature of the system implies a large transfer from younger to older generations, as officially confirmed in Table 24, Panel B.[108] A further reform is hence unavoidable and many proposals have been advanced. Although there seems to be a consensus among academics about the need to add some elements of a funded system to the current PAYG scheme, some political parties and labour unions advocate maintenance of a pure PAYG scheme.

Table 24. **A long way to go after the 1999 pension reform**

A. Pension liabilities and their finance for the Welfare Pension System
Tier I and II, March 2000, trillion yen

Liabilities	Existing liabilities 720		Future liabilities 1 420		Total 2 140	
	Case 1	Case 2	Case 1	Case 2	Case 1	Case 2
Finance						
Accumulated funds	170	170	0	0	170	170
Expected revenues from contribution	450	420	1 250	1 160	1 700	1 580
of which:						
Revenues at the current rate (17.35 per cent)	0	0	1 170	1 110	1 170	1 110
Revenues due to an increase in the contribution rate	450	420	80	50	530	470
Tier II related	330	330	50	40	380	370
Tax	100	130	180	270	280	400

B. Contribution and benefit by generation in the Welfare Pension System
Per household, million yen, present discount value in FY 1999 prices

Born in	Benefit	Employees' Contribution[1]		Total Contribution[2]	
		Case 1	Case 2	Case 1	Case 2
1929	68	7	7	13	13
1949	57	20	20	38	38
1969	50	31	29	61	58
1989	49	38	35	75	69
2009	49	39	36	78	71

Note: Case 1 assumes tax revenues finance a third of basic pension benefits, while Case 2 does a half from 2004 on. Other assumptions: Wage growth is 2.5 per cent, inflation is 1.5 per cent and interest rate is 4 per cent.
1. Employees' contributions include those from their wives, but not the effects of tax deduction.
2. Total contribution includes that from employers.
Source: Ministry of Health and Welfare.

Social insurance system or tax-based system: options for reforms of Tier I

Even with the 1999 reform, many of the problems afflicting the mandatory Tier I part of the public pension system are likely to persist. The most important of these seems to be that, despite extensive (but costly) administrative efforts to collect contributions, at least 13 per cent of the self-employed stay out of the Tier I scheme of the National Pension system. According to a MHW survey (1996 Survey on Actual Conditions of the Insured of the National Pension Scheme), this seems to be mainly due to the fact that people cannot afford to pay the contributions (55 per cent) but also do not count on benefit payments (21 per cent). The proposed increase in the share paid by the state from the current one-third to a half would attenuate these concerns. In order to ensure the effectiveness of Tier I as safety net (or national minimum),[109] some prefer a fully tax-financed system, although the leading Liberal Democratic Party and the government are against this idea. The choice of financing is hence clearly related to the philosophy of system design, *i.e.* what roles should Tier I play? If its role is to provide a "national minimum", a question arises as to whether the tax-financed Tier I is a replacement of or supplement to the current livelihood assistance (tax financed support with a means test). The former case is equivalent to the universal pension without means tests found in some countries.[110]

If the tax-financed system were adopted, the question remains as to which tax should be used to finance it (income, consumption, or any other taxes). Proponents of a tax-based system tend to support the consumption tax, though some (*e.g.* Ushimaru *et al.*, 1999) prefer the income tax. In addition to general arguments about merits and demerits of these taxes, the following considerations are pertinent, given the present Japanese tax system.[111] First, severe erosion of the income tax base (because of incomplete coverage of incomes of the self-employed, and many deductions and high tax threshold) implies that a higher rate would be required than otherwise and that horizontal inequality would worsen. On the other hand, a higher consumption tax rate would make the problem of evasion more serious, if the current system remains as it is.[112] The regressive impact on income distribution could be overcome by earmarking the revenues to Tier I benefits because that is almost equivalent to a consumption tax with lump-sum tax credits for the retired. Because the current system is effectively the same as an earmarked wage income tax, the shift of the tax base to consumption expenditures would allow spreading burdens more widely, increasing those on pension beneficiaries while reducing those on the working-age population.

Reforms in Sweden, Italy and Poland may suggest a possible direction of future reform if social insurance is to remain the basis of the system. In the reforms in these countries, contributors are given notional individual accounts and their benefits are linked to their contributions with returns equal to wage growth (see OECD, 1998*a*, 2000*a*). As a result, it is possible to make the system sustainable as well as transparent.[113] Although this line of reform could alleviate the current incentive problem in the system, it is uncertain whether it would be sufficient to solve it. Because wage growth (the return in the new system) is likely to be lower than returns on portfolio investment in capital markets, and some transaction costs are involved in changing pension plans, the problem would remain.[114] Low incentives are not the only reason for low participation: Chile, which has relied on a universal individual account system since 1980, also has low coverage of the self-employed, as well as incomplete coverage of employees.

Fully funded or PAYG: *options for reform of* Tier II

The consensus among academics on the desirability of a reinforced funded system for Tier II has led to diverse reform proposals. Some propose to shift to a fully funded system (Hatta and Oguchi, 1999). They proposed a kind of shock therapy, *i.e.* an immediate shift of both Tier I and II to a funded system by raising the contribution rate to 23 per cent (or some 7 trillion yen in total). Although the adverse effects on the economy could be minimal if confidence in the public pension system is regained, uncertainty may remain. The Economic Strategy Council (1998), Keidanren (1998) and Oshio (1998) went further, to propose privatisation of Tier II. An obvious focal point of the arguments is how to deal with double burdens in the transitional period.[115] The currently hidden liabilities (bequeathed from current to future generations) may amount to 330 trillion yen (66 per cent of GDP), according to the Ministry of Health and Welfare (MHW) (Table 24, Panel A). Although the figure is substantial, it may not be too costly to be insurmountable. For example, Poland chose to privatise its Tier II part in 1999 (OECD, 1998*a*) although the implicit liabilities were estimated to exceed 200 per cent of GDP.[116] Other countries' experience shows that not only "clean break" (*i.e.* Chilean) but also "partial" privatisation approaches are available as an option (Disney, 2000). The latter could take two forms, allowing individuals the choice of joining a funded or PAYG programmes[117] (as in the United Kingdom) and only allowing certain (young) people to join a funded scheme (as in Argentina, Hungary and Poland). These forms of partial privatisation could reduce and/or spread the transition costs. In any case, detailed discussion of specific ways to handle the problem is necessary if privatisation is pursued.

Parametric revisions in the current system cannot be completely disregarded but would involve substantial changes. Indeed, as Takayama (1999) argued, if tax revenues were to be allocated additionally to two-thirds of Tier I benefits, the resulting decline in contribution rates (about 4 percentage points), combined with various rationalisation of the benefits, would make it possible to keep future contribution rates below the current rate (17.35 per cent). In particular, as he emphasised, there is still (some) room for further cuts of benefits which may be acceptable because of their distributional consequences. For example, even if across-the-board cuts of benefits are difficult to implement, there are other options with the same effect such as lengthening the contribution period required to receive a complete pension (as in France). Therefore, it may be possible to keep the current PAYG nature intact, albeit with a significantly reduced size of Tier II benefits. Even so, this strategy still leaves the system vulnerable to unexpected demographic changes.

There are diverse opinions as to the desired role of the government in the pension system. Some proponents of both privatisation and maintaining the PAYG systems share a view that the role of the public pension system should be reduced.[118] Indeed, a successive slimming-down of benefits of the PAYG public pension system could be regarded as a gradual scaling back of its role to providing a minimum protection against old-age poverty (Takayama, 1999; Oshio, 1999).[119] On the other hand, the shift to a fully funded public pension system means much greater accumulation of financial assets in the hands of the government, which could make their management more prone to political pressures. In this regard it is appropriate that a recently enacted bill has included a new fund management scheme in line with the FILP reform (see Chapters II and IV). The obligation to deposit pension funds with the TFB is to be abolished, and the newly set-up fund is to deal with portfolio management under the responsibility of the Minister. Another consequence of the new law is that the Pension Welfare Service Public Corporation, which has been in charge of portfolio management within the FILP scheme, is to be dissolved.[120] In the new scheme, most of the funds are to be entrusted to private institutions to utilise their experience.

More private initiatives in Tier III

Corporate pension systems are under severe pressure from prolonged low returns in the market, resulting in increased dissolution of corporate pension funds.[121] Such a situation has made private pension funds reluctant to continue to assume some of the functions of the public pension systems for a few percentage points of contribution rates, which have been frozen at the current rate and hence are unlikely to compensate for the losses involved. Moreover, new accounting rules (see Chapter III) require all such liabilities (including those related to parts of public pensions) to be disclosed from March 2002. Complaints from private companies about the current amalgam nature of the systems – corporate pension systems are managed as a funded system, while undertaking a vicarious function of the PAYG public pension system – have led the Economic Strategy Council (1999) and some experts (Takayama, 2000) to propose the abolition of this agency role for public pensions.

An important consideration in private pensions is their portability. Currently, portability exists only among a limited number of large companies but should be increased to eliminate one of the obstacles to labour mobility.[122] This is easier under a defined-contribution scheme. The bill to introduce this new scheme from 2001 is to be reintroduced to the Diet. As private pensions move towards a contribution-based system, it becomes more difficult to justify limiting the favourable tax treatment to defined-benefit schemes alone (Takayama, 1999*b*). Some favourable tax treatment to be given to defined-contribution private pension plans from 2001, like 401(k) in the United States, is therefore welcome.

Reform of the health-care system[123]

The Japanese enjoy one of the best health status in the world judging from a set of commonly used indicators such as the life expectancy at birth, infant and perinatal mortality and the number of potential years of life lost before age 70. Even though factors other than health care, such as environment and life style, typically explain an important part of the inter-country differences in health indicators, the excellent health status in Japan has been obtained with a relatively small burden on the economy. At 7.6 per cent in 1998, the ratio of total health spending to GDP is well below the OECD average, and per capita health spending is below what would be expected from a cross-country regression on per capita income. The Japanese health-care system is not only relatively inexpensive but also offers universal coverage and total freedom of choice to both patients and medical service providers. It suffers, however, from relatively low patient satisfaction with the quality of services provided and underdeveloped patients' rights.[124] These problems are illustrated by extremely short consultation time, abnormally long duration of hospital stay, a very large volume of drug consumption, a lack of information and choice of treatment given to patients and the lack of accountability by physicians and hospitals. Many of these symptoms are the side-effects of the effective spending control mechanism which operates through price fixing by the Ministry of Health and Welfare (MHW), but more generally they reflect government regulation ill-adapted to modern, high income society and the relative lack of policy emphasis on consumer interests. The Japanese health-care system is also confronted with the problems of inequities stemming from the fragmented health insurance arrangements that need to change. Moreover, it is experiencing a serious problem of financing caused by a combination of low revenue growth and a persistent strong rise in benefit spending. Many of the problems mentioned above can only become more serious with population ageing, even though the introduction of nursing-care insurance was an important positive step. The system now needs a major overhaul.

Re-tuning the health-care system requires a reform of government regulation on both the demand and supply sides of medical services. Health care is an area where it is difficult for market mechanisms to work well – because of information asymmetry between doctors and patients, pursuit of equity objectives as well as moral hazard and adverse selection problems inherent in insurance arrangements – and hence government intervention is justified to correct the so-called "market failure". However, it has become clear that the current government regulation of health care in Japan leaves much scope for change in order for resources to be allocated more efficiently to maximise benefits to patients as consumers. The government has recognised the need to reform regulation in the health area, and some encouraging moves have been initiated. But legislative changes have been lagging, and further steps are necessary. Changes to correct symptoms of "government failure" are warranted in several respects.

First, rather than restricting information dissemination by medical service providers the government should promote it. Restrictions on advertising by doctors and hospitals should be eased so as to allow patients to learn more easily about the different characteristics and capacity of service providers. In this regard, an aborted bill, enabling medical service providers to publicise information about their treatment record, was a welcome step. As well, objective evaluation of hospital performance by an independent agency, which has started in 1997, should be encouraged and the results made public. As of March 2000, there were 318 hospitals which have opted for such an evaluation. Only the names of these hospitals are available on the web-site of MHW. Improved information about the quality of services offered gives a better basis for patients' choice of service providers, thereby promoting competition and functional specialisation among them.

Second, the functioning of markets for service provision can be improved by strengthening the role of insurers as an agent for patients. Currently, it is the governors of prefectures, and not insurers, who designate specific care providers as eligible for treating patients under medical insurance cover. This practice makes no sense and should be altered in due course as the consolidation of insurers advances. Even within the current framework, however, insurers can encourage or discourage the insured to use the service of certain providers, and greater disclosure of information about the quality of medical services rendered would help in this regard. Insurers should also reinforce their utilisation review of medical services provided through a more critical evaluation of treatment records submitted by doctors and hospitals for payment.

Third, many restrictions on new entry into the market for service provision should be eased substantially, as they guarantee rents to existing providers and prevent the exit of non-viable ones. These restrictions include notably the control of supply by MHW which sets the maximum number of beds for each region, the mandatory requirement for the top manager of hospitals to have qualification as medical doctors and the prohibition of for-profit enterprises to run hospitals.[125] Under the current payment arrangements, however, the control of the number of beds is necessary to deal with the problem of extremely long duration of hospitalisation. Hence this restriction should be eased progressively as the method of remunerating hospital services moves away from the mixed per diem/fee-for-service payment system. As for other restrictions, there are no justifiable reasons for their existence. Administration of modern, complex hospitals requires managerial capacity that medical doctors do not necessarily have, and many private hospitals are *de facto* effectively run like profit-making entities.[126] Doing away with these restrictions would contribute to the restructuring of the supply side of medical care services, which would improve its efficiency and quality.

Perhaps the most important government regulation is price control through the fee schedule which sets the price insurers pay to service providers. Some have observed that the government has been able to contain health-care spending growth through a judicious adjustment of fees (Campbell and Ikegami, 1998). This has, however, resulted in a large volume of, and an extremely short time for, consultation by doctors, as the frequency and duration of consultation are not regulated. One can therefore interpret the effectiveness of price control in restraining spending growth as suggesting that the volume expansion has reached the physical capacity limit of doctors with some of them treating over eighty out-patients in one day, or five minutes per patient.[127] The very short consultation times make it nearly impossible for doctors to provide adequate explanations of diagnosis and therapies to patients. Doctors are not in any case under strong pressure to practice using informed consent as they are rarely faced with the threats of the potential malpractice suits that exist in many other OECD countries. Moreover, there are few clinical-practice guidelines ensuring that high-quality and efficient medical examinations are performed with patients' consent.

Apart from having an undesirable impact on the quality of consultation, the fee schedule influences resource allocation. Relative prices between broad categories of care have remained rigid with fees for traditional ambulatory services mainly in primary care remaining high compared with in-patient services and high-technology medicine. This has made it difficult to introduce innovative services or improve comfort of hospital services through capital investment and higher levels of staffing. Greater flexibility in adjusting fees to better reflect these concerns is desirable, and an official review is currently underway.

The fee schedule also applies to drugs. High profit margins for doctors' drug dispensing (the difference between the reimbursement price and the purchase cost is estimated to be 7 per cent for hospitals and 12 per cent for physicians' offices in the mid-1990s) are widely believed to be causing over-prescription of drugs in Japan, the world leader in the quantity of drug consumption per head. The reimbursement price is determined for each brand and product as a weighted average of purchase prices plus a reasonable margin, the so-called R-zone. The R-zone has, however, been reduced substantially, from 15 per cent in 1992 to 5 per cent in 1998 and further to 2 per cent in 2000, making drugs relatively unattractive as a source of income for doctors. This is expected to increase further the share of prescriptions dealt with by pharmacies, which stood at 26 per cent in 1997. A further reduction of the R-zone would be desirable as this would lead to negative margins for some doctors, promoting the separation of prescription and dispensing functions. Finally, a reference pricing system has been implemented in several OECD countries. If it were to be adopted, the experience should be built upon to minimise its potentially negative impact on innovation while reaping the benefit of cost containment, even if only temporary.

The current financing arrangements, which are highly fragmented and complex, also need a major streamlining to deal with equity problems and to facilitate the strengthening of the role of insurers as an agent for patients.[128] Some equity problems persist despite government subsidies and cross subsidisation to reduce the difference in financial conditions among the insurers. It is difficult to say whether such problems exist between the broad categories of insurers, Government Managed Health Insurance (GMHI) and Society Managed Health Insurance (SMHI) on the one hand, and National Health Insurance (NHI) on the other, for two reasons. First, even though contributions are higher for the former than the latter, the benefits are also higher for the former. Second, incomes of NHI recipients are difficult to assess. Inequities exist rather within SMHI and NHI. In the case of SMHI the total contribution rate (in the form of a capped payroll tax) varies from 6 per cent to 9 per cent of wages, and the employers' share of this from 50 per cent to 80 per cent. Within NHI there is a difference as large as seven-fold in the average per capita contribution, for essentially the same medical benefits. To the extent that such uneven insurance premiums stem from incomplete equalisation mechanisms, a first step towards eliminating such inequities would be mergers of existing insurers to achieve greater risk pooling. Larger and stronger insurers should also be able to play more effectively the role of purchaser of medical services on behalf of the insured.

For the health insurance system as a whole a large and growing deficit is a serious problem. While to some extent it resulted from slow revenue growth due to the stagnant economy of the 1990s, the expansion of benefit spending has been driven by structural forces, notably the rising share of the elderly whose per capita medical spending is typically four to five times greater than that for the others. Containing the spending pressure in general, and in this area in particular, requires a significant move away from the current fee-for-service methods. A wider application of Diagnostic-Related-Groups-type payments, particularly to chronic illness and terminal care, would be desirable. GMHI has been running a deficit since 1993; about one-third of SMHI are facing financing difficulties; and about half of municipalities-managed NHI are in the red, even with subsidies from governments and transfers from SMHI to their Healthcare for the Elderly Programme (HEP). Indeed, such transfers are the main reason for the deteriorating financial situation of SMHI funds whose members resent a further increase in their contribution rates. How to deal with the rapidly increasing deficit of HEP is the major issue faced by the government, and various options are under discussion. As in the case of pensions, the rising scale of the financing needs is making the heavy reliance on payroll taxes problematical and would seem to call for a broadening of financing sources.

IV. Improving the performance of public spending

Background

The necessity to improve the performance of public expenditures is now more apparent than before. Recent fiscal stimulus packages have raised numerous questions about the value of the projects which have been undertaken, while population ageing is creating new demands for public expenditures and reducing the need for others. At the same time, the changing structure of family, society and the workplace (with greater mobility between enterprises) requires a reformulation of existing welfare and transfer programmes if social objectives are to be met. On the other hand, there is a pressing need over the medium term to pursue fiscal consolidation which will mean, *inter alia*, that aggregate spending will have to be closely controlled and even reduced in relation to GDP. To meet given policy objectives will therefore require greater cost effectiveness of expenditures. However, it will also be necessary to go beyond this limited goal and to ensure that the composition of expenditures is in itself allocationally efficient: whether the numerous goals and objectives determined by the governance/political process are being implemented with regard to the opportunity costs involved.[129]

Last year's *Survey* examined the tax system while the OECD *Regulatory Review* set out to identify the requirements of a modern, efficient, regulatory system. This chapter complements these two studies. Conclusions are, however, necessarily more general since the objectives of public spending are more numerous and diffuse, while efficiency criteria are more difficult to implement than in the case of tax systems. The chapter therefore focuses on broad, systemic, factors leaving specific questions of programme design in individual areas such as health care, pensions and debt management to other chapters. The first section examines the structure and determinants of public spending, identifying where efficiency and cost effectiveness problems appear most important and where expenditures might even have to be increased in the future. The second part discusses reform options to improve the cost effectiveness of public spending and which might also improve the efficiency of public choice.

Characteristics and determinants of public spending

This section first describes the size and structure of public spending in an international comparative context. In many respects, the structure of public spending is mid-way between the European model, with its high outlays on social programmes, and the North American model, with its emphasis on private provision. Automatic stabilisers associated with non-discretionary expenditures are comparatively weak due in part to the importance of nominal wage flexibility, long-term employment contracts and a buffer of discouraged female workers in stabilising unemployment over the business cycle. But public investment is significantly greater than in countries with a similar level of income and has been used for counter-cyclical policy. The second part examines the determinants of public spending and the efficiency and cost effectiveness of some of the programmes. Institutional factors associated with the budgetary and political process are clearly important. This part also seeks to highlight where and how pressures for increased spending might be evolving.

Size and structure of public expenditures

On a general government basis, public expenditure as a share of GDP is relatively low in Japan and its composition differs from that observed in other major OECD countries. Spending amounts to some 35 per cent of GDP, the sixth lowest ratio among the OECD member countries (Figure 27) and comparable with that of the United States and Australia. The low level of overall expenditure is due in great measure to final public consumption, which is only about half that of European G7 countries and even lower than in the United States (Figure 28). This feature is partly attributable to the low level of defence expenditures (Table 25). The low level of public consumption is partially offset by public investment, which is 2 to 3 times as large as in other G7 countries – even before recent stimulus packages. Social security benefits and property income payments (including interest paid) are still relatively low but increasing due to rapid population ageing and a substantial build up in government debt. By function, the most striking characteristic is the low share of consumption expenditures allocated to health although international comparison is difficult due to the differing classification of hospital employees (Figure 29). On the other hand, the share of public expenditure devoted to education is high.

Over the past three decades, the trend of public expenditures has varied widely reflecting different phases of fiscal consolidation. Up to 1980, expenditures rose rapidly from 26 per cent of GDP in 1975 to some 33 per cent in 1980 (Figure 30). At the same time, the general government deficit widened to some 6 per cent of GDP in 1980. Fiscal consolidation measures throughout the 1980s stabilised expenditures at around 32 per cent of GDP until 1990. Investment expenditures bore the brunt of the consolidation, the counterpart of which was

Figure 27. **Government spending and the level of income**[1]

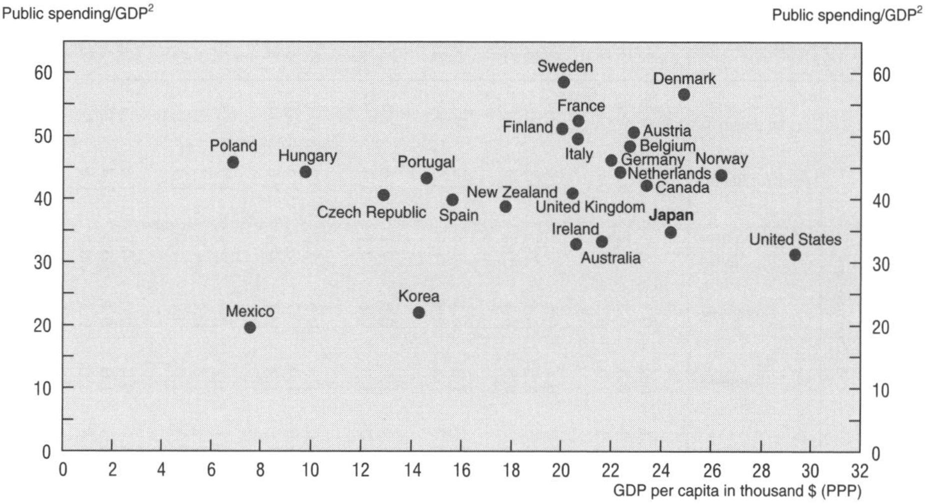

1. 1997 or nearest year available.
2. Public spending is defined as the sum of current outlays and net capital outlays.

Source: INEGI; OECD, *National Accounts.*

Figure 28. **General government spending by economic category in major seven countries**[1]

Per cent of GDP

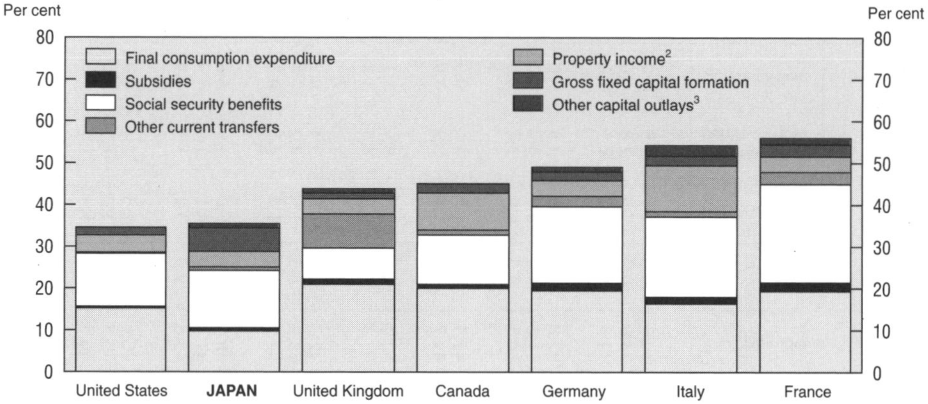

1. In 1997 or nearest year available.
2. Including interest payments.
3. Increase in stocks, purchases of land and intangible assets (net) and capital transfers to other sectors.

Source: OECD, National Accounts.

Table 25. **Structure of government outlays by function**

Per cent of GDP[1]

	Total expenditure	Public goods				Merit goods				Income transfers							Economic services	Public debt interest
		Total	Defense	General public services	Other functions	Total	Education	Health	Other social services	Total	Pensions	Disability	Sickness	Family cash benefit	Unemployment	Housing[1] and other benefits		
United States																		
1980	32.5	10.6	7.1	2.5	1.0	9.7	5.3	4.0	0.5	9.3	6.3	0.9	0.3	0.5	0.9	0.5	3.7	3.2
1990	34.9	10.9	7.0	2.8	1.0	10.8	5.3	5.2	0.3	8.5	6.2	0.8	0.3	0.2	0.7	0.4	3.1	5.1
1995	34.3	9.2	5.2	2.9	1.0	11.9	5.0	6.5	0.4	9.4	6.5	1.0	0.3	0.3	0.6	0.6	2.8	4.8
Japan																		
1980	32.8	4.1	0.9	3.3	0.0	9.9	4.9	4.6	0.4	9.6	4.0	0.4	0.1	0.2	0.0	2.4	6.0	3.2
1990	31.6	4.4	0.9	3.4	0.0	8.9	3.7	4.7	0.5	10.0	5.0	0.5	0.1	0.2	0.3	2.2	4.3	3.9
1995	36.5	4.5	0.9	3.6	0.0	10.1	3.8	5.6	0.6	12.8	6.2	0.5	0.1	0.2	0.5	1.5	5.3	3.8
Germany																		
1991	47.4	6.4	1.9	4.6	0.0	12.7	4.4	7.1	1.2	16.3	9.7	1.2	0.4	1.3	3.0	0.6	5.3	2.9
1995	49.7	5.2	1.4	3.9	0.0	13.9	4.5	8.0	1.3	18.2	10.7	1.4	0.5	1.2	3.7	0.8	4.5	3.7
France																		
1990	50.2	10.1	3.1	3.9	3.1	12.6	5.1	6.5	1.0	18.7	10.9	1.5	0.5	2.1	2.6	1.1	3.3	2.9
1993	55.4	9.2	2.9	4.5	1.8	14.1	5.9	7.1	1.1	20.9	12.0	1.5	0.6	2.2	3.3	1.3	3.1	3.5
Italy																		
1980	42.3	5.3	1.7	3.4	0.2	10.7	4.8	5.6	0.3	12.4	9.0	1.5	0.3	1.0	0.6	0.0	6.4	5.0
1990	53.2	6.5	1.9	4.2	0.4	12.4	5.8	6.3	0.3	16.3	11.9	1.9	0.2	0.6	1.5	0.0	6.2	9.4
1995	52.2	6.5	1.7	4.5	0.3	10.2	4.5	5.3	0.3	17.9	13.5	1.8	0.1	0.4	2.0	0.0	4.6	11.5
United Kingdom																		
1980	48.1	15.6	5.0	1.9	8.8	10.8	4.6	5.1	1.1	12.8	7.1	1.1	0.3	1.8	1.7	0.8	4.0	4.7
1990	41.4	9.9	4.1	1.9	3.9	10.2	4.3	5.0	0.9	13.7	7.1	1.8	0.4	1.6	1.3	1.5	4.1	3.4
1995	43.6	9.0	3.2	1.9	3.9	11.5	4.6	5.7	1.2	15.6	7.3	2.8	0.2	1.9	1.3	2.1	3.3	3.6
Canada																		
1980	39.6	4.0	1.6	2.4	0.0	10.5	5.0	5.4	0.1	8.1	3.1	0.7	0.0	0.7	1.6	2.0	2.6	5.4
1990	46.7	3.2	1.7	1.5	0.0	12.2	5.4	6.7	0.1	10.8	4.3	1.0	0.1	0.5	2.4	2.5	2.6	9.5
1995	46.3	2.9	1.4	1.5	0.0	12.3	5.8	6.5	0.0	11.5	4.8	1.0	0.1	0.8	1.8	3.1	2.4	9.6

1. Housing benefits are not available for the United States, Canada and Japan.

Source: OECD.

Figure 29. **General government expenditures on goods and services by functional category in OECD countries[1]**

Per cent of GDP

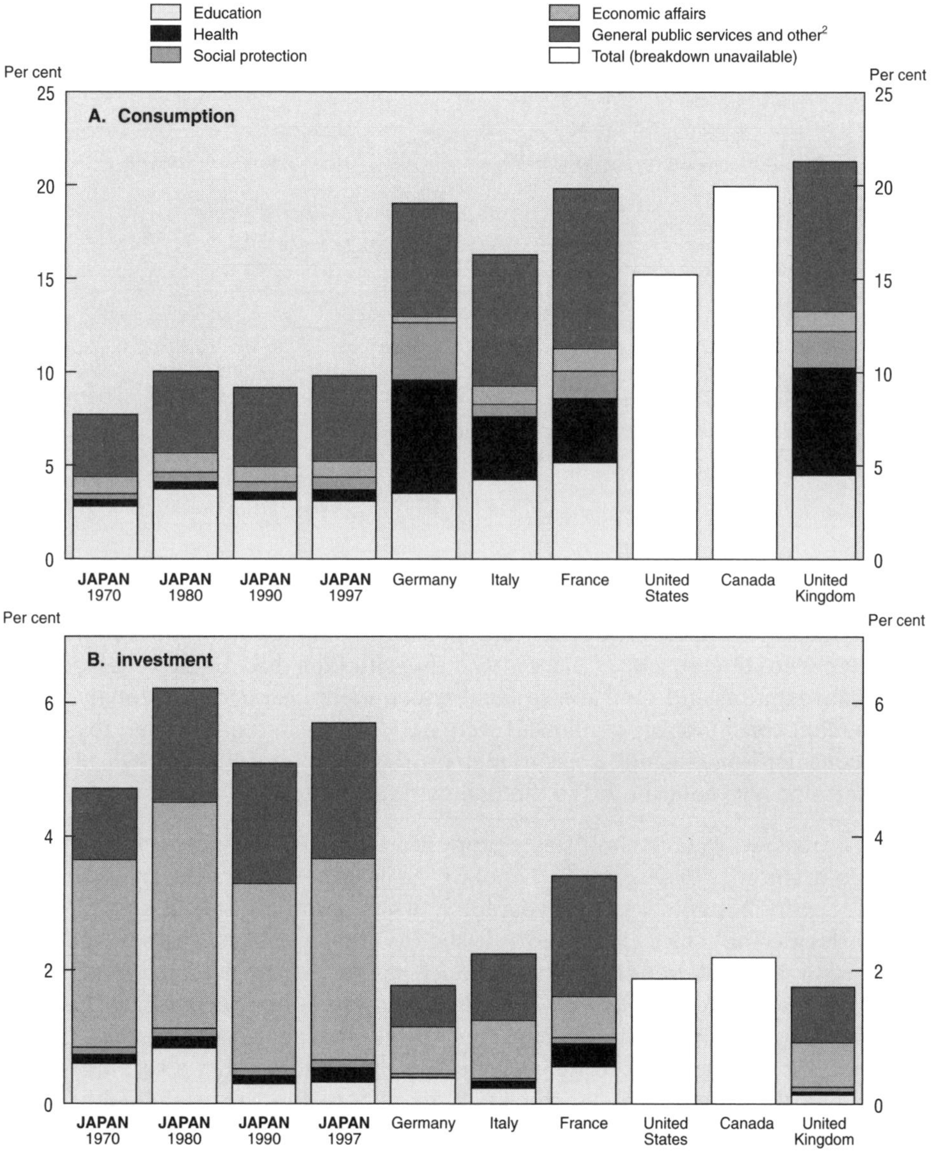

1. In 1997 or nearest year available.
2. Includes public order and safety, housing, cultural and unallocated expenditure.

Source: OECD, *National Accounts.*

Figure 30. **General government expenditures and receipts**
Per cent of GDP

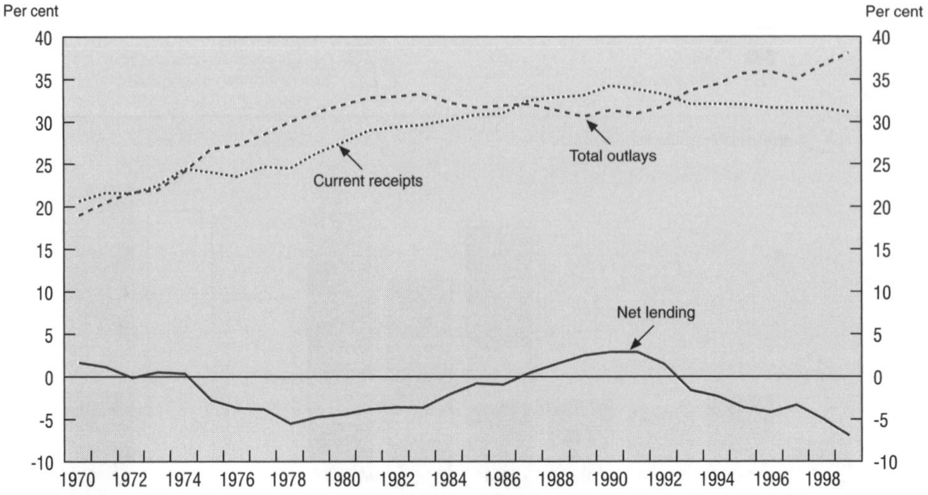

Source: OECD.

reduced transfers to local government, although final consumption expenditures also declined (Figure 29).[130] Since 1990 the situation has been reversed with public investment and transfers to local governments expanding strongly. As for government consumption, a renewed increase of wages in the 1990s led to government consumption reaching a record high of 10.2 per cent of GDP in 1998, although the recession also contributed to the rise by depressing GDP.

Transfers to households as a proportion of GDP have increased more than three-fold since 1970 (Figure 31, Panel C). As in other countries, an increase in social security benefits was a driving force, while social assistance grants[131] have been decreasing since the early 1980s as the pension system gradually matured.[132] Pension benefits showed much faster growth than those of health care[133] (Figure 31, Panel A and B). The sharp increase in pensions during the 1970s was the result of widening the coverage to all citizens. More generous benefit schemes and ageing reduced net payments to households from a surplus to near balance in the late 1980s. As the need to restore the financial health of the pension system became widely recognised, the government began to take reform measures from the beginning of the 1980s (Chapter III). As for health care, contributions have been insufficient to cover the payments over the last three decades, and the balance has tended to worsen due to the higher growth of the payments

Figure 31. **Transfers to households and financial condition of the social security fund**

Fiscal year, per cent of GDP

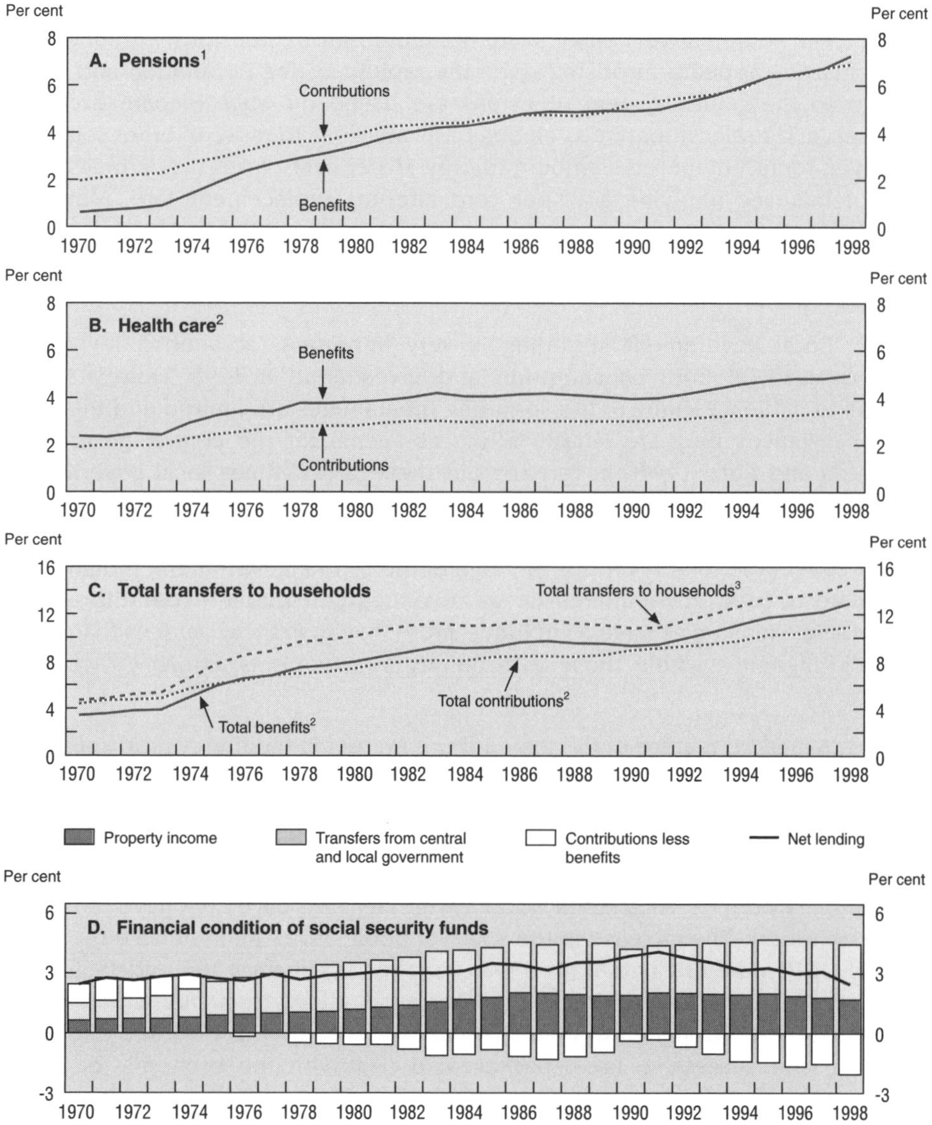

1. See footnote 119 of the text for a detailed explanation of which accounts are included.
2. Includes employment insurance accounts and others.
3. Sum of total benefits and social assistance grants.

Source: Economic Planning Agency.

for the elderly. As a result, net payments to households have been increasing to reach over 2 per cent of GDP in FY 1998 (Figure 31, Panel B), which was financed by property income generated by financial assets held by the health system and subsidies from the central and local governments.

The comparatively small share accounted for by pensions – around 6 per cent of GDP – appears surprising given the rapidly ageing population and is due in part to the bonus system. Pensions are based on wage income excluding bonuses, and replacement rates on this basis are close to those in other countries. However, replacement rates amount to only 51 per cent of pre-tax earnings inclusive of bonuses implying a 60 per cent after-tax replacement rate. Moreover, incomes for the retired are boosted by low taxation of benefits and by the practice of firms to make large cash payments when employees retire. There is thus in practice more private provision than is at first apparent.

Local government spending is very important, accounting for around three-quarters of both consumption and investment in 1998. However, their powers to influence many of the spending programmes are limited and in a number of instances they are simply acting as agents for the central government (Mochida and Lotz, 1999). In carrying out these programmes local governments depend on transfers from the central government: in fiscal year 1998, transfers from the central to local governments amounted to 7¼ per cent of GDP, about 40 per cent of the total revenues accruing to the central government. Judging from the share of local governments in tax revenues and public expenditures, this dependence may be as large as in Italy – more than in France, but less than in the United Kingdom – within those with unitary arrangements among G7 countries (Figure 32).

A marked feature of the expenditure system is the low cyclical sensitivity of discretionary expenditures such as unemployment benefits (Figure 33). In part this reflects the stability of the unemployment rate over the course of the business cycle. Counter-cyclical policy has, nevertheless, been important with public investment being used often as a tool to stimulate the economy during recessionary periods. As a result, local government expenditures have tended to fluctuate widely. The increase in the share of public investment in GDP by 2¼ per cent of GDP in the first half of the 1990s was the largest since the mid-1950s. This massive expansion took place in the context of a long-term public investment programme, the Basic Plan of Public Investment (decided in 1991 and expanded in 1994), and successive fiscal packages to deal with the economic downturn in 1993 and the following years. As a result, transfers to local governments have increased. On the other hand, as noted in Chapter II, fiscal policy *via* public works has been highly uncertain recently since the central government has little information about how local governments are reducing the public works for which they are fully responsible in response to their own financing problems.

Figure 32. **Local and central government shares in receipts and expenditures**

Per cent of GDP, 1998 or most recent year

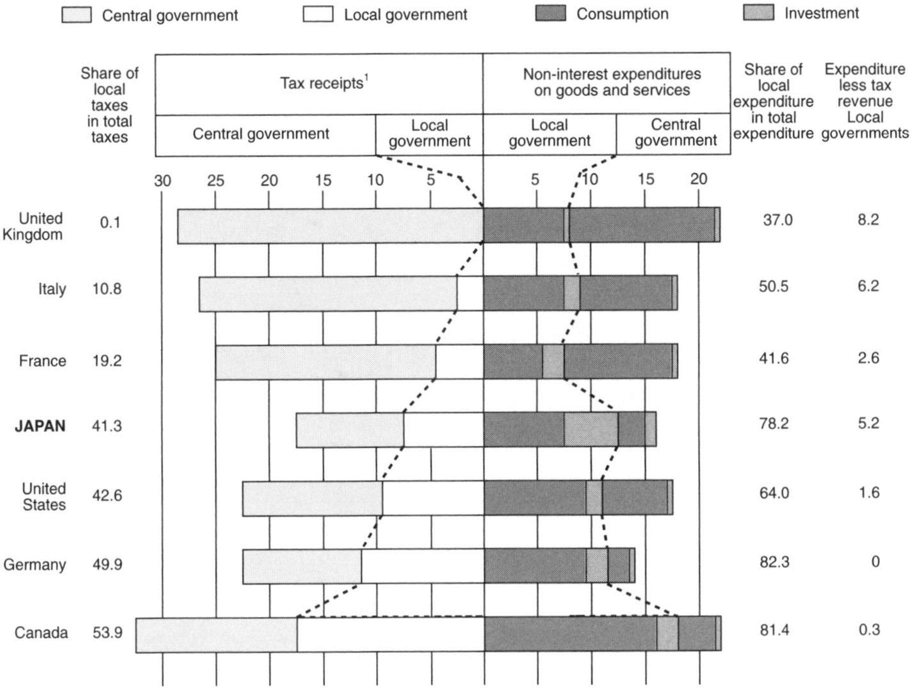

1. Indirect and direct taxes, excluding social security contributions.

Source: Economic Planning Agency and OECD, *Annual National Accounts.*

When viewed from the perspective of resource allocation, a striking feature of the public sector is its scale and complexity, which is not adequately covered by aggregate expenditure statistics. There are several dimensions, including loan guarantees which can substitute for expenditures, and a web of companies, entities and employment relations which reflects the fuzzy boundaries of the public sector.[134] Bank re-capitalisation and credit guarantees are not fully reflected in general government expenditures even though they have had a significant effect on the economy. Re-capitalisation has been undertaken by extending guarantees to the Deposit Credit Corporation to raise money in capital markets for buying convertible bonds from the banks. The full impact on general government expenditures and on debt service cannot be known until the banks have been rehabilitated,[135] but the cost is expected to be substantial. The presence of a large

Figure 33. **Cyclical sensitivity of the fiscal position and govenment size, 1999**

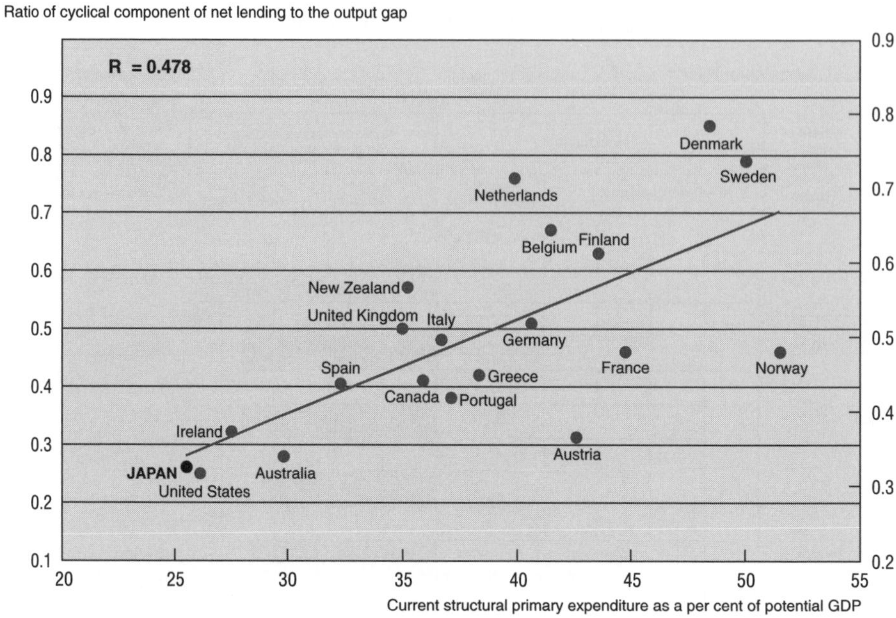

Note: In deriving cyclical effects on spending, investment has been classified as a discretionary item.
Source: OECD.

number of public enterprises means that general government expenditure can only be a rough guide to the impact of the public sector on resource allocation since, for one thing, liabilities might often need to be taken over eventually by the budget sector. Thus "privatisation" of the Japan National Railway contributed to the halving of subsidies from the early 1980s to ¾ per cent of GDP.[136] Nevertheless, ultimately the budget had to assume its liabilities – and those of the National Forest Special Account – in FY 1998 (OECD, 1998*b*), which amounted to 27 trillion yen (*i.e.* 5½ per cent of GDP). Another important aspect of the public sector not captured by expenditure statistics is the direct impact on the level of employment. In this respect Japan appears to compare favourably: employment in the general government sector is only half the OECD average and the absolute number has been declining (Table 26). The low level reflects a long tradition in Japan during the post war years of holding down public-sector employment and wage costs (Rao, 1998). On the other hand, a broader more realistic definition of the public sector than that encompassed by the national accounts points to a significantly higher level of employment and impact on resource allocation (Box 7).

Table 26. **Employment in the public sector**
Per cent[1]

	1988	1993	1997
Canada	7.4	7.8	6.5
France	29.4	31.0	31.8
Germany	n.a.	17.7	17.1
Italy	22.9	23.2	22.9
Japan	**8.0**	**7.2**	**7.0**
United Kingdom	23.9	19.5	n.a.
United States	15.8	15.8	14.4

1. Producers of government services as a proportion of total employees.
Source: OECD, Annual National Accounts,

In sum, although general government expenditures are low by international standards, the public sector is large and poorly defined. There has been a tendency for expenditures to expand during the 1990s and, as in many other countries, social benefits have been an important driving force. However, in Japan another key factor has been the expansion of public investment, in part for counter-cyclical reasons. A great deal of expenditure is undertaken by local governments acting as an agent for, and financed by, the central government. Clearly, the way in which these transfers and spending programmes are organised is important for understanding the dynamics and the overall efficiency and effectiveness of public spending.

Determinants of the performance of the public spending system

It is often difficult to generalise the objectives set for public expenditure programmes as they are quite specific and detailed and represent numerous competing constituencies. Nevertheless, general objectives have included: promoting growth (and in the 1950s and 1960s, reconstruction); achieving a high level of equality in income both by region and by urban/rural location; meeting social needs due to various forms of market failure; counter cyclical policy; and, more recently, decentralisation. This section first examines how the electoral system might have influenced the articulation of objectives for public spending, and then goes on to consider the budget process through which these spending objectives would usually be realised. The tentative conclusion is that the spending system is likely to exhibit important inefficiencies in the sense that objectives and the relevant tradeoffs have either not been identified or implemented *via* the budget process. The subsequent sub-sections consider two broad spending programmes, as examples, to examine the aspects of performance and to identify pressure for growth in the future. The spending programmes are: social security

Box 7. The extent of the public sector

Komiya (1999) portrays the broader public sector as a four-layer system with the first (central government) and second (local governments) layers rather slim, unless the direct employment effect of the large amount of public investment is taken into account. The third (public corporations and so-called third sector companies) and fourth layers are, however, large. At the local government level the situation is complex. According to the Ministry of Home Affairs (MHA), there were 10 135 local public corporations in March 1999 and about 58 per cent of these were jointly established with the private sector.[1] Many of these so-called "third sector" firms appear to be subject to insufficient public monitoring.[2] Whether and how they are favoured by local government action and the financial implications for local governments are unclear [(OECD (1999*a*), Box 3]. Between these three layers there are important inter-connections in staffing.[3]

The fourth layer is defined as private companies (based on the commercial code or the civil law) which have transactions (through public procurement, outsourcing, etc.) with the first three layers and also employ retired officials from the higher layers. There were about 26 000 such civil law companies (*koeki hojin*) in 1998 with 540 500 employees (about 1 per cent of the labour force), gross expenditures of 20.5 trillion yen (4 per cent of GDP) and assets worth 125.7 trillion yen (25 per cent of GDP).[4] Komiya also pointed out that the expansion of the fourth layer is being driven by the ageing of the workforce employed in the higher layers. Ageing tends to bloat the number of middle level managers in large private companies under the seniority-based employment system and these companies often transfer such employees to their subsidiaries to control costs. A similar mechanism appears to link the first three layers to the fourth in the public sector. Evidence of inefficiency in the fourth layer is ubiquitous. For example, *Koeki hojin* are often industry associations and are allowed to monopolise testing and certification of products in each industry.[5] Although public corporations usually can not establish their own subsidiary companies, there is a loophole: employee associations can. Public corporations sometimes have many such "quasi-subsidiaries". According to the Management and Co-ordination Agency (1999), in FY 1996 the Japan Highway Corporation (JHC) had 63 quasi-subsidiaries, which enjoyed a dominant market position in highway-related businesses (such as toll collection, maintenance, sales of prepaid cards, etc.) by receiving contracts which had not been the subject of open tendering procedures. This situation has improved since 1997 when the JHC introduced a competitive bidding system for these businesses.

1. At the central government level there has been some progress in reorganising and privatising the public sector: the number of central government public corporations has been reduced from 92 in 1995 to 78 as of October 1999.
2. Unless the government's share of equity is more than 25 per cent, the companies are subject to neither monitoring by the local Diets nor to review by the audit committee. Residents may, however, request disclosure.
3. The numbers are biased upwards since some of the third-sector companies are also *koeki hojin*.
4. According to a survey of the Prime Minister's office, 76 out of 78 central government public corporations have retired civil servants as executives, and overall they account for 309 out of 724 posts.
5. The FTC (1999) provides a survey of such business engaged by *Koeki hojin*. See various concrete examples in reports published by the Office of Trade and Investment Ombudsman.

and the provision of some merit goods, and public investment. The broad conclusion is that there is considerable scope for cost saving and for more effective expenditures and that it will be necessary to realise this potential since many programmes are under pressure to expand.

The electoral system: an important influence on resource allocation

It is axiomatic that within the OECD area, the setting of and the priority given to objectives for public spending occurs through the political process. However, the actual organisation of political activity and the role played by interest groups has an important bearing on the efficiency of this process. In this respect, a number of criticisms have been levelled against the system in Japan – at least the system up to the most recent changes in 1996. Multi-member constituencies with a strong weighting to the rural areas resulted in fierce intra-party competition, with success tending to be seen as the level of public resources which were obtained for the electoral area (Cox and Thies, 1998). The low level of votes required for election – combined with the need to avoid policy competition with fellow party candidates – led to tightly organised producer interest groups and companies having a strong political voice. The consequences of the system have been examined in a number of academic studies. For example, one study found that the affiliation and status of local politicians were important in attracting central government spending, including revenue sharing transfers, to an area.[137]

Widespread dissatisfaction with "money politics" led to the introduction of a new electoral system in 1996, which established single member electorates combined with proportional representation (Table 27).[138] Moving to single member electorates could in principle force Diet members to appeal to a broader coalition of interests than in the past. At the same time, the over-representation of the rural electorate was reduced although it still remains important. The extent to

Table 27. **Comparison of new and old Lower House electoral systems**

System	New system	Old system
Seats	500	511
District structure	300 single members 200 proportional representation	131 multi-members (2-6 seats)
Rural overrepresentation (per cent)	2.3	7.8
Percentage of votes to win	35.0	14.3

1. Rural overrepresentation is defined as the percentage of Lower House seats held by rural districts, minus their percentage of national population.
Source: Nikko Salomon Smith Barney Ltd., *Japan: Issues and prospects*, 8 June 2000.

which the new system brings about effective change remains to be seen, especially since the support groups for individuals remain intact and elections are expensive. It will also depend on other reforms – such as more rigorous project assessment, which would limit the potential for individual Diet members to channel government largesse to their local constituency.[139]

The political process has also set the framework for public spending through defining the treatment of private property rights and how these relate to the public interest. A key feature of public works activity in Japan has been the cost and difficulty of dealing with land rights, in part because land ownership is so fragmented. This has raised negotiating costs. Expenditures on land and compensation account for about 20 per cent of projects undertaken by the Ministry of Construction. Moreover, a number of projects such as airport construction have been retarded by only one or two individuals refusing to part with strategic land holdings. While the law formally recognises the right of compulsory acquisition for public projects, the political determination has not been present to exercise these rights. The Ministry of Construction has now decided that where 80 per cent of land has already been acquired by negotiation, the remainder could in principle be acquired compulsorily. However, it should also be noted that the political process is now turning against centrally-instigated public works projects in some areas, sometimes on environmental grounds.

The budgetary system: short term control lacking medium term perspective

Although the budget process exhibits a high degree of short-term parliamentary control, from the macroeconomic policy perspective, the potential to set the overall fiscal position is much weaker. Parliamentary control focuses on approving a complex structure of individual accounts for the central government (see Box 8). Since the level of borrowing is included in the general account of the central government there is a need for the passage of a supplementary budget when this limit is exceeded, and not just a simple lifting of the borrowing limit as is undertaken in most OECD countries. This new budget might also confirm expenditure controls taken in the meantime by the Ministry of Finance. Less attention is given to setting a consolidated budget or determining the stance of fiscal policy and indeed knowledge about developments at regional and local level is limited. The level of effective fiscal control is thus less than is at first apparent. Moreover, the tradition to base the initial budget for the following year on the initial budget for the previous year, thereby excluding decisions implemented by supplementary budgets also obscures the stance of fiscal policy and the nature of the decisions which are being taken.

The formulation of the central government budget is highly diffuse and this is thought to limit flexibility between different categories of expenditures. After the cabinet approves general guidelines, ministries and agencies formulate

Box 8. **The Japanese budget system**

The budget process is an important factor in ensuring expenditure efficiency since it influences the degree of control over the path of fiscal policy (*i.e.* the ability of the fiscal authorities to control future trends in spending) and how well the ultimate objectives of budgetary policy are defined in concrete spending programmes. Although the budget process is similar to those in many OECD countries (OECD, 1999*d*; Ishi, 1996; Bayoumim 1998), there are also significant differences which include the relatively minor role accorded to the consolidated budget.

The budget system of the central government is represented in Figure 34. Three types of budgets are discussed and approved by the parliament rather than the overall national budget as such: the general account (*Ippan kaikei*), the special accounts comprising 38 separate funds each with its own budget, and the budgets of government-affiliated agencies. The financial plan of these institutions is submitted to the Diet as the Fiscal Investment and Loan rogramme (FILP) only for discussion and information. A consolidated central government budget is presented but does not play a key role. Most of the central government's tax revenues (about 95 per cent) accrue to the "general account" out of which transfers are made to the special funds which in turn, *inter alia*, provide transfers to local governments. The FILP, which receives funds mostly from the postal savings system and pension contributions, is important for financing capital expenditures of local governments and public agencies and corporations. In addition, both the central and local governments provide transfers to the social security system which in turn is a major source of transfers to households.

Figure 34. **Flows of financial funds from the General account to other budgets (yen billion)**

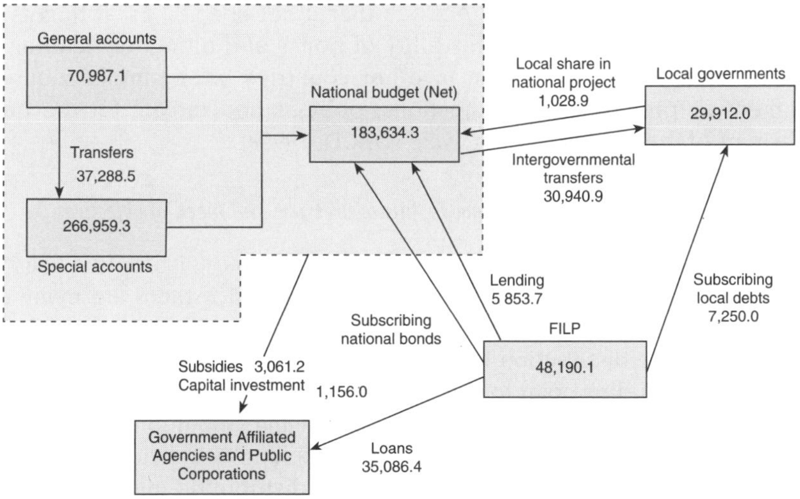

Notes: All figures are based on those of the initial budget and local public finance program in 1995.
Source: Ishi, 1995.

initial budget requests, which by their very nature tend to be based on past budget allocations. More detailed budget plans are then developed through negotiations between the Ministry of Finance and the relevant ministries, leaving them very little flexibility in making fund allocations and operational decisions. These negotiations are particularly important in the area of public works spending and may account for the tendency to observe incremental budget outcomes by which the share of resources received by ministries has remained relatively constant over a long period. For example, the allocation of public works funds between the Ministries of Construction and Agriculture has changed little.[140]

Unlike many other countries, Japan has no regular cycle of medium-term expenditure planning so that negotiations about expenditures focus almost exclusively on spending levels for the next financial year. This tends to lower pressure to consider the future fiscal consequences of policy actions and tends to subject the system to *ad hoc* across-the-board cuts during periods of consolidation (OECD, 1999*d*). The government does announce multi-year plans for investment, but these plans do not appear to be closely integrated with the annual budgetary process. The under-development of medium-term expenditure planning has been recognised as a problem for quite some time but has not been dealt with adequately.

The Fiscal Structural Reform Act in 1997, which was relaxed once and finally suspended in December 1998 (Box 9), was a first attempt to articulate fiscal targets over the medium term. However, even at that time it appeared that a more wide-ranging reform of the budgetary process was required, involving a comprehensive long-term expenditure programme integrated with revenue projections. A major weakness with the Reform Act was that it set specific fiscal targets in the legislation, thereby limiting the flexibility of policy and ultimately leading to the weakening of the law. Legislation in other countries often simply requires the government to provide fiscal projections, policies and targets for the next few years as part of the regular budget cycle (OECD, 1999*e*).

Social programmes and merit goods: future pressure and meeting objectives

Social equity, including an "equitable" income distribution, has represented an important policy objective although in practice there are many dimensions to this objective making any assessment difficult. Evidence about the evolution of income distribution in Japan is partial, often covering only the working population. Such studies point to some widening of the household income distribution over the period 1984 to 1994, mainly due to rising labour force participation by women (Nishizaki, Yamada and Ando, 1997).[141] Looking at individual elements, the tax system has been strongly progressive in its distribution effects. On the other hand, social expenditures appear to have had only a limited impact on income distribution since the programmes have been associated with only a small volume of expenditures: relative to GDP they are the smallest of the G7 countries (Figure 35).

Box 9. **The 1997 Fiscal Structural Reform Act: a first approach to articulating fiscal targets**

The law specified five basic principles or objectives:

- restoring the "golden rule", whereby net bond issuance is limited to the level of public investment, by FY 2003;
- reducing the general government deficit, excluding social security, to below 3 per cent by FY 2003;
- reducing discretionary general account spending in FY 1998 compared with FY 1997;
- 1998/2000 specified as a special reform term;
- ensuring that the sum of taxes, social security contributions and the fiscal deficit does not exceed 50 per cent of GDP.

Caps were also imposed on some individual expenditure lines. However, except for some limited objectives for spending on public works (which was to be cut by 7 per cent in FY 1998 and would not exceed the previous year's initial budget in the following two fiscal years), social security transfers and defence spending, no detailed expenditure plans were announced for future years (OECD, 1997).

The law was amended in May 1998 to allow deficit financing bonds (as opposed to those issued to cover investment under the golden rule) to be issued in the event of a sharp downturn or where GDP expanded by less than 1 per cent. The spending caps were not relaxed. Greater public works spending was therefore only possible *via* supplementary budgets. This law was finally suspended in December 1998.

Since social programmes have emphasised income replacement, their impact on a narrow concept of income distribution has been, if anything, negative. When considered from a more dynamic and future oriented perspective, the situation with respect to equity appears more complex. Social programmes are often earnings-related and not overly influenced by floors and ceilings: they are concerned with income replacement rather than income redistribution or poverty alleviation *per se*. To the extent that earnings might become more unequal as performance-related pay assumes a greater role, the transfer system will mirror this development. Above all, the pension system, with its emphasis on security of income in old age, contributes to increasing inequality, both intra- and inter-generational [Horioka (1999); Oguchi, Kimura and Hatta (1996)].

Social programmes will remain under pressure from both the changing structure of the economy as well as from ageing. To maintain efficiency and cost effectiveness will thus require continual revision and monitoring of the programmes. With respect to the needs of a changing economy, labour markets are a

Figure 35. **Public social expenditure in OECD countries**[1]
Per cent of GDP

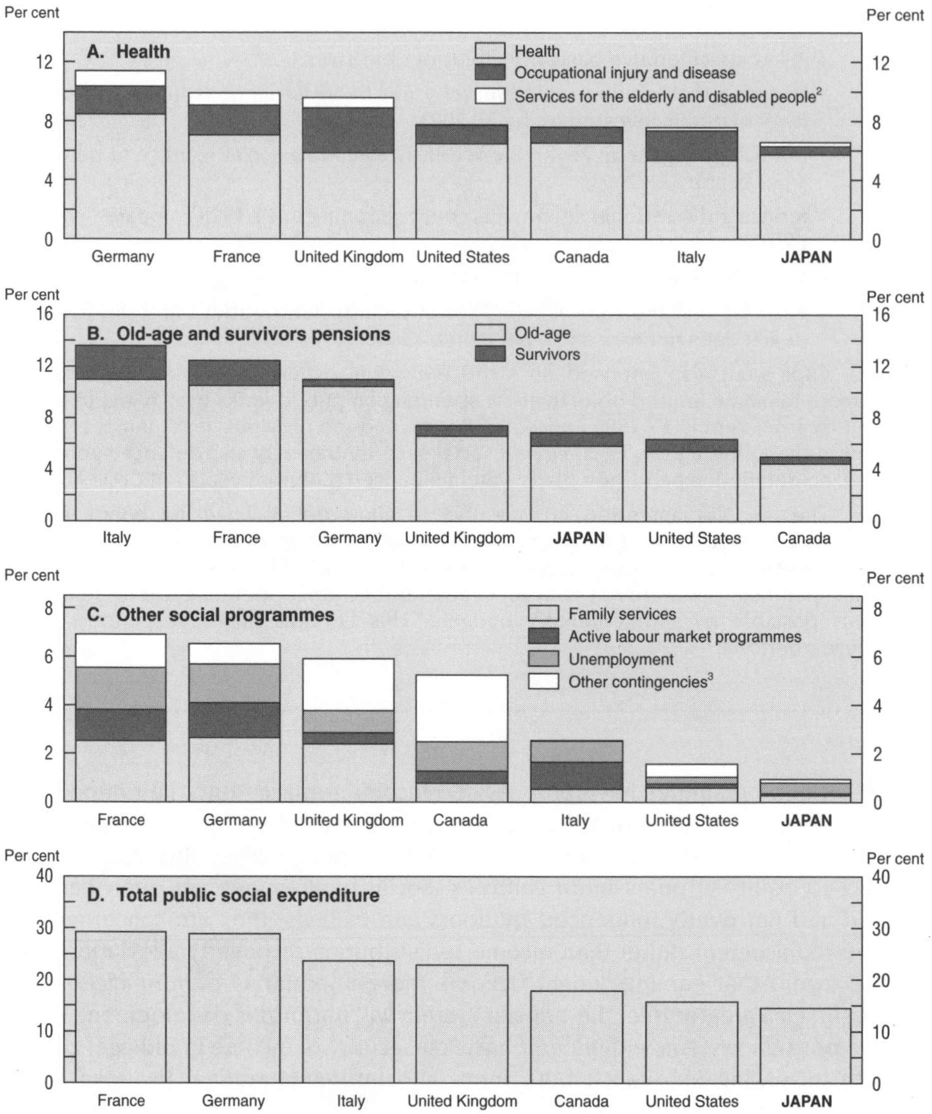

1. In 1997 for Japan and the United States; in 1996 for Canada, Germany and France; in 1995 for Italy and the United Kingdom. Spending on education is recorded separately.
2. Not available of Canada.
3. Housing benefits (except for Canada, the United States and Japan) and other contingencies.

Source: OECD, Social Expenditure Database.

good example. Higher unemployment rates than in the past, greater worker mobility and changing job requirements all suggest the need to restructure labour market spending perhaps even raising spending on youth training (Chapter III). Rising wage disparities across industries and occupations as firms restructure might also lead to a greater conflict between income replacement and income distribution objectives than in the past. A similar pattern has also been seen in Europe where social transfer programmes have been increasingly adjusted by ceilings and floors so as to reflect distribution objectives. However, ceilings and floors to programmes often result in distortions with respect to labour supply decisions.

For both pensions and health care, the major challenge is related to the ageing population. An official estimate from 1997 showed that the increase in national health care expenditures due to ageing might amount to 23 trillion yen (including patients' self payments and the possible effects of long-term care insurance which was launched in April 2000) in current prices over the next decade; increasing at an annual rate of some 8 per cent would boost the share of public health spending in GDP by around 2 percentage points. The challenge for public spending policy will be to keep the projected rise in health expenditures to a minimum through, *inter alia*, the efficient transfer of resources from the diminishing prime age group to the growing older population. A large number of elderly are at present hospitalised in acute care beds even though they do not need specific medical treatment, accounting for the long length of stay in hospitals: 39 days, way above the OECD average. The new long-term care scheme (for details see Chapter III) should result in the development of long-term care institutions and might also assist in providing even more economical in-home care. Reforms of healthcare and pension systems to meet the challenge for an ageing population are discussed in Chapter III. It is only necessary to note here that reforms will have to address minimum healthcare and income concerns directly if the negative effects on both intra- and inter-generational income distribution are to be avoided and labour force participation encouraged.

An important social programme concerns housing which is an example of a programme with unclear or conflicting objectives. Estimates of expenditures are not available but they are thought to be high. As noted in Chapter II, there are at present substantial tax benefits arising from buying an apartment or house before the end of June 2001 while a public financial institution, the Housing Loan Corporation, provides housing finance at below marker rates (Figure 36). According to an official estimate, the tax expenditure could amount to 1½ trillion yen per year on average over the next fifteen years. In addition, a lower bound estimate of the policy cost of the housing loans provided by the HLC places them at 1.2 trillion yen, and at 2.1 trillion when based on market interest rates.[142] These estimates compare with the 448 billion yen in FY 2000 budget. The fact that subsidy costs have only been recently calculated on a trial basis indicates the lack of a forward

Figure 36. **Housing market interest rates**

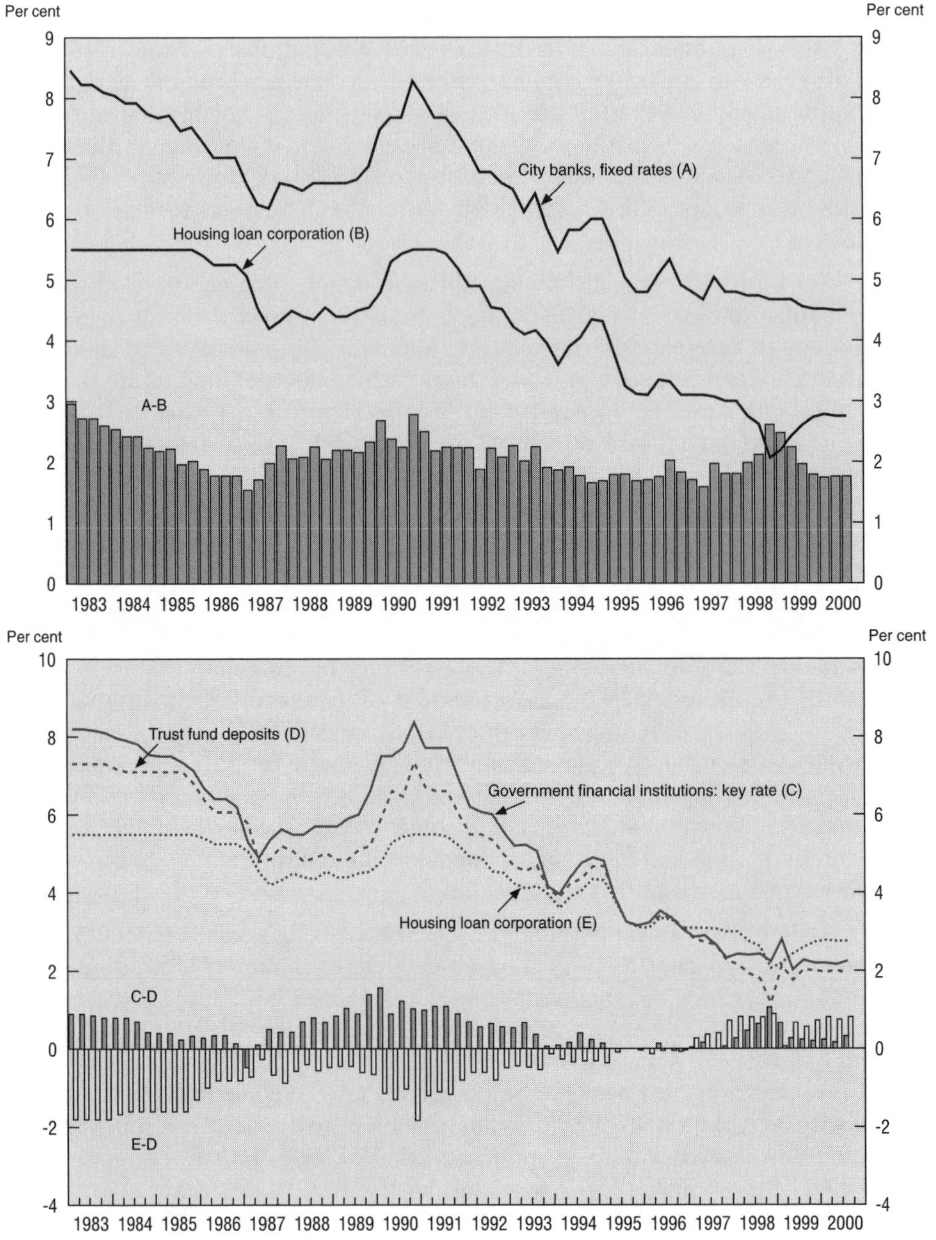

Source: Bank of Japan.

oriented budget process. Unlike many other countries which target support on social housing, the scheme in Japan is oriented to owner-occupied houses and so mainly support middle income groups. Indeed, since the number of houses exceeded that of households in the late 1960s, the policy objective shifted to support for the acquisition of *quality* houses. Thus the policy objective is quite regressive. However, there are some signs of change. Subsidies through favourable lending rates of the HLC were reduced when rate setting was reviewed in 1997. Although tax expenditure is currently high, this measure is of a temporary nature and, unless renewed, will decline over time. Moreover, the expected decline in population will undermine policies to stimulate new housing construction. Given the current (quantitatively) sufficient level of the housing stock[143] and different needs for accommodation according to the life cycle (which will be more apparent as ageing proceeds), it seems desirable to improve the functioning of the secondary housing market (see Chapter III for a discussion of the new rent law and financial market reforms). This could be a more cost-effective way of improving living conditions than the current policy.

With respect to the provision of merit goods, education is an example of a programme which appears to have been cost-effective although it will require modification in the future. Expenditure on education represents a high proportion of public expenditures (about 40 per cent of public consumption) although as a share of GDP it is somewhat smaller than in other G7 countries. However, participation of the private sector and effective targeting of public expenditure has made it possible to attain high levels of educational achievement with relatively low levels of government expenditures. In 1992, the share of public expenditures in total educational expenditures was around 60 per cent but it accounted for 70 per cent of expenditures in primary and secondary levels and only 40 per cent in colleges and universities. The focus on the basic level would seem cost effective as it is believed that this is where educational externalities are probably greatest. At the college level, where there is a greater possibility for returns to education to be captured by the individual, it is more efficient for individuals to carry more of the expenditure themselves.[144] Nevertheless, to maintain cost effectiveness in the education system will require further changes. For example, population ageing is already creating excess capacity in the primary school system, yet there are a number of difficulties in closing schools and relocating teachers to other activities.

Another key area of public sector activity has been technology and R&D spending and here there are tentative moves to improve cost-effectiveness which illustrates the need for close monitoring. The inflexibility of the R&D system has become more apparent in recent years leading to a number of structural reforms, *inter alia*, to improve incentives for university researchers and to spread research findings more effectively [OECD (1998*b*), Table 38]. Following the Science and Technology Basic Plan (decided in 1996), the government allocated 17.2 trillion yen in total to R&D for five years up to FY 2000,[145] aiming to lift its share toward the OECD average. Although a new scheme to allocate project funds through competition has been introduced, the share is still low (less than 10 per cent) in comparison with the United States (about one-third) and the United Kingdom (more than 40 per cent). The mid-term review of the Basic Plan (April 1999) pointed out that an improved evaluation system would be essential for a more extensive use of the new scheme. Indeed, evaluation in this area seems lax. Thus the Board of Audit noted that in 16 per cent (2 235 cases) of the cases inspected, the research results had not been reported within the pre-specified period. In 205 cases at twenty universities covering some 2 billion yen, the delay was more than two years, yet new funds were granted to 35 of these projects. Institutions will take some time to adapt themselves to the new environment but, with more budgetary resources available, greater cost effectiveness and transparency is needed.

A *high level of public investment with multiple objectives*

With such a large share of GDP devoted to public investment over a long period, the question arises whether this is due to institutional inertia (including interest group behaviour) or to special requirements (institutional or otherwise) of Japan. The remarkable constancy of public expenditure shares between ministries, and the slow change in the composition of expenditures would all point to considerable inertia. The nature of the political and budget process lends support to this judgement. In other words, there has been no effective policy process to enable global reallocation among areas so as to improve allocative efficiency. On the other hand, the geography of Japan does suggest that projects might be more costly than in other countries: the land is mountainous, the ground is soft (alluvial), it is an earthquake area and rainfall is high. The government places an emphasis on this aspect and considers that international comparisons with other developed countries of some infrastructure and amenities justify a continued high level of expenditures (Table 28). However, this evidence is not so clear. Because the comparisons cover only several kinds of infrastructure,[146] this "shortage" might have been compensated by other related investment or indeed might reflect inefficient allocation in the past, whose cause would need to be corrected before additional investment is undertaken. With overall indicators difficult to interpret, it is therefore necessary to examine the programmes in more detail to see whether public investment has been allocated efficiently and to determine whether demands for further investment are being properly assessed.[147]

The estimated rate of return to public investment, which has been derived from macroeconomic production functions, is low. Analysis of the rate of return indicates that it is positively related to prefectoral income, but that investment is higher in low return areas (Figure 37). Indeed, per capita investment in low income prefectures is four times greater than in high income areas. Put another

Table 28. **Comparison of infrastructure**

Sector	Japan		Other countries			
	At present	Early 21st century	United Kingdom	Germany	France	United States
Sewerage						
Sewerage diffusion rate (per cent)	60[1] (1999)[2]	90	97 (1995)	92 (1995)	81 (1994)	71 (1992)
Cities of more than 1 million inhabitants (per cent)	98	–				
Cities of less than 50 000 inhabitants (per cent)	24	–				
City parks						
City park area per resident (m²)	7.9 (nation) 3.0 (Tokyo ward area) (1999)[2]	20	26.9 (London) (1997)	27.4 (Berlin) (1995)	11.8 (Paris) (1994)	29.3 (New York) (1997)
Roads						
Length of expressways (km)	7 554 (1999)[2]	14 000	3 226 (1996)	11 309 (1997)	9 900 (1997)	88 601 (1996)
Length of expressways per 10 000 cars (km)	1.07 (1999)[2]	–	1.31 (1996)	2.58 (1997)	3.19 (1997)	4.32 (1996)
Flood control						
Flood control rates	57 per cent (1999)[2]	59 per cent	Probability of damage by tidal waves; once in 1 000 years	Probability of damage through flooding; once in 500 years	Probability of damage through flooding; once in 100 years	Probability of damage through flooding; once in 500 years
River			Thames, barrage completed (1983)	Rhein, completed (1993)	Seine, completed (1988)	Mississippi, 79 per cent (1993)

1. 69 per cent if sewerage system under the Ministry of Agriculture and the Ministry of Health and Welfare is included.
2. Fiscal year.

Source: Ministry of Construction.

Figure 37. **The level and return on government investment**
46 prefectures of metropolitan Japan, FY 1993

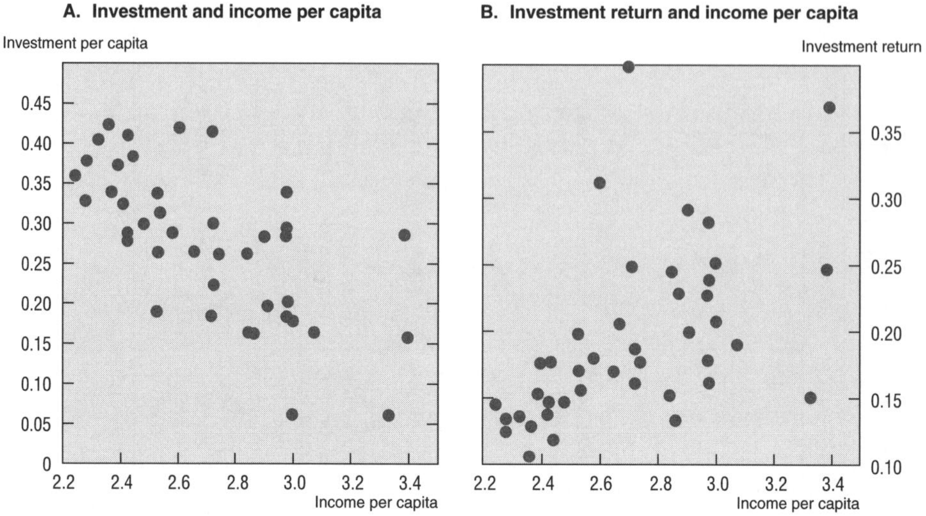

Source: Economic Planning Agency, Prefectoral income and spending.

way, the return to social capital in cities is roughly twice the rate of return in outlying regions[148] (EPA, 1997). The high level of investment in poorer areas has not stimulated self-sustaining growth as hoped, the areas simply becoming highly dependent on public construction – a similar result is also observed in regions of Germany and Italy. Clearly the main objective has been income distribution (Box 10) – and especially so in agricultural areas – so that it is difficult to say, *a priori*, whether the projects have been allocationally efficient or not (as opposed to having been implemented at least cost). However, two factors suggest that the investments may not have been efficient in this broader sense. First, the shadow price or valuation of income distribution objectives is a political question so that the question turns on whether the political process is efficient in articulating this objective. The analysis above suggests that this might not be the case in view of the high electoral weight of these regions. Second, a given project might help achieve temporarily a desired income distribution target, but an alternative method such as income transfers might have been more cost effective than public investment. The question revolves around whether the alternatives were examined at the basic policy making stage. Funding inertia, the ongoing importance of public construction and the political importance of attracting public projects to the electorate all suggest that this might not have been the case.[149]

Box 10. Public investment in agriculture

Social infrastructure investment is replacing land improvement

Public investment in agriculture, most of which concerns land improvement projects, accounts for about 10 per cent of total public investment.[1] A recent pick-up in spending has been due to Uruguay-Round-related measures, which amounted to 3.18 trillion yen (revised down from 3.55 trillion yen in 1997) out of 7.21 trillion yen covering eight years. Although government projects – large-scale ones in particular such as irrigation and drainage – are tending to decline over time, resources are being shifted to investment in social infrastructure (rather than the production base). Social infrastructure includes rural sewage facilities, roads (in villages as well as in production areas) and various public facilities.

Public investment has been used as an income transfer mechanism

Like in other areas, public investments in agriculture raise incomes through pure spending effects. In addition, some of these investments contribute to income growth through an increased production capacity. For example, the land extension project, whose main objective is to secure a stable food supply, had an effect of raising farm incomes through the expansion of rice production until 1969 when adjustment policy was introduced and the programme for paddy field was abolished. Since then all land extension projects have aimed at expanding upland farms. However, the exhaustion of potential areas for land extension has led to a further decline of these projects.

Project selection procedures need to be improved...

Despite the relatively long tradition of project analysis in agriculture, there still seems to be room for improvement. It is important to identify the social benefits obtaining from investing in a project and this is even more important when prices are distorted by support mechanisms. However, this point does not seem to be adequately taken into consideration by the cost-benefit analysis applied to farmland improvement projects (Okuno and Honma, 1998). With regard to the evaluation of environmental externalities, they pointed out that only the additional benefits from using the land for agricultural purpose, instead of keeping the land as greenfield, should be included in the calculation. Nakajima (1998) has argued that reduced agricultural production and progress in urbanisation in rural areas could complicate the calculation in the case of investment in existing facilities and for social infrastructure.

... and various measures besides public investment should also be considered

Measures other than investment in land should be effective in increasing productivity in agriculture. Larger farms could be facilitated by appropriate zoning regulations to eliminate expectations of gains from changing land use to another purpose while holding costs of idle farmland could also be increased.[2] Further easing of requirements for obtaining farmland would also be useful (see Chapter III).

1. The basic procedures for farmland improvement projects are: 1) producers apply for the scheme; 2) once the consensus among more than two-thirds is reached, all the members of the community are obliged to participate; 3) evaluation of costs and benefits is conducted; 4) funds are raised; 5) a management team is formed.
2. See OECD, *Economic Survey of Japan*, 1999, for the effect of such expectations on land use.

With respect to the effectiveness and efficiency of public investment, three inter-related questions are important: the nature and quality of project selection, the form of the financing constraint and the quality of project implementation.

- Project selection

Public investment takes place within the framework of long-term investment plans in most sectors (Table 29) and these are in turn related to the national development plan and to the medium-term economic plan. In addition there are also regional plans. However, the degree of linkage and coherence between these plans is not high. For example, although there is a legal consultation mechanism, the actual co-ordination between road and rail development, which concerns two different ministries, appears to be low. Implementation of these plans is decided through annual negotiations between the relevant spending ministry and the MOF, although the large number of supplementary budgets in recent years has led to almost continuous negotiations. Project selection takes place within this framework, but until the last two to three years the methods utilised have generally

Table 29. **Long-term public investment plans**
Trillion yen

	Current plans					Previous plans (reference)			
	Version	Start in	End in	Total costs	Costs per year	Start in	End in	Total costs	Costs per year
Flood prevention	9	1997	2003	24.00	3.43	1992	1996	17.50	3.50
Sloped area	4	1998	2002	1.19	0.24	1993	1997	1.15	0.23
Landslide prevention	9	1997	2003	3.77	0.54	1992	1996	2.76	0.55
Coast	6	1996	2002	1.77	0.25	1991	1995	1.30	0.26
Roads	12	1998	2002	78.00	15.60	1993	1997	76.00	15.20
Ports	9	1996	2002	7.49	1.07	1991	1995	5.70	1.14
Fishing ports	9	1994	2001	3.00	0.38	1988	1993	2.41	0.40
Airports	7	1996	2002	3.60	0.51	1991	1995	3.19	0.64
Housing	7	1996	2000	7.30[1]	1.46[1]	1991	1995	7.30[1]	1.46[1]
Sewage system	8	1996	2002	23.70	3.39	1991	1995	16.50	3.30
Waste disposal facilities	8	1996	2002	5.05	0.72	1991	1995	2.83	0.57
Urban parks	6	1996	2002	7.20	1.03	1991	1995	5.00	1.00
Land improvement	4	1993	2006	41.00	2.93	1983	1992	32.80	3.28
Forest creation	2	1997	2003	5.38	0.77	1992	1996	3.90	0.78
Coastal fishery	4	1994	2001	0.60	0.08	1988	1993	0.48	0.08
Traffic safety	6	1996	2002	2.69	0.38	1991	1995	2.02	0.40
Total				208.44[2]	31.31[2]			173.54[2]	31.33[2]

1. The planned number of housing units (in thousands).
2. Excluding housing.
Source: Ministry of Finance.

lacked a firm foundation in cost benefit analysis. This is particularly clear when it comes to considering the time path of costs and benefits. Thus it is only recently that estimates have been made of the future subsidy cost of various government institutions (Table 14). In the case of the Japan Highway Corporation, the potential cost to the budget is substantially greater than current budget subsidies indicate.[150] Another indication of past practices is illustrated by the project review which began in 1997. Projects not started five years after approval and those underway five to ten years after approval have been examined with respect to: progress toward completion, the social and environmental implications of the project, potential revisions to the cost benefit implications, and the scope for cost cutting.[151] One hundred projects were cancelled in FY 1999 under this review although the number has fallen to twenty-three in FY 2000. More recently, the three coalition parties agreed in August to step up the review, which may result in the termination of some 233 projects with total cost savings of 2.8 trillion yen. Annual budget savings would, however, only amount to around 1 per cent of budget allocations. In general, *ex ante* project selection has not been rigorous and has lacked a common methodology while *ex post* analysis has been underdeveloped until very recently.

- Project financing

There are three sources of financing for public investment – budget income, the FILP programme and earmarked taxes – each of which has an influence on project selection. With respect to budget funding, the situation is made complex by the nature of the fiscal equalisation system. As noted above, local governments undertake a great deal of investment. They have a major responsibility for local public goods such as city planning, environment, sanitation, education and welfare and cover a considerable proportion of the costs themselves from their general revenue grants. For other projects, the central government carries most of the costs and therefore is in effective control of the projects. Local governments have been executing many of the projects recently for which co-financing is available, while cutting back on their own projects (see Chapter II) because they work under a binding budget constraint.[152] Matching grants makes it likely that local governments have not been allocating investment funds according to the greatest benefit/cost ratio. The second source of finance is the FILP programme, which also covers a number of public expenditure programmes, and is particularly important for road finance. FILP lending has been mainly oriented to financing institutions rather than projects. With these institutions either covered by explicit or implicit state guarantees and often directly supported by subsidies, there has been little incentive for either the institutions or the lending body (the Trust Fund Bureau) to closely monitor cost effectiveness (Figure 38). Finally, some programmes, especially roads, are financed directly by earmarked taxes supplemented by budget revenues (Annex I). Earmarked taxes could enhance efficiency

Figure 38. **Core of the FILP system**

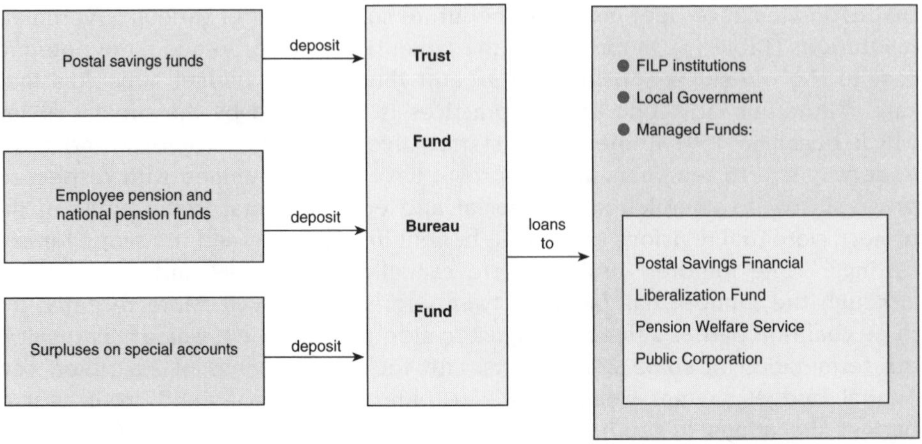

Note: In addition to the Trust Fund Bureau Fund, the financial resources of the FILP also include the Postal Life Insurance Fund, the Industrial Investment Special Account, and government-guaranteed bonds.
Source: « Summary of Discussions on the Fundamental Reform of the FILP », Sub-committee Study Group of the Trust Fund Council, August 30, 1999.

if properly designed by making beneficiaries pay part of the costs, but it would result in resource misallocation if the level of investment is determined by such tax revenues. In practice, however, this concern does not seem to be so relevant in Japan. In the case of road construction, which accounts for more than 70 per cent of earmarked national tax revenues,[153] tax rates have been regularly reviewed at the same time as a 5-year construction plan has been made and revised up, if judged to be necessary for financing the plan.

- Project implementation

A key element determining the effectiveness of public expenditures is the operation of the bidding/tendering system and in this area there is cause for concern. Miwa (1999) reported an important fact: local government officials have stated in an official meeting that more than 90 per cent of successful bids were awarded at prices quite close to the upper-bound. Local governments set upper and lower limits and argue that the lower one is intended to prevent "excessive competition" and to maintain the quality of construction work by ensuring reasonable profits. One interpretation of this distribution of successful bidding prices is a lack of competition, which raises the possibility of widespread bid-rigging (*Dango*) in public procurement (Box 11).[154]

Box 11. A case study of a recent *Dango*: agricultural projects in Hokkaido

In May 2000, the FTC issued a cease and desist order to 203 construction companies and 94 engineer surveying companies concerning bidding for agricultural projects handled by a local office of the Hokkaido local government. A remarkable fact was that the Agriculture Department of the Hokkaido government (including local offices) made a plan every year specifying a target for the value of public works to be awarded to each company. In order to achieve the target they suggested their preferred winner and bidding price to the industry associations. Would-be participants in the bidding co-ordinated their actions through the associations. Moreover, the Hokkaido government admitted that the headquarters and local branches of Agriculture Department adjusted allocation of public works to individual companies for quite a long time, at least three years according to the FTC. The number of ex-officials was an element taken into account when determining the allocation of public works, according to the Hokkaido government. The FTC cannot take any action against the Hokkaido government under the current Anti-monopoly Law. This case illustrates three issues in public procurement: lack of incentives to minimise costs, favourable treatment to SMEs, and the role of ex-bureaucrats.

Judging from publicly available information, *Dango* could be a deep-rooted problem in public procurement, although how extensive it is remains unclear.[155] The Fair Trade Commission (FTC) took legal actions against 20 cases in FY 1999 which concerned bid rigging in public procurement. Kanemoto (1998) even suggests that, by setting upper and lower limits and through other bidding arrangements, local governments seek to limit overcharging – *given* that *Dango* is widespread. Improvement of the public procurement system could bring large savings: if competition could push down successful bid prices to around the lower bound in all local bidding, it would imply a cost reduction by 15 per cent,[156] while maintaining the current volume of construction. This potential is sizeable,[157] compared with the 3-year programme, which aims for a 10 per cent cost reduction of public works in three years from FY 1997 to FY 1999.[158]

Local governments have not actively sought to improve the performance of the bidding system because one of their policy objectives is to support local SMEs. According to a survey by the FTC in 1998, about 90 per cent of municipal governments have the favourable treatment of local companies and locally produced goods and services as a policy goal. Such an objective appears to cost the local tax payers little because local governments rely heavily on transfers and subsidies from the central government. However, favourable treatment of SMEs is a policy goal of the central government as well. A special law, which was enacted in 1966, requires central government and governmental institutions to make efforts to ensure opportunities for SMEs in their procurement policy, and encourages local governments to follow.[159] Indeed, the Cabinet sets a guideline for public procurement contracts every year. The guideline specifies a target share of SMEs in total procurement by the central government, and the means to ensure this include reducing the size of orders.[160] The target for central government, about 40 per cent in recent years, has been almost achieved, while local governments (prefectures and cities with population of 100 000 or more) voluntarily allocate about 70 per cent of their orders to SMEs. Such a policy has resulted in many anomalies. First, each construction company is officially rated according to its capability, and a company rated highly is *not* allowed to participate in bids for "easy" public works. Second, small orders encourage *uwauke*, that is, subcontracting by winners of the actual construction to larger companies. This practice violates the Construction Business Law. Third, large construction companies are often required to form joint ventures with local SMEs in order to participate in bidding.

Another implementation problem concerns the execution of projects by public corporations, which have little incentive to minimise costs. Some of them are entitled to a special company status called "Koudan", which is a kind of project company and therefore is to be dissolved once its objective is achieved.[161] This concerns in particular the Japan Highway Corporation and three other special corporations. Taking the example of road construction (Annex I), increased profits would lead to earlier redemption of debt and, therefore, earlier dissolution of these corporations (Ohata and Imahashi, 1995).[162] Thus, this problem concerns a basic institutional arrangement of some public corporations. The incentive is also likely to be weakened by government subsidies granted to public corporations. In the case of road construction, government subsidies are provided to cover the difference between predetermined capital costs in the repayment scheme for toll roads and the actual borrowing costs (*e.g.* interest charged by the FILP and postal life insurance) depriving the JHC of incentives to minimise costs. It remains to be seen whether this will be corrected by the FILP reform (see below).

Issues in improving the effectiveness of public spending

Fiscal consolidation in the coming years will require close control over public spending but this does not necessarily imply a decline in public welfare since the current system exhibits significant inefficiencies. The above analysis suggests that inter-related measures are, however, required in order to realise the potential gains from improved efficiency and cost effectiveness of the public expenditure system. This section reviews the reform issues which arise in several key areas. At the most fundamental level, spending objectives need to be clearly defined in a medium-term budgetary perspective. In order to accelerate and deepen this process, the public sector should be more clearly defined, thereby subjecting more institutions to market disciplines. The public and the political leadership have to be made aware of the opportunity cost of expenditure programmes while the cost effectiveness of programme implementation must be improved. A summary of policy recommendations is presented in Table 30.

Improving coherency of policy: restructuring the decision making process...

A number of reforms are envisaged to reduce institutional deficiencies in the formulation and implementation of budgetary objectives. In order to enhance the transparency and efficiency of the central government and to facilitate decentralisation, the twenty-two existing ministries and agencies will be reorganised into ten ministries, two agencies and a new cabinet office starting in 2001 (see *Economic Survey*, 1999 for details).[163] The Council on Economic and Fiscal Policy, to be established under the new cabinet office, will deliberate and propose general economic/fiscal management and basic budget policies on the basis of work prepared by its Secretariat.[164] Thus the Cabinet will be formally responsible for the design of basic budget policies which should change somewhat the nature of the negotiations between the Ministry of Finance (MOF) and the other ministries. Moreover, the authority of the Prime Minister to propose basic principles for national policies at cabinet meetings has now been clearly stated in the Cabinet Law. Thus, in principle the overall political responsibility for determining public expenditure priorities will be improved.[165] The re-organisation would also be an appropriate moment to introduce multi-year budgeting in combination with multi-year spending plans, which will also serve to tighten the formulation of budget objectives. On the other hand, significant uncertainty still remains. Thus a council comprising government officials and ruling-party leaders has already been established to debate overall issues concerning the FY 2001 budget, including guidelines on budget requests by ministries. There have been proposals to make this forum permanent. How it would fit in with the intention to reform the process of government is unclear at this stage.

The merging of the Ministries of Construction, Transport, and the National Land Agency into the Ministry of Land, Infrastructure and Transport, together with the merging of Health and Welfare with Labour, offers potential for better co-ordination of policies, although larger ministries could reduce transparency unless measures are taken at the same time to improve accountability. Despite this appreciable effort, some of the overlapping responsibilities that have long been criticised for inhibiting efficiency remain.[166] Whether the new potential for more wide-ranging policy assessment will be utilised depends ultimately on the political will. However, as noted in the *Economic Survey of Japan*, 1998, any improvement in efficiency may be limited unless regulatory incentives, bureaucratic discretion and the lack of accountability and transparency in the decision-making process are changed.

Table 30. **Recommendations for improving the performance of public spending**

Based on the analysis presented in the chapter, the public spending system is associated with significant inefficiency in the sense that *i)* objectives are poorly defined; *ii)* programmes might not be cost effective because alternative possibilities to achieve the objectives at a smaller cost have not been investigated and; *iii)* programmes have not been implemented at least cost. These deficiencies affect different spending programmes in varying degrees. To improve the value for money of public spending will require broad reforms to the way the system operates and in its governance. The chapter identifies the need to move ahead in the following areas:

Improving coherency of policy

- *Restructure the decision making process.* Clearly establish the role of cabinet committees in setting budget priorities. Clarify relations between the government and the parties especially at ministerial policy-making level. Ensure that the move to larger ministries will improve policy coherency by creating strong policy assessment units in each ministry.
- *Clearly delineating the public sector.* Reduce the overlap between public and private activity so as to more clearly establish arms length transactions. Closely define the operating conditions and governance of the numerous public corporations and bodies. Pursue further reform of the FILP and re-examine the mission of the agencies and bodies receiving funds. Clearly establish subsidy programmes for those which will issue their own financing bonds. Control the use of government guarantees for the others.

Increasing budget transparency and strengthening public management

- *Introduce multi-year budgeting and a medium-term fiscal plan* so that implications of programmes both now and in the future are clarified. Present consolidated accounts and better estimates of fiscal impact on the economy.
- *Increase the flexibility of ministerial management and decision making* by moving from a detailed budget agreement between ministries and the Ministry of Finance to general expenditure caps.
- *Introduce accrual accounting.* Tighten accounting for guarantees and contingent liabilities.
- *Reduce the importance of earmarked funds.*

Tightening the reconciliation between public demands and economic trade-offs

- *Reforming financial relations between levels of government and devolving greater responsibilities to lower levels.* Give greater responsibility to local levels for spending decisions to match local needs and preferences. Reduce conditional grants from the central government. Shift part of the tax base to local level.
- *Increase use of user charges and experiment with vouchers.* Move to greater use of user charges in transportation in particular.

Improve cost efficiency

- *Greater use of cost-benefit/effectiveness analysis in ex ante evaluation.* New policy evaluation units in each ministry need to adopt these techniques with overall framework being set by a central body such as the Management and Co-ordination Agency.
- *More cost effective auditing.* Strengthen resources of the Board of Audit in this area as well as the new policy analysis units. Improve feed-back into policy making by, for example, reports on follow-up action or greater role for parliamentary committees.
- *Reform the bidding system especially at local level.* Widen the coverage of competitive bidding in public procurement and in public works. Review and reform policies which are aimed at supporting local SMEs through tendering arrangements.

Source: OECD.

Lacking up till now has been effective evaluation of policy, both *ex ante* and *ex post*, and how it relates to government objectives. The logical place for such work is the Management and Co-ordination Agency, which has already been involved in the evaluation of managerial efficiency of the Ministries. Unfortunately, with the reorganisation of the government the Agency is being integrated into the Ministry of Public Management, Home Affairs, Posts and Telecommunications together with the Ministry of Post and Telecommunications: an important spending ministry.[167] The role of the Ministry should also be to oversee and to set the cost/benefit framework for the evaluation units now being created in each ministry (see below).

... and more clearly delineating the public sector

If the decision-making process is to become more focused and oriented to improved efficiency, a clearer delineation of the government from public and private corporations and activities is essential. More arms length transactions would allow the social benefit to be more clearly distinguished from the benefits accruing to various public or private entities. This would involve action in several areas, including management practices and defining the scope and operations of public institutions. With respect to the former, the government has made an important start with the entry into force in April 2000 of a strict ethics code for civil servants. Moreover, capable retired civil servants may be re-employed up to the age of 65 years. However, this only partly deals with the problem, which is the apparent ability of retired civil servants in either public or private institutions to influence expenditure programmes – a problem which is not confined to Japan. It will also be important to more closely define the governance and operating conditions of the numerous public corporations and bodies – including their close business relationships with related firms – with a view to improving the cost effectiveness of their operations. The need to tighten the governance of public bodies has in part motivated the reform of the FILP system, which will come into effect in April 2001.

The objective of the FILP reform is to create greater efficiency among special public institutions termed FILP institutions – such as the Housing Loan Corporation, Japan Highways Public Corporation, the Japan Investment Policy Bank, the Finance Corporation for Small Business Enterprises and local governments – by forcing them to raise funds on the financial markets, thereby encouraging greater expenditure discipline (Figure 39).[168] Apart from funds borrowed by a new and much reduced FILP system, the institutions will either have to issue their own bonds (FILP institution bonds) or rely on government-guaranteed bonds. The demand for funds would thus be driven to some extent by their own needs rather than by the supply of postal savings and pension reserves as under the old system. These latter institutions will be free to invest more widely.

Figure 39. **The FILP system after April 2001**

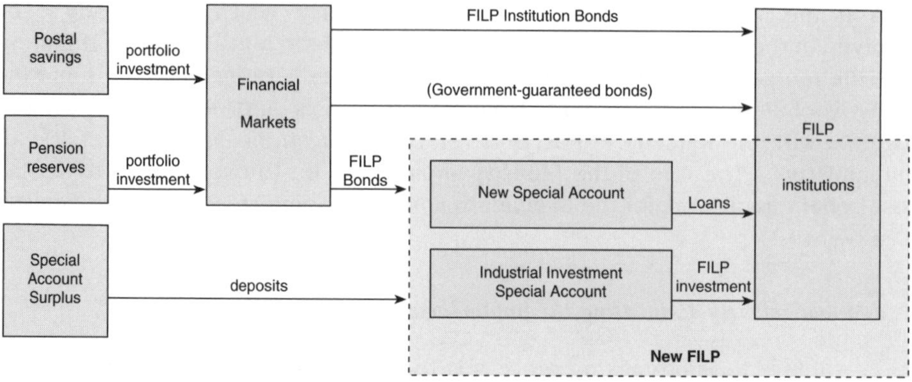

Source: « Summary of Discussions on the Fundamental Reform of the FILP », Sub-committee Study Group of the Trust Fund Council, August 30, 1999.

Although the reform is welcome and should serve to underpin moves to improve project selection and public expenditure efficiency, a number of issues remain to be resolved, quite apart from the macroeconomic issues discussed in Chapter II. For example, if they issue their own bonds, it will be difficult to form a market price unless the forward subsidy commitments of the government are known. If they rely on FILP bonds or on government-guaranteed bonds to undertake what in any case is government policy then little will change so that efforts to encourage institutions to issue their own bonds are desirable. In short, the problems with the FILP institutions need to be dealt with directly by reviewing the costs and benefits of the government policies they are implementing and by reviewing their governance: how they are managed, the incentive structures and the supervision.

Reconciling public demands with economic tradeoffs

Reforming financial relations between levels of government[169]

Heavy dependence of local governments on transfers from the central government and limited discretion in spending are likely to result in inefficient spending through two channels: reduced incentives to minimise costs and a limited ability to satisfy local preferences. The transfers take two forms: a general grant (*chiho kofuzei kofukin*) and matching grants (*kokko shishutsu-kin*), representing 24 and 15 per cent, respectively, of total expected revenues of local governments in FY 2000, according to the Ministry of Home Affairs. The local project to be subsidised is up to the spending ministry to decide and in order to obtain a matching grant, it is necessary to meet many conditions set by the ministry. Large facilities might be built so as to meet such conditions, but they sometimes result in low utilisation, thereby damaging local governments' financial position through high maintenance costs. Moreover, the local government has a reduced incentive to minimise project costs. When a project involves various subsidies from many ministries, the local government's discretion is likely to be quite limited in response to the needs of local residents.

The manner in which grants by central government for local budgets is organised leads to a divergence between tax payments and local expenditures among regions, thereby weakening incentives for local governments to select expenditure programmes efficiently as well as raise local tax revenues. In order to reduce these deficiencies, it is necessary to review the standard for various kinds of public services (*e.g.* the minimum number of elementary school teachers), which is the criteria for allocating these grants. The standard that is legally imposed by central government is likely to be too high. It is also necessary to raise local tax revenues. However, this will require changes to the present system since, in principle, an increase in local revenues reduces the level of the general grant from the central government.[170] Indeed, municipal governments only retain 25 per cent of the increase in revenues and the prefectures 20 per cent. A package of such reforms could enhance spending efficiency through "voting with the feet" and/or peer pressure (yardstick competition).

Increasing the accountability and responsibility of local politicians is an essential prerequisite to reducing the waste of public money at local level. The situation may improve because of progress in decentralisation. A new law to promote decentralisation has started to be implemented from April this year, leaving more decisions to local governments in areas like city planning and abolishing the role of the prefecture governor as an agent of the central government. The new law is also expected to increase expenditure efficiency by encouraging mergers of small municipalities: too many municipalities are smaller than the size needed for attaining the lowest unit cost of public services, which is likely to be a population of 120 000 (Kirishima, 1998). The MHA has planned to achieve a minimum population for municipalities of 10 000. The outlook for municipal mergers is likely to be clearer by the end of this year. Furthermore, in response to the Second Decentralisation Promotion Plan (decided in March 1999), some measures have been taken. First, the size criteria for defining national projects have been reviewed and revised upwards so as to shift responsibilities from the central to local governments in several areas. Second, the government set up two new types of "integrated subsidies" in the FY 2000 budget. They allow local governments more freedom, respectively, in deciding which project to adopt subject to a budget allocated by the central government, and in combining various subsidies for some specific purposes. Overall, although there has been some progress, the favourable effects may be limited unless more far reaching measures are taken to reduce the level of grants.

User charges

Public sector efficiency can be improved by greater resort to user fees, especially for transport infrastructure. However, setting charges to include concern for externalities and perhaps income distribution as well is far from easy and there are many practical difficulties, particularly in introducing peak load pricing of roads. It may be easier to introduce such pricing for railways, which play a larger role in commuting in large cities in Japan. This is because an automated ticket control system has been operating on most of the lines. Since discount tickets on weekends are available for railways, more sophisticated peak load pricing might be possible. Congestion in Tokyo needs to be tackled soon because, according to the current projection by the Ministry of Transport, transport demand in 2025 will be still as large as in 2000 despite falling population, and the situation may not improve for quite some time. A traditional way is to compensate railway companies' disincentive to invest due to regulated fares by granting investment subsidies. However, high investment costs as well as residents' objections often prevent sufficient supply. Therefore, introducing new fare policies merits serious consideration.

Vouchers as a means of widening choice

Vouchers have sometimes been proposed as a way of improving the cost effectiveness of public expenditure programmes. In particular, vouchers are considered to be a useful instrument in the allocation of merit goods while avoiding undesirable effects on income distribution associated with charging and private provision (OECD, 1998c). However, some general conditions need to be established for them to be effective, including (OECD, 2000*b*):

- competition between providers must exist;
- capacity of providers should be free to adjust;
- in some cases private payments to top up vouchers need to be allowed.

While the basic idea of vouchers is appealing, their application in practice has not been wide-spread and has tended to be confined to a supplementary role. For example, in the area of primary education only three states in the United States currently use vouchers.[171] In Ohio and Wisconsin vouchers have been adopted in one school district but are restricted to helping children from poor families. In Florida, vouchers were introduced to facilitate students in schools with problems to transfer to other schools. In Japan, the Prime Minister's Commission on Japan's Goals in the 21st Century (2000) proposed the introduction of vouchers for primary and secondary school students as one option for financial assistance, intended for the promotion of activities to enrich personal culture and vocational education outside the regular school hours, in the context of reforming the school curriculum. The school curriculum for compulsory education has been criticised as being too rigid (see, for example, Committee on Economics of Education, 1998). The limited application of vouchers likely reflects institutional and political difficulties in ensuring some of the conditions necessary for their effectiveness. In some areas other than primary education it might be easier to find conditions more conducive to the application of vouchers. For example, training vouchers have been introduced in several countries with a varying degree of success. The recent experience in Korea with a voucher scheme for training the unemployed revealed serious administrative difficulties and problems of fraud. In sum, lessons from the limited experience described above would seem to be that while in theory vouchers are a potentially powerful instrument in improving the cost effectiveness of public programmes, their practical application requires much prudence and hard thinking given the difficulties involved in ensuring the right conditions for their efficient operation.

Improving cost efficiency in implementation

Cost-benefit/effectiveness analysis

An important weakness of the public expenditure system noted above has been the relative neglect of the future costs of policy decisions and the inadequate attention given to systematic evaluation of projects. This is an area where the discipline of cost-benefit analysis could bring major improvements, even in those cases where externalities such as congestion, pollution and the environment are important. Where it is impossible to value external effects, non-financial quantitative information should be produced. Projects in rural areas have been carried out despite evidence from estimated production functions suggesting that the return to investment in cities is roughly twice the rate of return in outlying areas (EPA, 1997). Many have been selected on the grounds that they are in rural areas and would therefore contribute to achieving balanced regional development and an associated change in income distribution. In these cases, cost benefit analysis would need to specify explicitly the income distribution target, document the need and how the project could achieve these objectives. An analysis of alternative policies to achieve the same ends would also be needed to obtain a clear knowledge of the opportunity cost of the project. Such a process would help in resisting the political pressures to attract public works of dubious quality to a particular electoral district.

Cost-benefit analysis was applied on a trial basis to *ex ante* evaluation of some projects in FY 1997 and its application has been extended to more projects since the beginning of FY 1998. For projects not started five years following approval and those still underway five to ten yers after approval, re-evaluation is being conducted using cost-benefit analysis where necessary. Problems with the current practice include: 1) it has not been used to reallocate resources between different types of projects in the absence of a uniform rule such as a rate of return; and 2) benefits are sometimes overestimated. The administrative reform law states that ministries should strengthen the self-evaluation of their policy performance and that the results of such evaluation should be reflected in the decision making process. To this end, new units are now being formed. The mandate would thus appear to be *ex post* whereas what is required in the first instance to improve the efficiency of the public expenditure system is *ex ante* policy analysis. The capacity for *ex ante* analysis needs to be strengthened and this could best be achieved if, as suggested above, there is some central evaluation unit to specify the framework and standards such as a uniform rule to value consistently some costs and benefits.[172]

Improved cost effectiveness auditing

External auditing of cost/effectiveness by the Board of Audit (BOA) has a fundamental role to play not just with respect to projects but to government expenditures in general.[173] Audits are undertaken by the BOA to determine: 1) whether expenditures (settlement of accounts) fairly reflect implementation of the budget and its financial position (accuracy); 2) whether accounting is in conformity with the budget requirements, laws and regulations (regularity); 3) whether projects are implemented in economical and efficient ways, and 4) whether project goals are achieved. Traditionally, the first two objectives have been dominant, and the BOA detected many cases of improper accounting of government subsidies in the 1950s. As part of the administrative reform enacted in 1997, the law was amended so that the Board can carry out a specific audit requested by the Diet. At the same time, the amendment clarified the powers of the Board to conduct audits not only from the viewpoint of accuracy and regularity (its traditional role), but also with respect to economy, efficiency and effectiveness. Since the 1970s, efficiency and effectiveness audits have become an increasingly important task of the BOA.[174]

It is also an appropriate time to step up the process of *ex post* efficiency and effectiveness audits by the BOA, which would be an essential complement to the evaluations which the new assessment units in each ministry are expected to undertake. Such a process would be aided by improved *ex ante* project analysis, which would make slippage and effectiveness more transparent. To this end, resources devoted to such audits will need to be increased. Even more important though is the feedback from audit results to policy. The BOA has regular meetings with the Budget and Financial Bureaux of the MOF, which may lead to changes in either the budget of the central government or that of the FILP. The feedback process might be made more effective through a strengthened role for parliamentary committees.

Bidding, outsourcing and private/public participation

Public procurement and the associated bidding system is not fully delivering value for money. The central government has taken measures since 1994 to improve the system by using open competition more extensively and, for smaller projects, to use a designated bidding system in a more transparent manner. It is also trying to take advantage of more flexible bidding systems, such as VE (Value Engineering) methods (introduced in FY 1997), profit-sharing after the bidding, comprehensive evaluation method and the design-build techniques. These efforts have been reflected in changes in the bidding systems run by the central and prefectural governments. Despite the improvements, the Board of Audit has noted that only half the contracts by value are executed under the new system and that no marked difference had been observed in the price spreads between the new and old systems. They also noted that bidders were able to execute contracts even when contracted prices were beneath the minimum price which is usually 80 per cent of the government's estimated cost (Board of Audit, 1999). Municipal governments have been reluctant to move ahead. The 1996 WTO agreement obliges prefectural governments and designated cities to implement open competitive bidding for contracts above a threshold value.

It is important to press ahead with further reforms of the bidding system, particularly at the local government level, but for this to happen policy objectives need to be rebalanced. Governments at all levels will need to give more weight to cost effectiveness and less to policies favouring local companies or SMEs. As an intermediate measure preference could be made conditional on the price being within a certain margin of the preferred bidder, as happens in some European countries. However, incentives also need to change especially at the local government level by, *inter alia*, modifying the system of fiscal equalisation between the central and lower-level governments. Employment practices could also be altered to give incentives for cost saving by officials. Nishiguchi (2000) proposed, after examining problems in defence procurement, the introduction of a project team like in private companies. In this scheme, members are drawn from various departments and a "heavy-weight project manager" leads the cross-functional team and is responsible for the whole process from design to procurement. This procedure is also observed in the auto industry (Clark and Fujimoto, 1991). Although this idea could be applied to procurement of non-standardised goods, such as large-scale projects and special weapon systems, significant revisions to human resource management and regulations would be required.

There is a role for outsourcing and for private/public partnerships to improve the cost efficiency of the public expenditure system. Such outsourcing could include franchise bidding to permit more cost-sensitive private agents to construct and manage projects, while enabling the government to decide investment plans. According to Ohta and Imahashi (1995), the case of Tokyo Bay Crossing Road Inc. may be closest to such a system in Japan,[175] although how well this scheme functions has been a subject of debate. In order to make greater use of market incentives, the legal framework for private/public partnerships has been in place since September 1999, and several projects are underway at local government level. To ensure a successful outcome for these projects will require accompanying reforms such as clearer delineation of the public sector and its objectives if the problems which have arisen with third sector companies are to be avoided.

Transparency of the budget process and of public management

A key weakness of the public expenditure system is the lack of devolution of expenditure management and the underdeveloped transparency of the budget system. Even under the new cabinet system it appears that sectoral ministries will have very little flexibility in making final allocations of funds and in operational decisions. A better system would be to set overall expenditure ceilings and policy guidelines and let the ministry take its own decisions. This would be feasible if the reform of the cabinet system also leads to a tightening of political representation at each ministry. Fiscal transparency has a number of aspects including the medium-term perspective, comprehensiveness and the treatment of contingent liabilities and other off-budget commitments (OECD, 2000*c*).

In order to enhance efficiency of the expenditure system, it is important for the government to present its budget plan and its implication for financial balances both now and in the future in a transparent manner. Although there has been some progress, there still remains room for improvement. The issue is how the government should provide comprehensive information in a timely and reader-friendly manner. It is quite difficult to understand the overall picture of the budgets, comprising general and many special accounts as well as those of government institutions. Clearly, consolidated presentation of various budgets is desirable. Furthermore, the delay in publishing information about the financial plans of local governments needs to be shortened. Presentation of the overall fiscal position should also be consistent with the national accounts to obtain a comprehensive picture of macroeconomic policy. Above all, budgetary plans should be set out in terms of a medium-term framework so that the ongoing impact of government programmes and taxation decisions is made clear.

At the more micro level, subsidy cost analysis of FILP institutions on a trial basis has been quite useful (see Chapter II). Its coverage should be expanded to all the related institutions and publicised earlier so that it could be used as a material for the Diet's deliberation of the budget plan. Such an exercise could lead to an examination of the budget plan on an accrual basis and underpin a move to multi-year budgeting. Accrual accounting is important to evaluate policies whose effects extend over a long period. A good example is pension liabilities, which are expected to reach enormous proportions, as discussed in Chapter III.

Loan guarantees and other contingent liabilities are usually "off-balance sheet". However, it is clearly desirable to make them explicit, as is the practice in the private sector. In addition, some supplementary information, which is essential to assess the financial condition, such as past default rates in the case of loan guarantees, needs to be disclosed simultaneously. Because liabilities held by public corporations and other government-related companies (including third-sector companies) may be taken over by the government (even where they are not explicitly guaranteed by the government), disclosure should be as comprehensive as possible. These disclosures would indicate to what degree the credit risks are socialised in Japan.

An important feature of the budget system is the existence of a number of earmarked funds. In principle, unified management of funds is desirable. However, various justifications have been made to keep some of the funds separate. First, separate treatment could make it possible to charge beneficiaries for the costs they cause, thereby enhancing efficiency. This may also be a good way to finance the maintenance costs of infrastructure, which are expected to increase rapidly in the future. Second, some political economy arguments are used to justify the earmarking. For example, in response to strong pressure for a significant increase in an expenditure item, the increase could be contained within some limits by earmarking. In general, however, earmarked funds could lead to inefficient resource allocation to the extent that they influence spending decisions. It is therefore necessary to subject them to a review in the context of budget reforms.

Notes

1. The share of exports in consumption goods shipment is 10.4 per cent. This is the fixed weight from 1995 used to calculate the index.
2. It needs to be noted that the rapid growth of investment by small firms in the non-manufacturing sector is poorly understood and is hard to justify by reference to what is known about their overall financial condition. Anecdotal evidence points to the development of IT intensive small enterprises which could be an explanation.
3. The survey results are: 2 per cent of the respondents answered "less than 6 months", 13 per cent "less than 1 year", 43 per cent "less than 2 years", and 42 per cent "more than 2 years".
4. For an explanation of the stock market dispersion index see C. Calderwood and M. Matsuoka (2000). The EPA has also constructed a Herfindal index to show the variation of investment activity across sectors. It is now markedly higher than in other cycles and periods.
5. Of course, if they have been investing and reduce this level it will serve to lower aggregate demand.
6. Iron and steel, precision machinery and cement are those industries reporting a cut in capacity while also reporting a planned rise in investment this year.
7. To qualify for the tax credit buyers must be in residence by the end of the period and need a residence registration as proof.
8. The share of housing construction using HLC's loan programmes declined in the first half of 2000, which may suggest a weakened reliability of this leading indicator of residential investment. A reason for the decline in the share may be that conditions of loan programmes – interest rates, in particular – were made less favourable in 1998.
9. The impact on residential investment may be ambiguous even in the long term. The contracts should encourage the building of rental houses for families, which are effectively non-existent at present. Declining numbers of singles and students will lower demand for small rental accommodation, which is mainly associated with the older housing stock. This stock might be replaced by new family housing. On the other hand, more opportunities to rent houses for family use could discourage people to build (or purchase) their own house.
10. For example, in the manufacturing sector the share of companies adopting some kind of adjustment measures peaked at 46 per cent in the fourth quarter of 1998 and decreased to 30 per cent in the second quarter of 2000. These statistics also include companies which took only mild measures, such as restricting overtime and transferring workers.

11. The difference from the EPA estimate could be partly explained by the possible under-estimation of GDP in 1999.
12. Thanks to a decline in the labour force participation rate, the unemployment rate has remained in the range 4.6 to 4.8 per cent, despite a 0.5 per cent increase in the population of working age and a 0.8 per cent decrease in total employment. It is remarkable that the male participation rate declined by 0.8 percentage points from 1998 to 1999, which is as large as the decline in the rate for women. It may indicate that the traditional buffer role of women in dampening a cyclical increase of the unemployment rate now also extends to males.
13. A survey has shown that the official statistics on vacancies are biased downwards since many companies are not notifying vacancies through the labour office but are using other means.
14. In establishments with five or more employees summer bonuses rose ½ per cent, after falling by 3.7 per cent in 1999. For those with thirty or more employees, the summer bonus declined by around 1 per cent following a decrease in 1999 of 4½ per cent.
15. Household appliance sales were relatively favourable, led by PCs. Because of a high level of durable goods relative to disposable income, some stock adjustment mechanisms may have been at work (OECD, 1999*a*; EPA, 2000*b*). This is consistent with the observed increase in the period of use before replacement.
16. In 1999, capital goods had a larger share in import values than materials for manufacturing for the first time. See EPA (2000*b*) for the details.
17. This buffer function might have been enhanced by import liberalisation measures for oil products taken in March 1996. Nagaoka and Kimura (1999) argued that the announcement of the deregulation led to the collapse of an implicit cartel among domestic producers.
18. The projections are based on the unrevised GDP estimates for 1999 and 2000. Revisions will be released in December 2000, which will also incorporate the shift to 93SNA standards. See Box 1 for details of other changes which will be introduced at that time.
19. A special reserve for public works (0.5 trillion yen) was also set up in the same way as in FY 1999, and the allocation to programmes was decided in July.
20. For example, through suspending delayed projects, which is likely to save some 25 billion yen.
21. Employment measures in the package were provided with 274 billion yen in the second supplementary FY 1999 budget (192 and 173 for general and special accounts, respectively) and 722 billion yen (29 and 693 for each account).
22. Interest payments have almost levelled off at around 10 to 11 trillion yen since the early 1990s.
23. The bailing-out scheme allows the DIC to cash its holdings of government bonds of 7 trillion yen. The government has cashed 1.9 trillion yen in the third supplementary FY 1998 budget, 3.2 in the initial FY 1999 budget and 1.9 in the second supplementary budget for that fiscal year. As a result, the DIC held JGBs worth 2.2 trillion yen in March 2000. The provision of 5.9 trillion yen 4.5 trillion yen in general account and 1.4 in a special account) in the FY 2000 budget implies additional funds of 3.6 trillion yen, over and above the 7 trillion yen allocated when the scheme was set up in FY 1998. Another 6 trillion yen of JGBs were allocate to the DIC in FY 2000.

24. The general grant from general account of the central government – the Local Allocation Tax (LAT) and the Special LAT – increased by about 1.4 trillion yen to 14.9 trillion yen in FY 2000, compared with the FY 1999 initial budget. A predetermined formula to calculate the LAT resulted in an increase by some 0.9 trillion yen, which includes the following effects: an expected surge in income tax revenues due to maturing postal savings; and a change in the formula, which increased the share of local governments in national corporate tax from 32 per cent to 32.5 per cent in FY 1999 and once again to 35.8 per cent in FY 2000. In addition, two special measures were taken. One is intended to compensate for a cyclical decline in local tax revenues and the other is for a structural decline (due to permanent tax cuts). These measures increased transfers by 0.2 and 0.3 trillion yen, respectively. Furthermore, because of borrowing by a special account, the transfer received by local governments (22.3 trillion yen in FY 2000, see Table 10) is recently larger than that given by the general account of central government (14.9 trillion yen in FY 2000, see Table 8). With reduced borrowing by the special account, the transfer received by local governments increased by 0.8 trillion yen in FY 2000.

25. The FILP sets the ceiling of funding to various institutions, which might not be used. For example, although the FILP allocated some 10 trillion yen to the Housing Loan Corporation in FY 1998, only 6 trillion yen was actually committed.

26. Because the mid-term information suggested the equal amount of public works in FY 1997 and 1998, the settlement could be the same without any shocks. This conjecture implies that the net increase due to the November 1998 fiscal package could be as small as 0.6 trillion yen.

27. Virén (2000) estimates a VAR model for output growth, inflation and a fiscal indicator (therefore, no distinction between government consumption expenditures and public investment) in 21 OECD countries for the 1960-96 period. Although he did not find a positive effect of fiscal expansion on output growth in some European countries (Sweden, Denmark, France, the Netherlands, Greece and Spain), he detected similar positive effects in Japan as in the United States and Germany.

28. The liabilities held by these institutions are not available on a calendar year basis and are, therefore, not listed in Table 15. They are included in the central government liabilities of 441 trillion yen. They are estimated to amount to 72 trillion yen at the end of March.

29. Table 15 shows that the central government held short-term government securities worth 6.5 trillion yen. The table also shows that the social security funds held long-term bonds amounting to 16.6 trillion yen, of which central and local government bonds are estimated to be 5.1 trillion yen. In sum, about 12 trillion yen should be consolidated.

30. Subsidies include cash payment as well as implicit subsidies.

31. According to the Ministry of Health and Welfare, the system has accumulated funds worth 170 trillion yen or 34 per cent of GDP, which is included in the official net debt figures.

32. One trillion yen was provided to cover expected losses due to defaults of SMEs using the special guarantee scheme, assuming default and collection rates of 10 and 50 per cent, respectively. As for the additional 10 trillion yen (5 trillion yen up to March 2000 and 5 trillion yen for FY 2000), default rates are set at 8 and 10 per cent in the respective period and 450 billion yen in total was budgeted. The default rate since the start of the scheme is about 1 per cent. Because most of the users of the scheme have also

used some other schemes, and the total default rate for all guarantees outstanding is 2 per cent in FY 1998, the default rate for the special scheme may not rise above those assumed.

33. According to the appropriation account of non-financial public corporations on a SNA basis (including FILP and other institutions, such as local enterprises), they are incurring losses amounting to 0.9 trillion yen in FY 1998, although the aggregate number may mask difficulties of some institutions and is rather difficult to interpret. The overall situation seems to have improved, compared with an annual loss of around 1.2 trillion yen in most of the 1990s, mainly because the central government took over the debt from the Japan Railway Settlement Corporation and National Forest Special Accounts. With respect to financial public corporations, loans past due by more than 6 months amounted to 1.2 trillion yen or about 1 per cent of their loans outstanding as of March 1999, although reserves were provided against such loans.

34. The length of asset life is arguably another source of upward bias.

35. The "net" of the word, *net* fixed assets, means deduction of depreciation of fixed assets other than social infrastructure, such as machinery and equipment.

36. Items requiring consolidation are (see Table 15): currency (1.4 trillion yen), short-term government securities (31.6), long-term bonds (245.9), transfer from general government (4.7), and loans by general government (210.7). In total, consolidation amounts to 494.3 trillion yen.

37. Some more accurate consolidation is possible, if fiscal year numbers are used. Consolidation of non-financial public corporations could boost the gross debt of general government by 18 percentage points, and that of both non-financial and financial corporations by 15 percentage points in March 1999.

38. In May 2000, the Bank of Japan changed its definition of base money to include current account balances held by institutions not subject to reserve requirements, such as money market dealers (*tanshi*).

39. Thus M. Matsuoka (2000) argues that all the excess reserves would have to be absorbed which would amount to a strong tightening in terms of base money. However, there is no *a priori* reason why all excess reserves would need to be withdrawn since even with an overnight cost of .25 per cent there might be a demand for them. Indeed, if the BOJ statements are taken at face value, current excess reserves are just required to keep rates close to zero. Only a small absorption might be necessary to move rates up to the desired level.

40. In addition, there have been reports that banks have continued to liquidate their shareholdings ahead of their September interim balance date.

41. The TFB announced that it would cease its JGB repo operations and instead conduct three month reverse repo operations (about 300 billion yen per month) to gather funds to meet possible redemption needs. This caused worries about market liquidity, but the BOJ announced in November 1999 that it will act as the counter party for the TFB's operations under the condition that the market demand falls short of the TFB's offered amount or the size of a given TFB operation exceeds the typical size of market operations.

42. Rather surprisingly, recent research indicates that sterilised intervention might have had an impact in the past. The study also confirmed that co-ordinated interventions were more effective and that interventions have had a small but persistent effect on the yen-dollar rate. See Ramaswamy and Samiei (2000).

43. However, the corporate bond market has only been growing slowly since the major banks were re-capitalised in March 1999.

44. For example, the Flow of Funds shows that the increase of JGB outstanding in FY 1998 of 82.2 trillion yen was matched by increased holdings by public institutions (10 trillion yen in BOJ, 5 in postal savings, 5 in postal life insurance and 31 in the TFB), while private institutions accounted for 21 trillion yen.

45. The withholding tax was lifted for non-residents in September 1999 and the transaction tax was abolished in April 1999. On the other hand, the requirement that non-residents need to deposit JGBs with domestically-based custodians within the BOJ settlement system has been regarded as a burden by investors.

46. Although the Local Bond Plan compiled by the Ministry of Home Affairs (MHA) shows the TFB as a major subscriber, the settlement document of the TFB carries the transactions as loans. Therefore, BOJ's Flow of Funds and EPA's Annual Report of National Account show the outstanding amount held by the TFB to be nil. The description here is based on the information of the MHA.

47. Currently, only 28 out of more than 3 000 local governments are permitted to issue their bonds in the market.

48. The permission will not be required any more in FY 2006.

49. Others have argued that items in the CPI still show signs of demand weakness (Nikko Salomon Smith Barney, 2000b).

50. Some argue that such a monetary environment would constitute moral hazard dangers for firms which would reduce their efforts at restructuring. This is a danger but one that could be minimised if pressure is maintained on banks earnings and on the quality of their balance sheets.

51. With household financial assets mainly held in the form of cash and deposits the argument that they have suffered from low interest rates is important. However, it may be more of a problem for the future since around a tenth of their wealth has been held up till now as postal savings deposits carrying an interest rate of some 6 per cent. Now that these deposits are maturing, households will come under pressure to shift to higher risk assets if they are to offset the fall in income.

52. This assumes that technical issues such as the choice of the price index have been solved. The BOJ has conducted a study of potential problems in the different indices of prices. For some discussion of the issues in Japan see S. Shiratsuka, 1999.

53. The argument assumes that the current problems in Japan do not result from deflation *per se* nor from the response to normal shocks. Rather the balance sheet adjustment is a product of the bubble economy and the failure of monetary policy to adjust at an early stage.

54. For the importance of monetary aggregates see Orphanides and Wieland (1999). For the choice of unconventional instruments see Johnson, Small and Tryon (1999). The reasons for and experience with the BOJ buying and selling simultaneously at different maturities in 1998 are given in Saito and Shiratsuka (2000).

55. Forecasts are published in two forms: a range of highest and lowest figures, and a range of next highest and next lowest figures. In the latter, if there is more than one extreme value, only one of them is eliminated at either end.

56. See Okina and Oda, *op. cit*,. for a detailed discussion including practical examples.

57. There is also another independent organisation to monitor financial markets: the Securities and Exchange Surveillance Commission.
58. According to the report of the FRC, "risk-based insurance premium is, in principle, desirable in terms of supplementing market discipline. However, if adopted this time when the Deposit Insurance Corporation (DIC) needs to repay substantial borrowings as early as possible, the insurance premium of financially troubled institutions would inevitably be very high, further affecting their weakened conditions. Although the framework of a risk-based premium should be considered at an early opportunity, the application of the framework is not feasible at this juncture".
59. The maximum borrowing limit of the fund, which can be guaranteed by the government, has been increased from 460 billion yen to 960 billion. The fund can count on 400 billion yen from the government and an additional 100 billion yen from the industry.
60. The recovery rate of the Resolution and Collection Corporation is low, meaning that it will not finish its job in 7½ years, the time frame originally foreseen. In addition, it will have to buy the assets of failed life insurers and take on credits of prefectural credit associations in Tokyo, Osaka and Kanagawa.
61. Legally speaking, under the Commercial Code the bank must declare a defect in the asset which has been acquired.
62. In fairness to the authorities, it was difficult for the government in Germany to explain sales of large companies in eastern Germany for a low or even nominal price even if the owners were assuming important liabilities.
63. 22 per cent of outstanding loans are still in the real estate sector where conditions are difficult.
64. In addition, banks have transferred bad debts to a common holding, the Co-operative Credit Purchasing Company (CCPC). Fitch IBCA estimates that this company holds some 15 trillion yen in bad loans. It is reported to have sold some 1 trillion yen face value of debts in the last quarter of 1999 which was a marked acceleration in the rate of disposal.
65. It should also force an end to window dressing stock transactions at the end of the financial year. Bremer and Kato (1996) documented the end of fiscal year turnover (and later buy-back) despite the discouraging effects of capital gains tax.
66. Three major general contractors officially admitted such transfers, which reduced their holdings of real estate for sale by some 10 per cent at the end of the financial year in March 2000.
67. According to a survey by the Nikkei, a third of the respondents (major listed companies) are planning such a contribution, which should help meet an unfunded liability of some 10 trillion yen.
68. The breakdown of a restructuring agreement among Tokai, Asahi and Sanwa was reported to be caused by conflict over a choice of a merger or a holding company.
69. The law also requires the company to consult with labour in advance about the split. It did not, however, request prior consent for transfers of each employment contract from the labour side, as some feared it would on the basis of an article of the civil law. However, employees were granted some veto powers concerning transfer of their own employment contracts.
70. They include: ensuring more effective implementation of the agreed reorganisation plans; strengthening the say of creditors on assets; changing senior creditors' right on collateral; selling more easily companies' assets; and allowing more possibilities to pursue managers for mismanagement.

71. Ikeo and Seshita (1998) showed that the rescue operations of main banks could have the desirable characteristics of a new procedure proposed by Bebchuk (1988) and Aghion, Hart and Moore (1992). Shoji Homu Kenkyu-kai (1997) examined the applicability of the proposed procedure in Japan.

72. Nevertheless, it is interesting to note that the first case has produced a restructuring agreement within three months of the filing whereas under the old reorganisation mechanism it typically took one to two years.

73. The Industrial Revitalisation Law was described in the *Economic Survey*, 1999, p. 200. Among other things, the law provides for low interest loans and guarantees, and tax incentives such as an extended period for loss carry forward and accelerated depreciation allowances for firms whose business restructuring plans are approved by the government.

74. There are, however, other estimates. According to NLI Research, the percentage of cross shareholdings dropped to 15.39 per cent of all listed shares as of the end of FY 1998 from 18.62 per cent in FY 1990. Ownership of firms by individuals and foreigners is rising: individuals owned 26.4 per cent and foreigners 12.4 per cent of listed shares at the end of FY 1999.

75. See Komiya (1988). Miwa (1998) argues that the fundamental question is who makes up the controlling group which establishes the basic value criteria that will be employed in making decisions and choices about alternatives in an organisation. In a world of voluntary exchange rather than coercion, they will have to take account of other stakeholders but it is the composition of the group which is crucial for performance. On the basis of such analysis, he argues that employees constitute the major group in Japan with banks very much less important than in other studies.

76. The idea of a friendly shareholder has been utilised by Miwa, *op. cit.*

77. Tachibanaki *et al.* (1998) argues that use of the holding company scheme could allow easy restructuring of insurance companies which have a large number of sales staffs.

78. Demutualisation of AMP in Australia in 1998 and Norwich Union in the United Kingdom in 1997 have been estimated to have created windfall gains per policy holder worth 14 000 Australian dollars (US$8 600) and £1 450 (US$2 400), respectively, according to the Reserve Bank of Australia (1999) and Bank of England (1997). In addition to share allocations based on the capital value of the policies, there was also an allocation of a fixed number of shares per policy holder. This fixed part was worth 2 300 Australian dollars and £486, respectively. In Japan, the commercial code is unlikely to allow such fixed per policy-holder distributions. Moreover, according to the code allocation of shares to members holding policies with negative spreads is also not permitted.

79. Boards have traditionally been large and expanded in the 1960s and 1970s in order to provide places for promotion of insiders. For example, the size of the boards at Toyota and Sony grew from 18 to 55 and from 14 to 38, respectively, in the period from 1966 to 1996. The latter has now slashed the size of its board to ten members.

80. The statutory auditors should not be confused with external auditors who are required to check the accuracy of the company's financial statements and whether they have been complied according to accounting standards.

81. Insiders can become outsiders following a five-year cooling-off period. Tokyo Shoko Research's study of the audit boards of 116 banks and securities companies found that about a half of the auditors could be classified as outsiders but that a half of them used to be insiders.

82. According to a survey by the MITI, more than three quarters of the respondents pointed to prompt decision-making as a reason for introducing executive officers. Those who pointed to risks of derivative law suits accounted for only 4 per cent.
83. Some activities are not covered by the statistics such as agricultural corporations. The number of such corporations has risen over the last five years by 40 per cent to 5 600.
84. Some sociologists have coined the phrase "parasite singles" which covers young people living with their parents and relying on their support. While this might be a sociological phenomenon explaining some consumption patterns, it is hard to see how it might have caused increasing youth unemployment in recent years since the increase is faster than is usually associated with cultural changes. See Genda (2000).
85. As noted above, a new law was passed in May, which eased the conditions for the transfer of both assets and employees.
86. The authorities had the restructuring at Nissan in mind when this measure was adopted. Widespread expectations to the contrary, the labour force restructuring at this company is very traditional relying on natural attrition and on early retirement.
87. As noted in the above section, the laws on transferring workers during company splits and mergers were also revised.
88. Benefits are currently 60 to 80 per cent of prior wages, excluding bonuses, for a period of 90 to 300 days. People in their early 60s usually receive the maximum benefit for the longest time and 30 per cent of total benefits are paid to this group.
89. The maximum period for receiving benefits has risen from 300 to 330 days.
90. It is important to note that company surveys of views about the employment situation in Japan show about three-quarters in favour of completely or mainly performance-based pay but three-quarters also want to maintain or revise only partially the lifetime employment system (Hattori and Maeda, *op. cit.*).
91. In addition, one study finds significant positive welfare effects from liberalisation of the oil product market and notes that the industry had shown all the signs of an implicit cartel. See Nagaoka and Kimura (1999).
92. The authorities believe that this is an appropriate response to the suggestion that private parties have greater powers to initiate law suits against violations of the Anti Monopoly Act.
93. More specific developments include the introduction of a price cap from October for calls based on the CPI-x formula. The applicable CPI was set at –.3 per cent and x at 1.9 per cent. In June 2000, the Radio Law was amended to add procedures for issuing mobile licences for common carriers by examinations comparing applications.
94. The technicalities are complex although the fundamental argument is straightforward: who should pay for the equipment in the local loop which interconnects the optical cable with the copper wire, which is the final connection to the user. Under the so-called "LRIC case A", the new companies which are interconnecting pay the full price of the equipment even though NTT companies must also use the facility. Under plan B, the costs would be shared according to use but this would mean that NTT would have to raise its basic charge for a telephone connection by consumers.
95. At the same time the supply and demand balancing requirement was abolished for chartered buses and in March for railways. Prices were liberalised for chartered buses and for railways the system has shifted to a maximum tariff regulation. There is also a new law to encourage competition between ports by liberalising participation in the provision of services at Japan's twelve major container ports.

96. Until last year airlines were allowed to maintain unused slots at the busy Narita airport. A "use it or lose it" formula has now been introduced in line with international practice.

97. As part of the dialogue with the United States, the government has confirmed that "It will ensure that JFTC's independence in matters of personal recruitment, promotion and placement, including at senior levels, and in enforcement decisions or policy, will be preserved after the government reorganisation in 2001. In addition, the Government of Japan confirms that the discretion that JFTC currently has within the Prime Minister's Office in connection with procedures for developing its budget, deciding on appropriate expenditures and formulating, co-ordinating and conveying its position on legislative matters, will be preserved as well".

98. An independent regulatory body includes the institutional structure of an independent regulator which is used in some OECD countries. However, an independent regulator is a necessary though not sufficient condition for efficiency since regulatory capture cannot be excluded and there have been cases where the regulator (including a committee or commission) was not suitable for the task. To minimise these dangers, the regulator needs to be provided with a clear definition of objectives, which would also constitute a firewall if the regulatory body were to be formally located in a ministry. To guard against the danger of regulatory capture, the system also needs to be underpinned by competition policy and enforcement, which together forms a system of checks and balances.

99. In addition, regulations result in high construction costs, trenching costing some US$2 000 a meter, which is five times that in Europe and 10 to 12 times that in Latin America. The trench must be opened and closed each night with old soil carted away and replaced by new soil. The Ministry of Construction argues that the rules are necessary because of earthquakes and dense population.

100. For a review of the complex regulatory issues see Seki (2000).

101. Malfunctions of the judicial system have been apparent for some time leading to deliberations by the Judicial Reform Council (established in July 1999) which is to submit a final report by July 2001. The discussions include how to make the system more user-friendly, how to increase participation of people in the system and how to reinforce human infrastructure. The latter point includes how to increase the number of legal experts and to improve their training. See Fukui (2000).

102. As promised in the past fiscal packages, the code of civil execution was revised in 1996 and 1998.

103. These occupiers are often gangsters (called *yakuza*) colluding with debtors who want to obstruct the forced procedures and to keep these properties in their hands. Fukui and Kume (1999) give examples of various obstructions, which were reported by veteran legal practitioners.

104. Some observers have noted that the information does not include whether someone is actually occupying the property. Participants in the auctions cannot usually inspect the interior of the property in advance.

105. Toda and Ide (2000) confirmed this point empirically using micro data from the Osaka area.

106. Some legal experts argue that a reasonable solution could be abolishing the protection of short-term tenant rights, applying the Coase theorem to this problem. That is, because inefficiency of resource allocation increases in line with transaction costs, legal rights should be allocated initially so as to minimise these costs. Whereas it is

very costly for successful bidders to realise their property rights, it appears to be quite easy for good tenants to conclude contracts with new owners. A new allocation of the property right would allow new owners to skip lawsuits to realise their rights and simply to ask the courts to conduct forcible executions. Even so, according to Soejima and Yamaguchi (1999, 2000), the costs of forcible execution would remain sizeable, amounting to around 1 million yen.

107. The Japanese public pension system has two tiers. The first tier is a compulsory flat rate scheme with minimal coverage and is one-third tax financed. The second tier has two elements: The Employee's Pension Insurance (also known as Welfare Pension Insurance) for private-sector employees and a voluntary scheme, the National Pension Fund, for the self-employed. For the first of these, both contributions and benefits are related to income, while for the second benefits are proportional to contributions. For further details of the Japanese pension system, see OECD (1997). In addition to the public schemes, there is a third tier, offered by about 90 per cent of private companies, which provides benefits at retirement, lump sum and/or pensions.

108. Hatta and Oguchi (1998) estimate that in the case of the Employees Pension scheme, those born in 1935 will receive benefits greater than contributions by about 25 per cent of their lifetime wage income, while those born in 2010 receive benefits less than contributions, amounting to 11 per cent of wage income. This is the historical legacy of the initial decision to use the pension system rather than means-tested livelihood assistance as the main means for protecting the 1935 generation from old-age poverty.

109. Other merits of the shift to a tax-financed system include: 1) it is possible to avoid the regressive nature of flat-rate contributions; 2) it could correct the situation where working females have to pay contributions while house wives do not.

110. It may be relevant to note here that many of the Nordic countries which initiated universal basic pensions now do reduce basic pension entitlements for those with sufficient earnings-related pension entitlements.

111. See OECD (1999*a*) for details of the Japanese tax system.

112. The problems, which were examined in detail in last year's *Survey*, include: a high tax-exempt threshold for paying VAT; the lack of an invoice system, and the absence of taxpayer identification numbers.

113. Disney (2000) expresses two concerns. First, there is no enforcement mechanism of such an "actuarially fair" benefit growth in case of developments which are unfavourable to beneficiaries. For example, if a positive inflation rate (and hence positive wage growth on a per employee basis) is accompanied by a decrease in the number of workers, no growth of total wage payment and pension benefits may result. Second, absence of inter-generational re-distribution effects could undermine a major rationale for a public pension system.

114. In Poland, the low but stable returns on Tier I are to be compensated for by high but volatile returns on privatised Tier II.

115. Hatta and Oguchi (1999) support a bond issue and repaying the bonds through progressive income taxation.

116. The number is an estimate for hidden debt for all the public pension system, not for Tier II only.

117. An obvious objection to this option is the problem of adverse selection.

118. According to one expert, how to bring the current Tier II to "euthanasia" is the issue (Ihori, 1999).

119. For example, Takayama and Yamaguchi (1999) calculated the impact of joining a private pension scheme using funds made available by a 4 per cent reduction in the contribution rate due to a shift to 100 per cent tax financing of Tier I. They found that returns net of administrative costs of 3 per cent could be sufficient to maintain the income replacement ratio at around 75 per cent.

120. The corporation recorded a surplus on portfolio investment in FY 1999 after having cumulative losses through most of the 1990s. In addition, the corporation was engaged in supplying accommodation services in some resort areas to promote welfare of the insured, which turned sour. In response to a request from the Diet, the Board of Audit inspected the situation of the accommodation activities of the Corporation and other public institutions, and recommended withdrawal from such operations in 1999. In the context of administrative reform and in response to a decision by the Cabinet in 1997, the corporation will withdraw from this line of activity.

121. This was despite the abolition of a requirement to use a fixed discount rate of 5.5 per cent for actuarial calculations in 1997. Although it may be possible to cut the planned rate, the demerit of such a measure is to increase the amount of hidden debts.

122. See Kaneko (1999) for the empirical evidence of the effects of pension portability on labour movement.

123. Japan's health care system, which is highly regulated by the government, combines a mainly private provision of services and a mandatory health insurance. Payments are made by insurers directly to service providers (the third payer system) largely on a fee-for-service basis with the fees set by the government. Between 20 and 30 per cent of the fees are born by patients with a ceiling. Health insurance is highly decentralised, with employees of large companies covered by an insurance society at each company, those of SMEs by a subsidised central government insurance scheme and most others by schemes run by local governments. For more details, see OECD (1997).

124. Opinion surveys carried out by MHW indicate that those who responded as satisfied were 51 per cent for ambulatory care and 55 per cent for in-patient care. International comparisons in this area are difficult, but these figures appear to be low in relation to over 65 per cent in France and Germany and 85 to 90 per cent in Finland and Denmark.

125. This second regulation has been eased somewhat. It should also be noted that as of 1997 71 per cent of all hospitals are private hospitals set up as a special status (non-profit) corporation, the so-called *Iryo Hojin* (medical legal pension).

126. A major restriction on *Iryo Hojin* is that it cannot redistribute the surplus. This restriction thus limits equity as a financing source.

127. Another major reason for the short consultation time is the limited supply of doctors. At 1.9 per thousand population, the density of practising physicians is among the lowest in the OECD. Concern about excess supply of doctors in 20 years or so may well be exaggerated if the average consultation time is to be increased substantially.

128. The system of medical insurance comprises over five thousand health insurers: 3 249 local governments and 166 societies for the NHI which covers mainly the self-employed and the elderly, one big insurer of the central government for GMHI which covers employees of SMEs, 1 813 health societies for SMHI which covers employees of large companies, and another 80 Mutual Aid Associations and one Seamen's Insurer.

129. Efficiency is here used in the sense of allocational efficiency: whether the marginal social utility associated with an objective is equivalent to its marginal opportunity cost. Efficiency is often used in the literature in the more narrow sense of technical efficiency: least cost in achieving the objective. In this chapter the term cost effectiveness is used which also incorporates the possibility that a programme might have only a little impact

– or even none at all – on the objectives with which it is associated. Cost effectiveness is a necessary though not sufficient condition for allocational efficiency.

130. In addition, public investment by public corporations diminished in the 1980s because of privatisation of three major corporations. Nippon Telegraph and Telephone (NTT) and Japan Tobacco (JT) were excluded from public corporations in FY 1985 and Japan Railway (JR) in FY 1987.
131. The social assistance system is characterised by a very low take-up rate. Central government spending (about 75 per cent of welfare benefits) covers medical, housing and living costs for those under a social minimum (and from FY 2000 will also include nursing care services) and reached only some 1.5 trillion yen in 1999 (0.3 per cent of GDP).
132. The high proportion of social assistance grants in earlier decades was due to elderly people who had not accumulated pension rights. As the system matured, pension payments rose while grants declined. In addition, implementation was tightened as part of fiscal consolidation efforts.
133. Pension benefits are calculated as the sum of benefits from the following accounts using Economic Planning Agency, *Annual Report on National Accounts* 2000: Welfare pension, National pension, Mutual benefit associations, Pension funds and Seamen's insurance (pension account). In a similar manner, health care benefits include payments from the following: health insurance run by central government, national health insurance, medical services for the elderly, mutual benefits for societies, health insurance run by private mutual associations and seamen's insurance (health insurance).
134. The cost of guarantees put in place at the end of 1998 to protect SMEs – and extended by a further 10 trillion yen in November 1999 to 30 trillion yen – will only be fully reflected in general government expenditures as losses are paid to the credit guarantee associations and/or the Japan SME Corporation. The risks of the guarantee associations are shared with the Japan SME Corporation. The government money was disbursed to these organisations in the third FY 1998 supplementary budget, assuming the default rate would be 10 per cent. Therefore, a higher default rate would require additional money.
135. The FY 2000 budget recognised 4.5 trillion yen as costs from the bank bailout this year.
136. The decline in budget subsidies was also due to reduced financing for the price support system in the rice market and for other public corporations, which resulted from greater utilisation of market mechanism in general.
137. Steven Meyer and Shigeto Naka (1998). The study confined itself to the numerous supplementary budgets up to 1990 and investigated whether party affiliation and status were important in changing budget priorities from the initial plans approved by the Cabinet, which was assumed to reflect more the priorities of the Ministry of Finance. Other factors have also been at work even though they are closely related to political determinants. Thus, reducing regional income inequality has also played an important role in the allocation of central government resources at certain times, depending on the stage of development. See also Kimiyoshi Kamada, Nobuhiro Okuno and Ritsuko Futagami (1998).
138. On the other hand, the introduction of the mixed system of voting appears to have increased the disproportionality of the electoral system. New Zealand also reformed its electoral system at the same time, but as in Germany, the proportional lists are explicitly intended to correct for any disproportionality introduced by results in the first-past-the-post single member electorates. See Michael Gallagher (1998) and the extensive Japanese references.

139. Echoing criticisms in Japan, Gallagher, *op. cit.*, notes that Diet members have shown a preference for election *via* the single member electorates where their support groups are extensive and where they believe they can directly deliver benefits to their constituents.

140. However, within each ministry there has been a greater shift in the composition of expenditures. For example, the Ministry of Agriculture has re-allocated expenditures from irrigation to roads and rural infrastructure (see also Box 10).

141. Tachibanaki (1998). The distribution of personal income might also have widened.

142. The calculation assumes that the Housing Loan Corporation makes no new loans from FY 2000 and does not include lending by the FILP to the corporation of 10 trillion yen in FY 1999. See T. Tomita (2000).

143. The number of houses was 13 per cent greater than the number of households in 1998.

144. One study has calculated that the private rate of return to college education was around 6½ per cent in 1995 (H. Ono (1999)). Cost effective it may not be however. EPA (1998) has estimated that if all subsidies to private universities were converted to scholarships, the coverage could be more than doubled from the current 10 per cent. However, the social rate of return could be lower since the private rate of return reflects to some extent wage profiles not closely related to productivity. EPA (1998) has calculated that the social rate of return to education in Japan is less than that in the United States due to inefficiencies in the education system.

145. Because the budget in FY 1995 was 3.18 trillion yen, the average annual growth during the period was about 2.6 per cent.

146. For example, the table indicates only the length of expressways. There are many general roads under the control of the Ministry of Construction (MOC), and the Ministry of Agriculture also builds and manages roads for agriculture, which are often used for non-agricultural purposes as urbanisation progresses in rural areas. Moreover, the share of roads in public investment in agriculture has been increasing (see Box 10). In addition to the lack of comprehensive data, substitutability between different intrastructure makes interpretation of the indicators difficult.

147. Nemoto *et al.* (1999) estimated an "optimal" level of social infrastructure and argued that the shortage of infrastructure for industry almost disappeared in the early 1980s.

148. There is an argument in Japan that, with land prices lower in rural areas, it would be rational to favour projects in these areas when allocating budgetary resources. From the perspective of resource allocation, this argument does not necessarily hold. Land prices do not at present reflect relative opportunity costs but are also strongly influenced by the land tax system and by government support for land prices in some areas. In the absence of detailed social cost/benefit analysis, the only clear conclusion which emerges is that land-intensive projects should be located in non-urban areas.

149. Public choice theory would suggest that politicians would tend to favour allocations to their regions with which they could be closely identified (such as public works) rather than through a general rule such as regional tax allowances.

150. A conservative estimate showed a subsidy cost of 4.3 trillion yen which is fourteen times greater than the current budget subsidy. The cost is even greater when using private sources of finance, which is officially estimated to be 5.1 trillion yen. See also Tomita, *op. cit.*, 2000.

151. Projects where the socio-economic basis for their viability has changed drastically are also subject to review.

152. The constraint takes the form of a limit on borrowing which if exceeded results in the Ministry of Home Affairs assuming control of the local government.

153. There are some other earmarked national taxes. These include taxes on: *a*) aviation fuels, *b*) electricity, and *c*) oil and liquefied natural gas, which are earmarked for airport construction, electric power development, energy conservation and promotion of energy use other than oil, respectively.

154. With regard to public works, because the government's method of calculating costs is well known in the industry and the unit prices they use are available as public information, it is possible for companies to make a good guess about the upper bound. The distribution of successful bids is therefore only suggestive and is not in itself evidence of collusion (*Dango*).

155. For example, two local governors and an influential LDP politician were arrested in 1993 because they were bribed in exchange for arranging favourable treatment in bidding. The FTC has stated that 31 general contractors, many of them listed companies, were involved in *Dango* concerning public works in six prefectures in the *Kinki* area – around Osaka – for ten years until 1997, although the FTC could not take any legal actions in one case because of the expiry of the time limitation.

156. The Ministry of Construction believes that pushing down prices to around the lower bound would imply an unacceptably high risk of poor quality public works.

157. Construction and related companies capture this rent at present. McMillan (1991) estimated that excess profits attributable to collusion in Japan's construction industry could be worth 16 to 33 per cent of the successful bid price based on his theoretical collusion model with some plausible values for parameters.

158. The cost reduction achieved is cumulatively 9.6 per cent in the three years to FY 1999.

159. Many OECD countries have similar policies although there are often also safeguards. Thus in several federal countries, there are limits on the extent to which local suppliers may be favoured and in the EU, at the end of the day, there is always the restriction that the free movement of goods and services should be ensured. For a review see OECD *Small and Medium Enterprise Outlook*, Paris, 2000.

160. The MOC and the FTC jointly issued a notice warning local government against dividing a project into "excessively" small orders in December 1999 to prevent *uwauke* (see below). The government also decided to increase the size of orders to improve efficiency as part of the 3-year Deregulation Plan. These are seemingly inconsistent with the policy to treat SMEs favourably.

161. This is not "Kousha", a status to which three privatised corporations (JT, JR and NTT) were entitled, and which means a permanent concern.

162. Ohta and Imahashi (1995) argue that privatisation of these corporations will allow them to roll over liabilities corresponding to land values out of the total construction costs (because land is non-depreciable assets), thereby improving cash flows. On the other hand, the possibility of a return to free access to the roads in the future will disappear.

163. Moreover, the number of bureaux in central ministries and agencies will be reduced from 128 to 96, the number of government advisory panels from 211 to 90 and the total panel seats to 1 800 from the current 5 300.

164. It includes the White Paper on the Economy and short- and medium-term forecasts.

165. It is also important to note that parliamentary procedures have been altered so that ministers rather than high-level civil servants must now answer questions about policy before the Diet. A deputy minister system has also been introduced.

166. While the building of sewage systems for residential areas falls under the jurisdiction of the Ministry of Construction, the Ministry of Agriculture, Fisheries and Forestry is responsible for the construction of sewage systems for farms. Also the divisions between the Ministry of Health and Welfare, which oversees nursery schools, and the Ministry of Education, which is responsible for Kindergartens, will continue to exist even under the new organisation.

167. However, it has been announced recently that a new committee for policy evaluation comprising independent experts will be set up to ensure the objectivity of evaluations conducted by the Ministry.

168. As Tomita (2000) observes, the reform seeks to mitigate political failure by establishing financial discipline on government institutions.

169. See OECD, *Economic Survey of Japan*, 1999, pp. 123-130, for more detailed information than given in this section.

170. There are two exceptional cases where an increase in local tax revenues will not lead to a decrease in general grants from central government: the situation where the increase in tax revenues is due to a higher tax rate than stipulated in a law, and to non-statutory taxes. Where the local governments (like Tokyo Metropolitan government) do not receive the general grant, the exception does not apply.

171. Vouchers were also utilised in pre-school education in England. Decisions were made in 1997 to phase them out.

172. Such a central function is also important since a ministry could hardly be expected to give up funding for projects simply because its own project unit believed that the internal rate of return was too low.

173. Under the constitution the Board of Audit (BOA hereafter) is independent from the cabinet. The most important objective of the audit is to validate the settlement of accounts of the annual budget, as in the case of private auditors treating company settlements. More specifically, the audit is conducted in order to: 1) ensure appropriate accounting and, if necessary, to request corrections of inappropriate accounting and to further institutional changes to prevent any recurrence; 2) confirm the accuracy of the settlement numbers and validity of the accounts. The scope of audit includes government institutions and local governments, with financial assistance from the central government, in addition to ministries and agencies. The BOA exchanges information with the Administrative Inspection Bureau of Management and Co-ordination Agency (MCA) and audit offices of local governments to use its resources more efficiently.

174. The BOA has stated that audits of effectiveness started around 1965. For examples of the findings of cost effectiveness audits see *Audit report tells us...*, Board of Audit of Japan (in English), Tokyo, various issues.

175. The Tokyo Bay Crossing Road Inc. is a special private company established by private sector, local governments and JHC. Based on a contract with JHC, the company was in charge of a major part of the construction of the Aqua line over Tokyo bay and, after its completion, sold it to JHC for about 1.2 trillion yen. The company is now engaged in maintenance work of the road based on a new contract with JHC. This company is currently suffering from losses due to overestimation of demand: actual traffic is about 40 per cent of the estimation.

Bibliography

Abe, Yasutaka and Yukio Uehara (1999),
"A proposal to abolish protection of short-term rental right" (in Japanese), NBL, No. 667, 15 June, Shoji Homu Kenkyu-kai, Tokyo.

Agion, P., O. Hart and J. Moore (1992),
"The Economics of Bankruptcy Reform", *Journal of Law, Economics and Organisation*, Vol. 8, pp. 523-46.

Ban, Kanemi (1996),
"Multiplier effects of public investment in macroeconometric models: overview and evaluation" (in Japanese), in *Research on effects of public investment on the economy*, Zaisei Keizai Kyo-kai, Tokyo.

Bayoumi, Tamin (1998),
"The Japanese Fiscal System and Fiscal Transparency", in B. Aghevli *et al.*, *Structural Change in Japan*, IMF, Washington.

Bebchuk, Lucian A. (1988),
"A New Approach to Corporate Reorganisation", *Harvard Law Review*, Vol. 101, pp. 775-804.

Board of Audit of Japan,
Audit report tells us…, The Board of Audit's activities and fiscal year 1997 *Audit Report* (in English), p. 56, Tokyo.

Bremer, Marc and Kiyoshi Kato (1996),
"Trading volume for winners and losers on the Tokyo Stock Exchange", *Journal of Financial and Quantitative Analysis*, Vol. 31, No. 1, March.

Calderwood, C. and M. Matsuoka (2000),
"Economic Quarterly Q3 CY00", *Jardine Fleming Research*, Tokyo, July.

Campbell, J.C. and N. Ikegami (1998),
The Art of Balance in Health Policy: Maintaining Japan's Low-Cost, Egalitarian System, Cambridge University Press.

Clark, Kim B. and Takahiro Fujimoto (1991),
Product Development Performance, Harvard University Press, Boston.

Coate, Stephen and Stephen Morris (1999),
"Policy Persistence", *American Economic Review*, Vol. 89, No. 5, December.

Cox, Gary and Michael Thies (1998),
"The cost of intra-party competition: the single non-transferrable vote and money politics in Japan", *Comparative Political Studies*, 31.

Disney, Richard (2000),
"Crises in Public Pension Programmes in OECD: What Are the Reform Options?", *Economic Journal*, Vol. 110, pp. F1-23, February.

Economic Planning Agency (1995),
Economic Survey of Japan, 1994-1995, Tokyo.

Economic Planning Agency (1997),
Economic Survey of Japan, 1996-1997, Tokyo.

Economic Planning Agency (1998),
Economists' Proposal to Reform the Education System, Research Institute of EPA, Tokyo.

Economic Planning Agency (2000*a*),
Annual Report on National Accounts 2000.

Economic Planning Agency (2000*b*),
Economic Survey of Japan, 1999-2000, Tokyo.

Economic Planning Agency (2000*c*),
Surveys on Corporate Behaviours: Restructuring Efforts to Raise Profitability and After, Tokyo.

Economic Planning Agency (2000*d*),
Price Report 2000, Tokyo.

Economic Strategy Council (1998),
Final Report to Prime Minister, Tokyo.

Fair Trade Commission (1999),
Regulations and Bidding System by Local Governments from a Viewpoint of Competition Policies (in Japanese), Tokyo, June.

Fitch (2000),
Newsletter, Hong Kong, China, 20 June.

Franks, Jullian R. and Walter Torous (1993),
"Lessons from a Comparison of US and UK Insolvency Codes", *Oxford Review of Economic Policy*, Vol. 8, No. 3, pp. 70-82.

Fukao, Mitsuhiro (ed.) (2000),
Non-performing Loans and Financial Markets, Japan Centre of Economic Research, Tokyo, March.

Fukui, Hideo and Yoshiaki Kume (1999),
"Failure of Judicial System in Forced Auction Managed by the Court" (in Japanese), NBL, No. 671, 15 August and 672, 1 September, Shoji Homu Kenkyu-kai, Tokyo.

Fukui, Hideo (2000),
"Regulatory reform of Judicial System" (in Japanese), in Naohiro Yashiro (ed.), *Economic Analysis of Social Regulations*, Nihon Keizai Shinbun-sha, Tokyo.

Gallagher, Michael (1998),
"The political impact of electoral system change in Japan and New Zealand, 1996", *Party Politics*, 4.

Genda, Y. (2000),
"Youth unemployment and parasite singles", *Bulletin of Labour*, Vol. 39, No. 3, Tokyo.

Hamori, Shigeyuki, and Kazumi Asako (1994), "Government Consumption and Fiscal Policy: Some Evidence from Japan", *Applied Economic Letters*, Vol. 6, pp. 551-555.

Hatta, Tatsuo (ed.) (1994),
Economic Analysis of Resource Concentration Mechanism in Tokyo, Nihon Keizai Shinbun-sha, Tokyo.

Hatta, Tatsuo and Noriyoshi Oguchi (1999),
Pension Reform, Nihon Keizai Shinbun-sha, Tokyo.

Hattori, Ryota and Eiji Maeda (2000),
"The Japanese Employment System", BOJ *Monthly Report*, January.

Hayakawa, H. and E. Maeda (2000),
"Understanding Japan's financial and economic developments since autumn 1997", Bank of Japan, Working Paper Series, 00-1, Tokyo.

Heinrich, R. (1999),
"Complementarities in Corporate Governance", Kiel Working Paper, 947, September.

Honda. Masaaki and Naozumi Atoda (1991),
"Increasing Interdependence in Inter-government Public Finance" (in Japanese), in Kaizuka, Ishi, Noguchi and Honma (ed.), *Public Finance in the Era of Devolution*, Yuhikaku, Tokyo.

Honma, Yoshihito (1999),
Reflection on National Development Plans: Future of Development-oriented Policies (in Japanese), Chuo Koron-sha, Tokyo.

Hori, Masahiro, Susumu Suzuki and Masaru Kayasono (1998),
"The EPA Short-run Macroeconometric Model of Japanese Economy: Basic Structure, Multipliers, and Economic Policy Analyses" (in Japanese), *Economic Analysis*, Economic Research Institution, Economic Planning Agency, Tokyo.

Horioka, C.Y. (1999),
"Japan's public pension system in the 21st Century", *Institute of Social and Economic Research Discussion Paper*, No. 482, Osaka.

Hoshi, T. (1998),
"Japanese corporate governance as a system", in K. Hopt *et al.*, *Comparative Corporate Governance – The state of the art and emerging research*, Oxford.

Ihori, Toshihiro, Takeo Doi and Hiroki Kondo (1999),
"Japanese Fiscal Reform: Fiscal Reconstruction and Fiscal Policy", mimeo.

Iimura, S. (1999),
"The latest wave of consolidation in Japan's financial sector", *Capital Research Journal*, Vol. 2, No. 4, Tokyo, winter.

Ikeo, Kazuto and Hiroyuki Seshita (1998),
"Institutional Framework for Corporate Bankruptcy in Japan" (in Japanese), in Miwa, Yoshiro, Hideki Kanda and Noriyuki Yanagawa (ed.), *Economics of Company Law*, University of Tokyo Press, Tokyo.

Ishi, Hiromitsu (1996),
"Budgets and the budgetary process in Japan", *Hitosubashi Journal of Economics*, 37.

Iwata, Kikuo (1994),
"Pollution by Auto Transport in Tokyo" (in Japanese), in Hatta (ed.).

Johnson, K., D. Small and R. Tryon (1999),
"Monetary policy and price stability", International Finance Discussion Papers, 641, Washington.

Kamada, Kimiyoshi, Nobuhiro Okuno and Ritsuko Futagami (1998),
"Decisions on regional allocation of public investment: the case in Japan", *Applied Economics Letters*, Vol. 5, pp. 503-506.

Kanemoto, Yoshitsugu (1999),
"Procurement of Public Works" (in Japanese), Kanemoto (ed.), *Construction Industry in Japan*, Nihon Keizai Shinbun-sha, Tokyo.

Keeler, Theodore and Kenneth A. Small (1977),
"Optimal Peak-load Pricing, Investment, and Service Levels on Urban Expressways", *Journal of Political Economy*, Vol. 85, No. 1.

Keidanren (1998),
Restructuring Public Pension System to Restore Its Credibility, Tokyo.

Kirishima, Kazutaka (1998),
"Expected Cut of Expenditures by 3.6 trillion yen due to Mergers of Municipalities" (in Japanese),*Toyo Keizai*, Tokyo, 14 November.

Komiya, Ryutaro (1988),
"Structural and Behavioural Features of Japanese Firms" (in Japanese), *Journal of Economics*, University of Tokyo.

Komiya, Ryutaro (1989),
"*Seiho* as a firm", Komiya and Imai (ed.), *Japanese Firms*, University of Tokyo Press, Tokyo.

Komiya, Ryutaro (1999),
"Declining population, the size of the government and the burden of public debt: some economic policy issues in Japan", in Craig Freeman (ed.), *Why Did Japan Stumble?: Causes and Cures*, Edward Elgar, Cheltenham, United Kingdom, and Northampton MA, United States.

Kume, Yoshiaki and Hideo Fukui (1999),
"Law and economics of protection of short-term rental rights" (in Japanese), NBL, 1 August, Shoji Homu Kenkyu-kai, Tokyo.

Kunihisa, Sotaro and Michihiro Kaiyama (1998),
"The Economic Effect of Highway Construction: A Comparative Analysis for the UK, Germany and Japan", *Review of Urban and Regional Development*, Vol. 10, No. 1, pp. 28-41, spring.

Matsuoka, Mikihiro (1999),
"Reconsidering Effectiveness of Fiscal Policy" (in Japanese), mimeo.

Matsuoka, M. (2000),
"Intentional monetary tightening", *Jardine Fleming Research*, July.

McKinnon, R. and K. Ohno (1997),
Dollar and Yen: Resolving economic conflict between the United States and Japan, MIT.

McMillan, John (1991),
"Dango: Japan's Price-fixing Conspiracies", *Economic and Politics*, Vol. 3, No. 3, pp. 201-218.

Meyer, Steven and Shigeto Naka (1998),
"Legislative influences in Japanese budgetary politics", *Public Choice*, 94.

Ministry of Labour (2000),
White Paper on Employment.

Missale, Alessandro and Olivier Blanchard (1994),
"The Debt Burden and Debt Maturity", *American Economic Review*, Vol. 84, No. 1, pp. 309-319.

Miwa, Y. (1998),
"The economics of corporate governance in Japan", in K. Hopt *et al.*, *Comparative Corporate Governance – The state of the art and emerging research*, Oxford.

Mochida, N. and J. Lotz (1999),
"Fiscal federalism in practice: the Nordic countries and Japan", *Journal of Economics*, 64 (4).

Mohring, Herbert (1970),
"The Peak Load Problem with Increasing Returns and pricing Constraints", *American Economic Review*, Vol. 60, No. 4, pp. 693-705, September.

Morichi, Shigeru (1999),
"Building-up of High-speed Transport System" (in Japanese), in Shigeru Morichi and Tetsuo Yai (ed.).

Morichi, Shigeru and Tetsuo Yai (ed.) (1999),
The Future of Social Infrastructure (in Japanse), Nihon Keizai Shinbun-sha, Tokyo.

Miyajima, Hiroshi (1989),
A study of Fiscal Consolidation: On Expenditure-cutting Policies (in Japanese), Yuhikaku, Tokyo.

Nagaoka, Sadao and Fukunari Kimura (1999),
"The competitive impact of international trade: The case of import liberalisation of the Japanese oil product market", *Journal of the Japanese and International Economies*, 13.

Nakajima, Yasuhiro (1998),
"Projects of Agriculture and Village Improvement and Subsidy Programmes" (in Japanese), in Masahiro Okuno and Masayoshi Honda (ed.), *Economic Analysis of Issues on Agriculture*, Nihon Keizai Shinbun-sha, Tokyo.

Nemoto, Jiro, Kimiyoshi Kamada and Makoto Kawamura (1999),
"Estimate of optimal public capital stocks in Japan using a public investment discount rate framework", *Empirical Economics*, Vol. 24, pp. 693-710.

Nikko Salomon Smith Barney (2000*a*),
"Credit spreads: Back to the future?", *Japan: Issues and Prospects*, 1 June.

Nikko Salomon Smith Barney (2000*b*),
"The price is right for the BOJ?", 3 August.

Nishiguchi, Toshihiro (2000),
"Toward a Better Design of Public Procurement for Defence Force" (in Japanese), *Business Review*, Vol. 47, No. 4.

Nishizaki, F., Y. Yamada and E. Ando (1997),
"Income distribution and poverty in Japan", *Economic Research Institute Discussion Paper*, No. 80, Tokyo.

OECD (1997),
Economic Survey of Japan, Paris.

OECD (1998*a*),
Economic Survey of Poland, Paris.

OECD (1998*b*),
Economic Survey of Japan, Paris.

OECD (1998*c*),
Voucher Programmes and their role in the distribution of public services, PUMA/SBO(98)7/Final.

OECD (1999*a*),
Economic Survey of Japan, Paris.

OECD (1999*b*),
Economic Outlook 67, Paris, December.

OECD (1999*c*),
Economic Survey of Germany, Paris.

OECD (1999*d*),
Budgeting For Results, Paris.

OECD (1999*e*),
Budgeting for the Future, Paris.

OECD (1999*f*),
Budgeting in a Surplus Environment, Paris.

OECD (2000*a*),
Economic Survey of Italy, Paris.

OECD (2000*c*),
Best Practices for Budget Transparency, Paris.

Oguchi N., Y. Kimura and T. Hatta (1996),
"Redistribution effects of the Japanese Public Pension system", *Review of Social Policy*, No. 5, March.

Ohira, Sumihiko (1996),
"An examination of effects of public investment using input-output tables" (in Japanese), in *Research on effects of public investment on the economy*, Zaisei Keizai Kyo-kai, Tokyo.

Ohta, Kazuhiro and Takasi Imahashi (1995),
"Road Policies" (in Japanese), in Yoshitsugu Kanemoto and Hirotaka Yamauchi (ed.), *Transport: Public Regulations and Industries* 4, NTT Press, Tokyo.

Ohta, Souichi (2000),
cited in Tachibanaki *et al., op. cit.*

Okano, Yukihide (1994),
"Commuting Congestion and Transport Measures" (in Japanese), in Hatta (1994).

Okina, Kunio and Nobuyudi Oda (2000),
"Further monetary easing policies under non-negativity constraints of nominal interest rates", Paper presented at the Ninth International Conference, *The role of monetary policy under low inflation*, Bank of Japan, Tokyo, 3-4 July.

Okuno, Nobuhiro (1988),
Public Economy: Theory and Policies of Social Infrastructure (in Japanese), Toyo Keizai Shimpo-sha, Tokyo.

Okuno, Masahiro and Masayoshi Honda (1998),
"The Future of Japanese Agriculture and Agricultural Policies" (in Japanese), in Masahiro Okuno and Masayoshi Honda (ed.), *Economic Analysis of Issues on Agriculture*, Nihon Keizai Shinbun-sha, Tokyo.

Ono, O. (1999),
Does examination hell pay off? The cost benefit analysis of college education in Japan, Paper presented at the NBER, Japan Project Meeting, Tokyo, December.

Orphanides, A. and V. Wieland (1999),
"Monetary policy in a low inflation environment", Paper presented at the NBER/CEPR/TCER Conference on *Monetary Policy in a Low Inflation Environment*, Tokyo, December.

Oshio, Takashi (1998),
A Plan of Privatising Public Pension System (in Japanese), Nihon Keizai Shinbun-sha, Tokyo.

Owoye, Oluwolfe (1995),
"The Causal relationship between taxes and expenditures in the G7 countries: cointegration and error-correction models", *Applied Economic Letters*, Vol. 2, pp. 19-22.

Packer, Frank (2000),
"Credit ratings and the Japanese corporate bond market", Institute for Monetary and Economic Studies Discussion Paper, 2000-E-9, Tokyo.

Ramaswamy, R. and H. Samiei (2000),
"The Yen-Dollar rate: have interventions mattered", IMF Working Paper, WP/00/95, Washington.

Rao, M.G. (1998),
"Accommodating public expenditure policies: the case of fast growing Asian economies", *World Development*, 26, 4.

Saito, M. and S. Shiratsuka (2000),
"Financial crisis as the failure of arbitrage and monetary policy: Evidence from the Japan premium phenomenon", Paper presented at the Ninth International Conference, *The role of monetary policy under low inflation*, Bank of Japan, Tokyo, 3-4 July.

Seki, Y. (2000),
"Japan debates the introduction of real estate investment trusts", *Capital Research Journal*, 3, 1, spring.

Shiratsuka, S. (1999),
"Measurement errors in the Japanese consumer price index", *Monetary and Economic Studies*, Vol. 17, No. 3, Tokyo, December.

Shogenji, Shin-ichi (1998),
Economic Analysis of Contemporary Agricultural Policies (in Japanese), University of Tokyo Press, Tokyo.

Shoji Homu Kenkyui-kai (1997),
An Investigation of New Bankruptcy Laws to Promote More Active M&A Activities (sponsored by Economic Planning Agency), Shoji Homu Kenkyui-kai, Tokyo.

Soejima, Takahiko and Hiroshi Yamaguchi (1999),
Secrets of the Courts (in Japanese), Yosen-sha, Tokyo.

Soejima, Takahiko and Hiroshi Yamaguchi (2000),
Verdict of Guilty on the Judicial System (in Japanese), Kodan-sha, Tokyo.

Tachibanaki, Toshiaki (1998),
Economic inequality in Japan.

Tachibanaki, Toshiaki, Kouichi Sunada and Hideo Nomura (1998),
"Economic Effects of Allowing Holding Companies", *Financial Review*, No. 47, Research Institute of the Ministry of Finance, Tokyo, October.

Tachibanaki, Toshiaki, Hiroshi Fujiki and Sachiko Kuroda Nakada (2000),
"Structural Issues in the Japanese Labor Market – An era of variety, equity and efficiency or an era of bipolarization?", Paper presented at the Ninth International Conference, *The role of monetary policy under low inflation*, Bank of Japan, Tokyo, 3-4 July.

Takahashi, Ryoko and Tsuyoshi Ohyama (2000),
"Backgrounds of recent pick-up in inward direct investment", BOJ *Monthly Report*, August.

Takayama, Noriyuki (1999*a*),
"Issues in Public Pension Reform" (in Japanese), *Business Review*, Vol. 47, No. 1.

Takayama, Noriyuki (1999*b*),
"Introducing 401(k) type pension scheme in Japan and its tax treatment" (in Japanese), *Zaikei Tsushin*, November.

Takayama, Noriyuki and Kotaro Yamaguchi (1999),
"Effects of Introduction of Defined Contribution Scheme with Contribution Rate Equal to 4 per cent of Monthly Wage" (in Japanese), *Operations Research*, September.

Takayama, Noriyuki (2000),
Class for Pension (in Japanese), PHP Shinsho, Tokyo.

Takeda, Fumio (1989),
"Road Transport Policies" (in Japanese), in *Interim Report of Japanese Transport Policy in Post-world-war Era*, Research Centre for Transportation Economy, Tokyo.

Toda, Yasushi and Takako Ide (2000),
"Real estate forced auction markets and legal status of evacuation" (in Japanese), *Quarterly Journal of Housing and Land Economics*, No. 37, summer.

Tomita, T. (2000),
"Reform of Japan's fiscal and loan programme", *Capital Research Journal*, Vol. 3, No. 1, p. 25, spring.

Ushimaru, Satoshi, Masuo Araki, Hideaki Kitaki, Atsushi Yoshida, Hiroshi Ito and Yasushi Iiyama (1999),
Towards Construction of A New Basic Pension System (in Japanese), Research Institute of Economic Planning Agency, Tokyo, January.

Virén, Matti (2000),
"Measuring effectiveness of fiscal policy in OECD countries", *Applied Economic Letters*, Vol. 7, pp. 29-34.

Washimi, Eiji, Noburou Akai and Hiroki Tanaka (1999),
"An Evaluation of Fiscal Conditions of the Japanese Government Based on Assets and Liabilities: Formulating a Balance Sheets on an Accrual Basis", Kobe University of Commerce Working Paper No. 169, October.

White, Michelle J. (1996),
"The Cost of Corporate Bankruptcy: A US-European Comparison" in Jagdeep S. Bhandari and Lawrence A. Weiss (ed.), *Corporate Bankruptcy: Economic and Legal Perspectives*, Cambridge University Press.

Annex I

Investing for an efficient road system

Road construction accounts for about a quarter of public investment. There are toll roads (invariably highways) constructed and managed by special corporations with finance from the FILP, and non-toll roads run by central and local governments (Figure A1). The latter are divided into those directly constructed or subsidised by the central government (*Ippan doro jigyo*) and those under the responsibility of local governments (*Chiho tandoku jigyo*). Investment

Figure A1. **Road construction and its finance**
Trillion yen, FY 1998

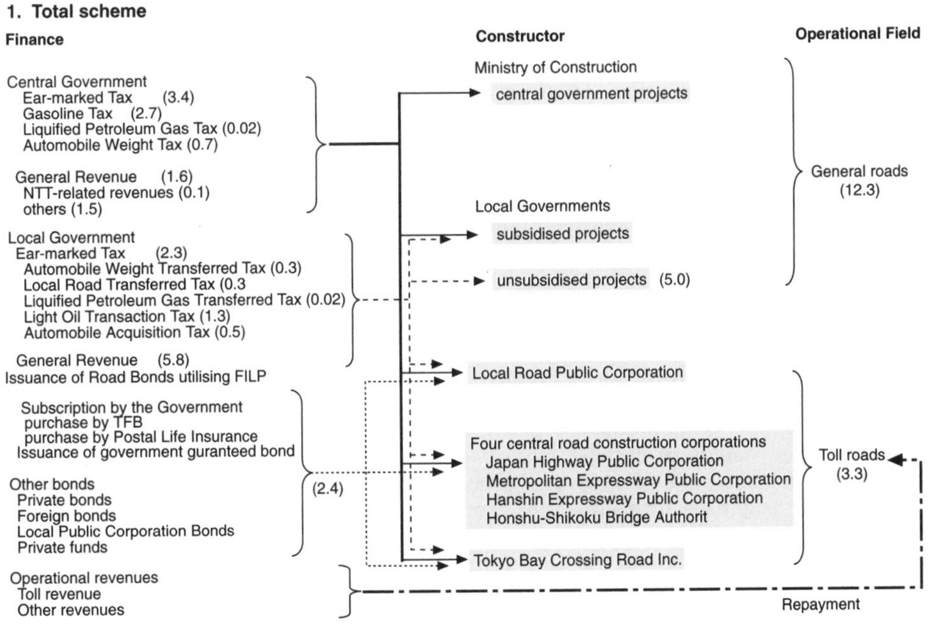

Source: Ministry of Construction.

plans are decided by the central and local governments as in other countries, operating and construction companies such as Japan Highway Corporation and other public corporations are not involved in this process. The Ministry of Construction (MOC) has a long-term construction programme, but projects are initiated *via* the annual budget. Auto and gasoline taxes are earmarked to finance road construction, but expenditures are often greater so that general revenues have been injected through supplementary budgets.

Where to build: setting priorities

While investment decisions need to satisfy both the need for alleviating congestion in urban areas and the promotion of balanced regional developments with rural areas, the choice of specific projects should be guided by consideration of costs relative to benefits which reflect policy objectives. In any country, a large amount of tax revenue is generated in urban areas where congestion is severe, but this does not by itself justify city road construction.[1] Congestion in Tokyo is largely attributable to delayed construction of circular roads:[2] according to the Ministry of Transport (MOT), daily traffic of 460 000 cars on the only circular road in central Tokyo could be reduced by a half if other circular roads were completed as planned. Although the Fifth Road Investment Plan (1967 to 1971) incorporated a construction plan for nine radial roads from and three circular roads around Tokyo, the completion rate of the circular roads is still about 20 per cent. In the past, the delay has encouraged construction of over-head highways in Tokyo because they did not require land acquisition. The completion of circular roads in other urban areas is also long overdue.

Highway building in some rural areas is likely to prove allocationally inefficient: traffic volumes would have to be significant to justify such construction. But social needs and other factors would also have to be taken into account at the planning stage. Kunihisa and Kaiyama (1998) estimated that the marginal productivity of highways in Japan declined more sharply than in Germany and the United Kingdom and by 1990 reached a level roughly comparable to that of these two countries, reflecting the rapid pace of highway construction and low utilisation rates of newly built routes. The MOC envisaged 14 000 km major trunk roads in the early 21st century, about half of which have been built (see Table 28). Now that less costly projects on either the Pacific Ocean or Japan Sea side are almost complete, the remaining projects connecting both coasts through mountainous areas are likely to be expensive and stretch the finances of the JHC. Such investments damage the natural environment more than in the urban areas at the margin, while stimulating regional economies to some extent.

Considering alternatives: other transport modes

Road construction needs to be evaluated in the context of the overall system of transportation, the development of which should reflect properly the benefits to users and their preferences through inter-modal competition. In addition, consideration also needs to be given to proper charging of road users. Such an evaluation is not, however, straightforward as different modes and parts of the overall transportation network act both as substitutes and complements. Highways are a substitute to other means of long-haul transportation, such as railways and air transport, to a varying degree. On the other hand, improving road access to major trunk roads and air, water and rail terminals is complementary to different modes of long-haul transportation and hence increases the substitutability between them. Despite such difficulties highway construction should in the first instance be evaluated as an alternative to developing other means of long-haul transportation where substitutability between them is considered to be high.

Enhancing efficiency by reinforcing connection between costs and benefits

Earmarked taxes provide a framework similar to some market mechanisms. However, taxes on car weight and purchase taxes, which account for about one-quarter of earmarked taxes[3] (Figure A1), are less tightly related to road use than fuel taxes. The system could be improved by raising taxes closely related to car use, while lowering others. Iwata (1994) also argued that preferential tax treatment of trucks over passenger cars, business over family cars and diesel over gasoline cars are exacerbating damages to the environment caused by traffic congestion. Different tax rates depending on vehicle types could also be utilised to contain such negative externalities.

Easier excludability of highways (*i.e.* toll roads) enables a closer link in principle between costs and benefits. The current system is based on some cross-subsidisation between routes.[4] The government tries to finance the construction of the network of highways envisaged in the current five-year plan in part through the toll revenues from the roads constructed earlier. The government also justifies the current cross-subsidies on the grounds that a uniform toll in the network, regardless of construction cost, is fair.

The current uniform toll could be seen as a compromise between: *a)* Ramsey pricing which sets a higher price where the price elasticity of demand is lower, and *b)* pricing based on repayment schedule of each route from its own revenues (as adopted before 1972),[5] as Ohta and Imahashi (1995) argued. A similar observation can be made as to tolls on different types of vehicle. Toll revisions in 1989 took account of the damage to roads and the price elasticity of demand. But they left tolls for heavy vehicles almost unchanged relative to others, since more damage called for higher prices but higher price-elasticity of demand justified lower prices. Therefore, according to Ohta and Imahashi, there is little room for improvement of the toll system, apart from peak load pricing. This last would be a theoretical solution to congestion, but in metropolitan areas this is likely to aggravate congestion on ordinary roads and might be too costly to implement in the short run.[6]

Notes

1. According to Takeda (1989), road investment was 1.3 to 2.3 times as large as car-related tax revenues raised in rural areas (such as Hokkaido, Hokuriku, San-in, Shikoku), while 60 to 70 per cent in three metropolitan areas (Tokyo, Osaka and Nagoya) and their neighbouring prefectures.
2. According to Morichi (1999), the situation is similar in many urban areas because the MOC places priority on construction of by-passes rather than circular roads, unlike in other OECD countries. Morichi argues that such a policy has not alleviated congestion because of free access to the by-passes: by-passes have become just like other roads and subject to congestion.
3. Taxes related to cars are not always earmarked for road construction. For example, auto tax and light auto tax are imposed on holding of cars. They are local taxes, and their revenues (1.6 trillion yen in FY 1998) are not earmarked for road investment.
4. In order to partially reduce the demerits of cross-subsidisation, cross-subsidies have been allowed only up to a half of construction costs of a new highway.
5. Suppose there are two highways, a highway earlier constructed in urban area with high demand and another one constructed later in rural area with low demand. As for the former, Ramsey price is the highest and the repayment-schedule price is the lowest, with the current price in the middle. As for the latter, the ordering of prices is the reverse.
6. It will be worth monitoring how load pricing will work in Hyogo and Kanagawa prefectures, which is likely to be implemented in FY 2001 at the earliest in response to strong local demands for improved air quality.

Annex II

Chronology of main economic events

1999

November

The Ministry of Finance and the Bank of Japan (BOJ) agreed that the Trust Fund Bureau would sell its JGBs under repurchase agreements in the financial markets to finance as necessary the outflow of postal savings, and that the BOJ would provide temporary liquidity to complement this measure.

The government announced special measures related to the newly introduced long-term nursing care insurance, including a reduction of contributions for the elderly aged 65 or above.

The Economic Planning Agency announced a fiscal package worth approximately 18 trillion yen (on a project cost basis, inclusive of the measures for long-term care) and also released a slight revision to the government's GDP forecast for FY 1999 from about 0.5 to 0.6 per cent.

The government decided the draft second FY 1999 supplementary budget to implement the announced fiscal package and submitted it to the Diet.

December

The cabinet approved the official forecast of about 1 per cent real GDP growth in FY 2000.

The government decided the draft initial FY 2000 budget.

The three parties in the coalition government agreed that the lifting of the universal guarantee for bank deposits be postponed from 1 April 2001 for a further year.

2000

January

The government submitted the Fiscal Investment and Loan Programme as part of the budget to the Diet.

The Prime Minister's Commission on Japan's Goals in the 21st Century submitted its final report to Prime Minister Obuchi.

The government decided the outline of FY 2000 tax reform.

February

A revised law to liberalise price setting in domestic airline markets became effective.

The Diet passed a law to cut the number of Lower House members by 20 to 480.

March

The Long Term Credit Bank was sold to a foreign investment consortium and its public management ended.

The Governor of the Bank of Japan, Mr. Hayami, announced that the BOJ would examine the issues regarding the measurement and definition of price stability.

The Diet passed the draft initial FY 2000 budget.

Three banks, Sanwa, Tokai and Asahi, announced that they would merge through establishing a joint a holding company.

The Diet passed draft laws related to pension reforms.

Tokyo Metropolitan Diet passed a bill to introduce a new tax on major banks, which is expected to raise 110 billion yen per year for five years.

April

The long-term care insurance scheme was implemented.

A new bankruptcy law, the Private Revitalisation Law, which aims to streamline procedures and encourage corporate restructuring, came into force.

Following the illness of Mr Obuchi, Mr. Mori was elected Prime Minister in the Diet.

Three banks, Tokyo Mitsubishi Bank, Nippon Trust Bank, and Mitsubishi Trust Bank, announced that they would establish a joint holding company in April 2001 and Nippon Trust Bank, Mitsubishi Trust Bank and Tokyo Trust Bank would merge by October 2001.

Sakura and Sumitomo banks announced that they would speed up their merger by a year to April 2001.

May

The Financial Supervisory Agency ordered the First Fire and Marine Insurance to terminate its operations, the first case in the non-life insurance area.

Emergency Employment Measures aiming to create 350 000 jobs a year, were approved by the Cabinet.

The Diet passed bills to postpone the lifting of full deposit insurance by a year, to facilitate the disposal of failed financial institutions and to ease de-mutualisation of insurance companies.

The Diet passed a bill to revise commercial codes to enable corporate splits.

The Law on Securitisation of Specified Assets by Special Purpose Companies (SPC Law), the Securities and Exchange Law and other related laws were revised in the Diet.

The Bill for the Amendment to the Trust Fund Bureau Fund Act and other related laws passed the Diet.

June

Shinsei Bank, ex-Long-Term Credit Bank, started operations.

FRC decided to sell Nippon Credit Bank to a consortium comprising three Japanese companies.

EPA provisionally dated the trough of the current business cycle as April 1999.

The three coalition parties maintained a majority in Lower House elections.

FRC and DIC approved the buy-back of loans from Shinsei Bank to Sogo, a major retailer, at their net book value and to forgive the amount of the loan already provisioned by the bank.

July

The Financial Services Agency was launched, integrating the Financial Supervisory Agency and the Financial System Planning Bureau of the Ministry of Finance.

A new Cabinet was formed under Prime Minister Mori.

Toyo Trust Bank announced that it would join a holding company to be set up jointly by Sanwa and Tokai banks in April 2001.

A major retail chain, Sogo, gave up restructuring outside the court, and filed bankruptcy under a new law.

The Government Tax Council released its report on medium-term policy directions, pointing out that fiscal consolidation would be required in the near future.

Agreement was reached between Japanese and US governments over inter-connection charges of NTT which would be lowered by about 20 per cent over a two-year period.

The Administrative Reform body submitted a report to the Prime Minister recommending that 140 government institutions should be obliged to improve their disclosure of information.

FRC postponed the sale of the nationalised Nippon Credit Bank to a consortium until September.

August

The Cabinet approved the guideline for the initial FY 2001 budget, envisaging general expenditure (*i.e.* total expenditure less debt servicing and transfers to local governments) of 48.4 trillion yen, up slightly from 48.1 trillion yen in the previous initial budget.

The National Personnel Authority recommended that the government should lower effective salaries for government officials.

The Bank of Japan decided to lift the so-called zero-interest rate policy and announced a rise of the target call rate to 0.25 per cent.

The three coalition parties submitted a list of 233 public works projects to Prime Minister Mori, which should be re-examined if they are to be continued.

The FSA ordered Taisho Life Insurance to terminate its operation.

September

The government decided the outline of the supplementary budget with disbursements amounting to 3.5 to 4 trillion yen.

A holding company was established jointly by three banks, Industrial Bank of Japan, Daiichi-Kangyo and Fuji Banks.

October

Chiyoda Life Insurance filed for bankruptcy, which was the first application of the special reorganisation scheme for financial institutions to an insurance company.

BOJ released a report, *On Price Stability*, and decided to issue its Policy Board members' outlook and risk assessment of the economy and prices twice a year, in April and October.

The government announced a fiscal package worth 11 trillion yen on a project cost basis, emphasising four key areas, IT, environment, ageing and urban infrastructure. EPA revised upwards its official forecast for FY 2000 by 0.5 percentage point to 1.5 per cent.

Kyoei Life Insurance filed for bankruptcy with liabilities amounting to around 4.5 trillion yen.

BASIC STATISTICS

BASIC STATISTICS:

INTERNATIONAL COMPARISONS

	Units	Reference period[1]	Australia	Austria
Population				
Total	Thousands	1997	18 532	8
Inhabitants per sq. km	Number	1997	2	
Net average annual increase over previous 10 years	%	1997	1.3	
Employment				
Total civilian employment (TCE)[2]	Thousands	1997	8 430	3
of which:				
Agriculture	% of TCE	1997	5.2	
Industry	% of TCE	1997	22.1	3
Services	% of TCE	1997	72.7	6
Gross domestic product (GDP)				
At current prices and current exchange rates	Bill. US$	1997	392.9	2
Per capita	US$	1997	21 202	25
At current prices using current PPPs[3]	Bill. US$	1997	406.8	18
Per capita	US$	1997	21 949	23
Average annual volume growth over previous 5 years	%	1997	4.1	
Gross fixed capital formation (GFCF)	% of GDP	1997	21.5	2
of which:				
Machinery and equipment	% of GDP	1997	10.3 (96)	8.8
Residential construction	% of GDP	1997	4.4 (96)	6.2 (
Average annual volume growth over previous 5 years	%	1997	7.3	
Gross saving ratio[4]	% of GDP	1997	18.4	
General government				
Current expenditure on goods and services	% of GDP	1997	16.7	1
Current disbursements[5]	% of GDP	1996	34.8	
Current receipts	% of GDP	1996	35.4	4
Net official development assistance	% of GNP	1996	0.28	0
Indicators of living standards				
Private consumption per capita using current PPP's[3]	US$	1997	13 585	12
Passenger cars, per 1 000 inhabitants	Number	1995	477	
Telephones, per 1 000 inhabitants	Number	1995	510	
Television sets, per 1 000 inhabitants	Number	1994	489	
Doctors, per 1 000 inhabitants	Number	1996	2.5	
Infant mortality per 1 000 live births	Number	1996	5.8	
Wages and prices (average annual increase over previous 5 years)				
Wages (earnings or rates according to availability)	%	1998	1.5	
Consumer prices	%	1998	2.0	
Foreign trade				
Exports of goods, fob*	Mill. US$	1998	55 882	61
As % of GDP	%	1997	15.6	2
Average annual increase over previous 5 years	%	1998	5.6	
Imports of goods, cif*	Mill. US$	1998	60 821	68
As % of GDP	%	1997	15.3	3
Average annual increase over previous 5 years	%	1998	7.5	
Total official reserves[6]	Mill. SDR's	1998	10 942	14 628 (
As ratio of average monthly imports of goods	Ratio	1998	2.2	2.7

* At current prices and exchange rates.

1. Unless otherwise stated.
2. According to the definitions used in OECD Labour Force Statistics.
3. PPPs = Purchasing Power Parities.
4. Gross saving = Gross national disposable income minus private and government consumption.

EMPLOYMENT OPPORTUNITIES

Economics Department, OECD

The Economics Department of the OECD offers challenging and rewarding opportunities to economists interested in applied policy analysis in an international environment. The Department's concerns extend across the entire field of economic policy analysis, both macroeconomic and microeconomic. Its main task is to provide, for discussion by committees of senior officials from Member countries, documents and papers dealing with current policy concerns. Within this programme of work, three major responsibilities are:

- to prepare regular surveys of the economies of individual Member countries;
- to issue full twice-yearly reviews of the economic situation and prospects of the OECD countries in the context of world economic trends;
- to analyse specific policy issues in a medium-term context for the OECD as a whole, and to a lesser extent for the non-OECD countries.

The documents prepared for these purposes, together with much of the Department's other economic work, appear in published form in the *OECD Economic Outlook, OECD Economic Surveys, OECD Economic Studies* and the Department's *Working Papers* series.

The Department maintains a world econometric model, INTERLINK, which plays an important role in the preparation of the policy analyses and twice-yearly projections. The availability of extensive cross-country data bases and good computer resources facilitates comparative empirical analysis, much of which is incorporated into the model.

The Department is made up of about 80 professional economists from a variety of backgrounds and Member countries. Most projects are carried out by small teams and last from four to eighteen months. Within the Department, ideas and points of view are widely discussed; there is a lively professional interchange, and all professional staff have the opportunity to contribute actively to the programme of work.

Skills the Economics Department is looking for:

a) Solid competence in using the tools of both microeconomic and macroeconomic theory to answer policy questions. Experience indicates that this normally requires the equivalent of a Ph.D. in economics or substantial relevant professional experience to compensate for a lower degree.

b) Solid knowledge of economic statistics and quantitative methods; this includes how to identify data, estimate structural relationships, apply basic techniques of time series analysis, and test hypotheses. It is essential to be able to interpret results sensibly in an economic policy context.

c) A keen interest in and extensive knowledge of policy issues, economic developments and their political/social contexts.

d) Interest and experience in analysing questions posed by policy-makers and presenting the results to them effectively and judiciously. Thus, work experience in government agencies or policy research institutions is an advantage.

e) The ability to write clearly, effectively, and to the point. The OECD is a bilingual organisation with French and English as the official languages. Candidates must have excellent knowledge of one of these languages, and some knowledge of the other. Knowledge of other languages might also be an advantage for certain posts.

f) For some posts, expertise in a particular area may be important, but a successful candidate is expected to be able to work on a broader range of topics relevant to the work of the Department. Thus, except in rare cases, the Department does not recruit narrow specialists.

g) The Department works on a tight time schedule with strict deadlines. Moreover, much of the work in the Department is carried out in small groups. Thus, the ability to work with other economists from a variety of cultural and professional backgrounds, to supervise junior staff, and to produce work on time is important.

General information

The salary for recruits depends on educational and professional background. Positions carry a basic salary from FF 318 660 or FF 393 192 for Administrators (economists) and from FF 456 924 for Principal Administrators (senior economists). This may be supplemented by expatriation and/or family allowances, depending on nationality, residence and family situation. Initial appointments are for a fixed term of two to three years.

Vacancies are open to candidates from OECD Member countries. The Organisation seeks to maintain an appropriate balance between female and male staff and among nationals from Member countries.

For further information on employment opportunities in the Economics Department, contact:

Management Support Unit
Economics Department
OECD
2, rue André-Pascal
75775 PARIS CEDEX 16
FRANCE

E-Mail: eco.contact@oecd.org

Applications citing ''ECSUR'', together with a detailed *curriculum vitae* in English or French, should be sent to the Head of Personnel at the above address.

For more information about all OECD publications contact your nearest OECD Centre, or visit
www.oecd.org/bookshop

Pour plus d'informations sur les publications de l'OCDE, contactez votre Centre OCDE le plus proche ou visitez notre librairie en ligne :
www.oecd.org/bookshop

Where to send your request:
Où passer commande :

In Central and Latin America / En Amérique centrale et en Amérique du Sud

OECD MEXICO CENTRE / CENTRE OCDE DE MEXICO
Edificio INFOTEC
Av. San Fernando No. 37 Col. Toriello Guerra
Tlalpan C.P. 14050, Mexico D.F.
Tel.: +525 281 38 10 Fax: + 525 606 13 07
E-mail: mexico.contact@oecd.org Internet: www.rtn.net.mx/ocde

In North America / En Amérique du Nord

OECD WASHINGTON CENTER / CENTRE OCDE DE WASHINGTON
2001 L Street N.W., Suite 650
Washington, DC 20036-4922
Tel.: +1 202 785-6323
Toll free / Numéro vert : +1 800 456-6323 Fax: +1 202 785-0350
E-mail: washington.contact@oecd.org Internet: www.oecdwash.org

In Japan / Au Japon

OECD TOKYO CENTRE / CENTRE OCDE DE TOKYO
Landic Akasaka Bldg.
2-3-4 Akasaka, Minato-ku
Tokyo 107-0052
Tel.: +81 3 3586 2016 Fax: +81 3 3584 7929
E-mail : center@oecdtokyo.org Internet: www.oecdtokyo.org

In the rest of the world / Dans le reste du monde
DVGmbH
Birkenmaarsstrasse 8
D-53340 Meckenheim
Germany
Tel.: +49 22 25 9 26 166/7/8 Fax: +49 22 25 9 26 169
E-mail: oecd@dvg.dsb.net

OECD Information Centre and Bookshop/
Centre d'information de l'OCDE et Librairie
OECD PARIS CENTRE / CENTRE OCDE DE PARIS
2 rue André-Pascal, 75775 Paris Cedex 16, France
Enquiries / Renseignements : Tel: +33 (0) 1 45 24 81 67
E-mail: sales@oecd.org

ONLINE BOOKSHOP / LIBRAIRIE EN LIGNE : **www.oecd.org/bookshop**
(secure payment with credit card / paiement sécurisé par carte de crédit)

OECD PUBLICATIONS, 2, rue André-Pascal, 75775 PARIS CEDEX 16
PRINTED IN FRANCE
(10 2000 03 1 P) ISBN 92-64-17503-2 – No. 51571 2000
ISSN 0376-6438